Household Crowding and
Its Consequences

Household Crowding and Its Consequences

John N. Edwards
Theodore D. Fuller
Sairudee Vorakitphokatorn
Santhat Sermsri

Westview Press

BOULDER • SAN FRANCISCO • OXFORD

Copyright © 1994 by Westview Press, Inc.

Published in 1994 in the United States of America by Westview Press, Inc., 5500 Central Avenue, Boulder, Colorado 80301-2877, and in the United Kingdom by Westview Press, 36 Lonsdale Road, Summertown, Oxford OX2 7EW

A CIP record for this book is available from the Library of Congress.
ISBN 0-8133-8802-3

Printed and bound in the United States of America

The paper used in this publication meets the requirements
of the American National Standard for Permanence of Paper
for Printed Library Materials Z39.48-1984.

10   9   8   7   6   5   4   3   2   1

Contents

List of Tables and Figures   vii

Acknowledgments   ix

1   **Population, Crowding, and Human Behavior**   1

Views of Urban Life, 1
What Is Crowding, 3
What This Study Is About, 4
On the Meaning of Pathology, 6
A Preview, 7

2   **The Effects of Human Crowding: A Theoretical**   11
and Empirical Review

A Short History Lesson, 11
Early Theorizing, 15
The Research Traditions, 18
The Bangkok Study, 34

3   **A Research Odyssey: Methodological Considerations**   39

The Focus Group Interviews, 40
The Survey, 48
Crowding and Culture, 56
Major Scales and Measures, 57
The Mode of Analysis, 61

4   **The Feeling of Being Crowded**   63

Background, 63
The Analysis, 65
Conclusions, 83

5   **Crowding and Psychological Well-Being**   87

     Some Prior Studies, 90
     The Analysis, 92
     Conclusions, 100

6   **The Impact of Crowding on the Family**   105

     Background: The Thai Family, 105
     Prior Studies on Crowding and Family Relations, 110
     The Analysis, 112
     Conclusions, 129

7   **Sexual Relations and Reproductive Behaviors**   131

     Background: Prior Research, 131
     The Analysis, 137
     Conclusions, 147

8   **Crowding and Health**   149

     Background: Previous Studies, 149
     The Analysis, 152
     Conclusions, 161

9   **Conclusions and Implications**   163

     Summary of Major Findings, 165
     Crowding and Culture: Theoretical Implications, 174
     Implications for Public Policy, 176

Appendix A: Questionnaire   179
Appendix B: Description of Scales   205
References   213
About the Book and Authors   223
Index   225

Tables and Figures

Tables

3.1   Bangkok and Sample Characteristics   51-54

4.1   Zero-order Correlations of Objective and   71
      Subjective Crowding Measures
4.2   Effect of Objective Crowding on Perceived   73-74
      Crowding for Three Different Models,
      Unstandardized Regression Coefficients
4.3   Effect of Objective Crowding on Lack of   75-76
      Privacy for Three Different Models,
      Unstandardized Regression Coefficients
4.4   Explained Variance for Perceived Crowding   79-80
      and Perceived Lack of Privacy: Summary
      Results for Various Subgroups
4.5   Standardized Regression Coefficients for the   82
      Effects of Objective Crowding and Other
      Exogenous Variables on Subjective
      Crowding

5.1   Zero-order Correlations Among Crowding   96
      and Measures of Psychological Well-Being
5.2   Relationship Between Measures of   97-98
      Psychological Well-Being and Objective
      and Subjective Crowding, with Controls:
      Standardized Regression Coefficients

6.1   Zero-order Correlations and Crowding   117-118
      and Family Relations Measures
6.2   Relationship Between Measures of Marital   119-120
      and Family Relations and Objective and
      Subjective Crowding, with Controls:
      Standardized Regression Coefficients
6.3   Relationship Between Sibling Conflict   124
      and Objective and Subjective Crowding,
      with Controls: Standardized Regression
      Coefficients

6.4   Relationship Between Measures of Violence   128
        and Objective and Subjective Crowding,
        with Controls: Standardized Regression
        Coefficients

7.1   Frequency of Sexual Relations Per Month   140-141
        by Selected Characteristics
7.2   Zero-order Correlations Among Crowding,   142
        Sexual Relations, and Reproductive Behavior
7.3   Relationship Between Measures of Reproductive   143-144
        Behavior and Objective and Subjective
        Crowding, With Controls: Standardized
        Regression Coefficients

8.1   Effects of Housing, Crowding, and Psychological   156-157
        Distress on Physical Health: Standardized
        Regression Coefficients
8.2   Sex Differences in Health for Married Men   159
        and Women in Bangkok

9.1   Summary of Major Findings   166-169

Figures
2.1   The General Model   37

4.1   Four Potential Nonlinear Relationships   72
        Between Objective and Subjective Crowding
4.2   Subjective Crowding by Persons Per Room   77

Acknowledgments

Carrying out a research project of the scope we discuss here, one incurs many debts. We are especially indebted to the National Science Foundation (SES-8618157), whose funding made possible the collection of the data on which this study is based. This funding was supplemented by additional support from the Institute for Population and Social Research, Mahidol University, Bangkok. We are most grateful to Dr. Pramote Prasartkul, the former director of the Institute, and Dr. Aphichat Chamratrithirong, the present director, for their sustained encouragement during the data-gathering phase of the project.

Valuable assistance in drawing the Bangkok sample was received from several sources, the National Statistical Office, the Bangkok Metropolitan Authority, and the National Housing Authority. In particular, our thanks go to Sophon Pornchokchai, Aporn Chandcharoaensook, and Juree Vichit-Vadakan for their cooperation and help.

Mr. Yothin Sawangdee ably served as the moderator of the male focus groups, which were conducted prior to undertaking the Bangkok survey. The groups' discussions were critical to the formulation of the survey instrument. On the U.S. side of the Pacific, the project greatly benefited from the expertise and technical assistance lent to us by Ms. Kristi Hoffman and Ms. Qing Wang. Their aid was crucial in expediting our quantitative analyses. Finally, but hardly least, we are most grateful and greatly indebted to Ms. Barbara Townley. Her technical expertise and cheerful cooperation were vital in assembling the manuscript and in enabling us to meet the publisher's deadlines.

The timely completion of this project would not have been possible without the unhesitant assistance of all of these individuals. Our thanks are small recompense for the amount of aid we received.

We thank Pergamon Press for permission to reproduce two tables that previously appeared in *Social Science and Medicine*, Vol. 36, pages 1425-6, 1993. We also appreciate the permission to reproduce one table from the *Journal of Health and Social Behavior*, Vol. 34, page 260.

John N. Edwards, Theodore D. Fuller,
Sairudee Vorakitphokatorn, and Santhat Sermsri

1

Population, Crowding, and Human Behavior

As we move into the twenty-first century, the effects of human crowding loom as an ever larger and more pressing issue. World population stands at over five and a half billion people. In the next ten years alone, it is estimated that 1.1 billion will be added to this figure (Todaro, 1989). Compounding the problem of numbers, much of this increase will take place in the less developed regions of the world, most notably increasing in Asia, Africa, and Latin America. In these regions, the provision of housing is especially problematic, for land-use is becoming more intensified and needed capital outlays for housing continue to escalate. With a tendency toward primate cities that dominate countries in these regions, the result, in all likelihood, will be cities of ever higher density. As city density increases, more intense crowding at the household level is likely to come about. All of this greatly amplifies the concern as to what consequences crowding has for the quality of life and individual well-being.

Views of Urban Life

This concern is by no means a new one. Cities, it seems, have always had their critics, regardless of their actual size or speific densities. Starting with the writers of the Old Testament forward, a list of the city's critics is a venerable one. It is a long list of philosophers, writers, and intellectuals, not to mention various social reformers and politicians. The list includes Plato, Machiavelli, Thomas Jefferson, Ralph Waldo Emerson, Thoreau, along with de Tocqueville and Edgar Alan Poe (White and White, 1962). In all, they saw the city, with its concentration of people in a limited area, as the source of sinfulness, lack of restraint, crime, alienation, and conspicuous waste. Particularly in America, and especially with the disappearance of its frontiers, the anti-urban litany has been loud and persistent. Perhaps no one put it more bluntly than de

Tocqueville (1835, 1945:289) in writing: "I look upon the size of certain American cities, and especially on the nature of their population, as a real danger which threatens the future security of the democratic republics of the New World; and I venture to predict that they will perish from this circumstance, unless the government succeeds in creating an armed force which ...will be independent of the town population and able to repress its excesses."

Echoes of the concern about urban living continue to be heard. In the 1960s, in *The Death and Life of Great American Cities*, Jane Jacobs – though a proponent of high density and diversity – argued that residential crowding was a crucial source of city decay and a contributory factor to increased social disorganization. Today, Paul Ehrlich reiterates the message he first put forward in his book *The Population Bomb* (1968), contending that the world is overcrowded and that there are too many people and too few resources to serve their needs. Reverberations of the concern are at the heart of the environmental movement, with its focus on overpopulation, resource depletion, pollution, and continued industrial growth. "No growth," "managed growth," and "small is beautiful" are slogans that encapsulate a rethinking of the desirability of urban life and urban growth.

For most critics of urban life, the number of people involved and their sheer concentration in a limited area are the core of the problem. "Each kind of animal," Desmond Morris maintains (1968:39), "has evolved to exist in a certain amount of living space. In both the animal zoo and the human zoo this space is severely curtailed and the consequences can be serious." Speaking of the contemporary city, Lewis Mumford (1968:210) goes even further, asserting: "No small part of this ugly urban barbarization has been due to sheer physical congestion: a diagnosis now partly confirmed by scientific experiments with rats – for when they are placed in equally congested quarters, they exhibit the same symptoms of stress, alienation, hostility, sexual perversion, parental incompetence, and rabid violence that we now find in Megapolis."

Our book bears on one aspect of the more general concern with urban life. In these pages, we deal with the issue of crowding at the household level, or what Stokols (1978) refers to as a "primary environment." Primary environments, he suggests (1978:235), "are those in which an individual spends much time, relates to others on a personal basis and engages in a wide range of personally important activities." The household is a primary environment *par excellence*. Except for the homeless, everyone resides in some sort of dwelling, usually living with others, relating to them personally, and unavoidably interacting with other household members and becoming involved in the various activities that take place there. If crowding has serious effects, as the urban critics and Stokols maintain, we should detect its most severe manifestations in the household itself. While a city in general may be very densely populated, one's "encounters with others are relatively transitory, anonymous, and inconsequential," as Stokols puts it (1978:235). Although one might perceive deficiencies in the more general or "secondary" environment, deficiencies in one's personal environment are more intensely experienced and longer felt.

What Is Crowding?

As reviewed in the chapter to follow, there are several disparate and relatively long traditions of crowding research. Each tradition approaches the subject of crowding somewhat differently. One tradition of research concentrates on animals other than humans. Another tradition focuses on humans, but is experimental in nature. Still another line of research looks at humans as an aggregate. Other investigators inspect what happens at the individual level. As a result of this diversity in approaches, the meaning of crowding has become rather muddled. So, let us clarify what it is we intend to discuss in the subsequent pages.

The animal research tradition of crowding emphasizes the concept of territoriality. This is the tendency of a group of animals to stake out a space and roam within it. Crowding occurs when the number of animals increases to the point that their food supply or reproduction is threatened. Under crowded conditions, some species of animals have been observed to undergo population crashes, whereby their numbers are reduced to a level that permits the remaining population to sustain itself (Christian, Flyger, and Davis, 1960). Territorial behavior appears to be biologically-driven, and there is no credible evidence that there is any such counterpart among humans.

Density refers to the number of persons in a defined spatial area. Typically it is a concept used to describe more macro-levels of crowding, such as the population per acre. However, as Gove and Hughes (1983) point out, density is in actuality a composite of different measures of the use of space, and it may be calculated in several different ways. In addition to referring to the population per acre, density can denote the number of dwelling structures in a given unit of land area, the number of dwellings per structure, the number of rooms per dwelling unit, and the number of persons per room. Because of its multi-dimensional character, two neighborhoods could have the same density but for very different reasons. Measures of density thus may or may not reveal a great deal about what happens at the interpersonal level. Density is useful, though, in telling us something about the objective level of crowding. Persons per room – the most disaggregated density measure -- is, in fact, the most commonly used measure of objective crowding. Persons per room has the advantage of dealing with the more microenvironment in which a person resides and indicates the potential for primary interaction between household members. It is, if you will, a measure of "social density," as opposed to higher-order aggregate indicators of "physical density" (Hawley, 1972). Because of this advantage, we will make extensive use of this measure in our analyses as an objective indicator of crowding.

Obviously, there is a subjective side to crowding as well. Logically, we would expect people in objectively congested circumstances to perceive the situation and to have some feelings about it. Admittedly, some individuals may feel crowded more intensely than others, even when there is the same level of objective crowding.

Subjective crowding has been approached by researchers in two fundamentally different ways. Stokols, for example, defines subjective crowding "as an experience in which one's demands for space exceeds the supply" (1978:222). In short, there is a mismatch between one's demand for and the supply of space. Altman (1974), on the other hand, suggests that the experience of crowding results when a person is unable to achieve some desired level of privacy, that is, when an individual is exposed to more contact with others than he or she desires. Each of these approaches, we think, is valuable in that they complement one another in tapping into the total experience of crowding. Accordingly, in our analyses, we use two different scales of subjective crowding, one we call "perceived crowding" and the other labelled "lack of privacy."

As even this brief discussion would suggest, crowding is a complex concept. When we treat it as a variable, it is necessary to distinguish between its objective and subjective components, for there is no one-to-one relationship between how objectively congested a situation may be and how people may perceive the circumstances. The perceptual component of crowding may manifest itself in either the feeling that there is too little space available or in the sense that one's privacy has been violated.

What This Study Is About

The present study focuses on crowding in the household, looking at its effects both as objectively and subjectively measured. As an example of a primary environment, the household provides us with a natural laboratory in which we can examine what, if any, effects crowding may have. Most past investigations have stressed the "costs" to close social bonds, which we are most likely to find among household members, when density and crowding reach certain proportions. Overcrowding, in brief, is generally viewed as leading to disturbed social relations and to social pathologies (Milgram, 1970; Galle, Gove, and McPherson, 1972; Gove, Hughes, and Galle, 1979; Gove and Hughes, 1983). Some investigators, though, have argued otherwise, providing data that crowding has little, if any, effects on family life and other aspects of social behavior (Booth, 1976; Choldin, 1978; Freedman, 1975). There is, thus, a continuing debate concerning the impact of crowding, a debate to which we seek to contribute through both methodological and conceptual refinements. In doing so, we inspect multiple measures of family relations and a variety of indicators of individual well-being.

Building on prior research, the present study is guided by a stress model of crowding. In basic outline, this model suggests that the more households are crowded, the more stressful the situation. The greater the stress experienced, the more likely disturbances in family relations and decrements in well-being are to occur. In other words, stress is hypothesized to be a crucial intervening variable between crowding, both as objectively and subjectively measured, and a set of dependent variables having to do with family relations and the well-being of individuals. Diagrammatically, the basic model looks like this:

Objective   Subjective   Decrements in
Crowding ⟶ Crowding ⟶ Stress ⟶ Family Relations
                    and Well-being

This constitutes, of course, a highly restricted model of crowding, for there are numerous known and theoretically relevant factors that influence each of the model's components. We elaborate on these factors in a later chapter, and suggest how they may relate to the components of this basic model.

Much of what is known about the effects of human crowding is based on research that has been conducted in Europe and North America, particularly the latter. One of the fundamental difficulties in interpreting the results from this research, and perhaps a major reason for the inconclusive findings it has produced, is that these locales have densities and household crowding which are relatively low by world standards. In the United States, for example, the average number of persons per room is 0.5 (Gove and Hughes, 1983). Belgium, West Germany (prior to reunification), Sweden, and Switzerland have an average persons per room of 0.6. The average number of persons per room is 0.7 in Norway, with Finland and France having an average of 0.8 (United Nations, 1985). In Asia, Africa, and Latin America, by contrast, household crowding is three to four times these levels. The bulk of the world's population lives in circumstances far different than those of Europeans and North

Americans. One of the innovative aspects of the present study is that we have chosen as the research site a place more typical in terms of household crowding than that found in Western societies. The data reported here come from Bangkok, Thailand, where the average number of persons per room is 2.1, or four times that in the United States. On the face of it, and in view of the mixed results of prior studies, the effects of crowding, if any, should be more intense. These data, we contend, provide a more critical test of the crowding-pathology relationship.

On the Meaning of Pathology

The literature on crowding effects, that dealing with humans as well as non-humans, is replete with references to pathology and abberrent behavior. Studies variously refer to, among other things, infant mortality, poor maternal care of the young, deficient mental health, disturbances in social interaction, atypical sexual practices, or poor physical health as manifestations of pathology. In labelling these phenomena as pathological, the connotation, of course, is that these deviate from normal and that they have deleterious or adverse consequences for those involved. Pathology implies we know what is "normal" and "good," and any behavior or event that departs from these is necessarily "deviant" or "bad." Pathologies represent departures from the norm and, therefore, are dysfunctional to individuals and, more broadly, to the groups of which they are members. At the most extreme, pathology implies the demise of individuals and their groups. This, we believe, is an unfortunate label, although it is perhaps unavoidable in some instances. We say unfortunate, for the term "pathology" suggests a judgment in value.

It is plainly the case, however, that we do not always know what the norm being violated is. Or even if the norm is known, it is not obvious in all instances that a departure from the norm is invariably adverse in character. Some so-called pathological behaviors may merely represent unusual, but innovative, responses to crowded conditions. They actually may be adaptive for individuals and/or the groups to which they belong. Therefore, in making later reference to pathology, we do so only under two circumstances: (1) when the phenomenon under discussion represents a clear-cut departure from a cultural norm and/or (2) when consistency with existing research literature dictates it.

A Preview

In Chapter 2, we begin our discussion of the effects of crowding by providing an overview of the theoretical and empirical underpinnings of crowding research. There is now a relatively long history of crowding research. We trace this from some of the early theorizing about population density resulting from urbanization to various contemporary empirical investigations. Over the course of this history, researchers have taken a variety of approaches to the subject. Some, as mentioned, have focused on the behavior of lower animals under compressed conditions. This ethological research tradition has been, in fact, a significant impetus for the examination of human crowding consequences, for many of the findings concerning lower animals have been very dramatic, documenting a wide range of pathologies and aberrant forms of behavior when animals live in a confined space.

The research on humans can be divided into three different traditions. Consistent with early sociological theorizing about the effects of urbanization, one strand of research is essentially ecological in nature, looking at aggregate population statistics and their relationship to various rates of phenomena, such as juvenile delinquency, mortality, and admissions to mental hospitals. Psychologists interested in crowding eschew such an approach. The psychological research tradition is based almost entirely on running experiments, where the investigator has control over extraneous factors that may affect the behavior being observed. The third research tradition, of which our study is a part, is one that focuses on residential arrangements and examines data collected from individuals. As we will see, these different theoretical and methodological stances sometimes produce very different results.

Chapter 3 details the methodology of the present study. What you have before you is the end-product of a research odyssey, starting with some initial ideas about the possible effects of crowding, leading to the collection of data, finally resulting in the analyses contained in this book. For the two senior authors, who initiated this investigation, doing research in a culture very different than their own presented special and numerous challenges. It is one thing to design a piece of research to be conducted in one's native land where there is great familiarity with the language and customs, but it is quite another when the language and culture are foreign.

To overcome the cultural gulf necessitated an international team of investigators, leading to the addition of two Thai nationals who were trained in the United States and were fluent in English. A second strategy used to bridge the cultural differences involved conducting focus group research, a qualitative research technique that complemented the survey discussed in Chapter 3.

The analyses of the survey results begin in Chapter 4. One unresolved issue in crowding research concerns why people feel crowded. While other studies of residential overcrowding have reported a link between objective and subjective crowding, the correlation between the two is much smaller than one might anticipate. Consistent with prior studies, we, too, find a modest relationship between objective measures of crowding and the actual experience people have in feeling crowded. In this chapter, we examine several reasons why this is the case and analyze why there is no one-to-one relationship between one's objective circumstances and the way one feels.

Psychologists, in particular, have argued that while we may perceive our broader environment (neighborhood, community) as containing too many people for the space available, individuals are more likely to be reactant to what is termed "the primary environment," the household constituting a prime example of this type of environment. It is an environment where an individual may find it difficult to escape the attention of and the need to interact with other people. This could elevate the level of stress experienced, eroding a person's ability to cope. One of the first manifestations of the impact of crowding may not be some departure in one's behavior, but instead it may manifest itself in various psychological reactions. Drawing on a broad array of measures having to do with psychological well-being and psychological disturbances, we look at this issue in Chapter 5.

Since the family forms the core of the household, we would expect that any behavioral disturbances created by overcrowding would be exhibited in how family members interact with each other. Some of its most severe and adverse consequences could bear on the husband-wife relationship and be displayed in the sort of relations that prevail between parents and their children. In Chapter 6, we empirically examine the relationship between objective and subjective crowding and a number of measures designed to assay the qualitative character of husband-wife relations and the relationships parents have with their children. The analysis also includes an assessment of how household crowding may influence the relations siblings have with one another. Rounding out this chapter, we present some findings bearing on the incidence of violence, one of the more extreme signs of pathology that crowding may precipitate.

Chapter 7 continues our examination of the consequences of crowding for family life. In this case, the discussion focuses on sexual and reproductive behavior. Ethological research has documented a variety of sexual aberrations among lower animals that come about when they live under crowded conditions. These departures from normality include everything from interrupted copulation to hypersexuality, homosexual behavior, and pansexuality. Crowding also disrupts normal reproductive behavior, resulting in a higher incidence of spontaneous abortion, ineffectual maternal care, higher infant mortality, and, ultimately, lower fertility. We test whether there are similar patterns among humans, paying particular attention to the implications of a lack of privacy in crowded households.

There are several compelling theoretical reasons that suggest crowding may adversely affect a person's health, an issue we address in Chapter 8. First, crowded living conditions can constitute a source of chronic stress, which eventually may be manifested in certain physiological symptoms. Secondly, if anyone in a crowded household contracts an infectious disease, it may be more readily transmitted to other household members, given the finite amount of space they occupy. Thirdly, crowded households tend to be of a poorer quality, having deficiencies that could bear on the state of one's health. In particular, they may lack proper sanitary facilities and an adequate water supply, exposing the occupants to the greater possibility of contracting various infections. We inspect several indicators of ill-health to examine if, and how, crowding may affect an individual's health status.

The final chapter, Chapter 9, contains our general conclusions. There, we first present a summary of the major findings from the Bangkok survey and discuss their theoretical implications, detailing their bearing on the stress model of crowding. We also take up the issue of the cultural relevance of crowding, addressing how its impact may vary in different cultural settings. As a final note, we point out some of the implications our findings have for housing policy and housing design, suggesting policy and design alternatives that may alleviate the effects of household crowding.

2

The Effects of Human Crowding: A Theoretical and Empirical Review

Objectively conceived, household crowding is hardly a new phenomenon. Looking at times past, household crowding appears to have been very commonplace in various societies and subcultures around the globe. No precise figures exist, of course, but historical evidence is highly suggestive. One might even conclude that crowding, at least as measured by today's standards, was the norm, rather than the exception.

A Short History Lesson

Take the Iroquois Indian as one example. Lewis Morgan, in his classic study of the Iroquois Indian (1965:64), describes their villages as having houses up to 100 feet (33 meters) long "with a passageway through the center, a door at each end, and with an interior partitioned off at intervals up to about 7 feet (two meters). Each apartment or stall thus formed was opened for its entire width upon the passageway." Each long-house could accommodate up to 20 families. Morgan also cites the reports of Lewis and Clark of their exploration of the northwest United States, coming on Indian settlements where a single house was sometimes as much as 150 feet long and contained as many as 400 to 500 inhabitants. Ethnographic accounts of long-houses in Borneo report structures up to a quarter of a mile long accommodating 600 people. Social historians estimate that in the early colonial United States the average size dwelling was on the order of 600 square feet (57 square meters), usually consisting of but one room and providing shelter to an average of about seven people (Demos, 1970). The colonial household often included boarders, apprentices, dependent strangers, and servants if the family was wealthy enough to afford them.

Writing of even an earlier era, Aries (1962) points out that up to the 1600s, houses lacked specialized rooms. "In the same rooms where they ate," Aries indicates (1962:394), "people slept, danced, worked and received visitors." Homes, he adds, "were obviously shelters for sleeping and sometimes (not always) eating." Not even the elite were exempt. "The king," Aries notes (1962:392), "was never left alone. But in fact, until the end of the 17th century, nobody was ever left alone. The density of social life made isolation virtually impossible, and people who managed to shut themselves up in a room for some time were regarded as exceptional characters." It was not until the eighteenth century, Aries contends, that housing design was drastically altered and specialized rooms with particular functions came into being. However, as late as the 1880s in Europe, a sizeable proportion of the population still resided in one-room households. Twenty-eight percent of Hamburg's population did so, 49 percent of Berlin's, 55 percent of Dresden's, and a high 70 percent of Chemnitz's population was confined to a one-room dwelling (Shorter, 1977).

People in rural areas may have been even more cramped, although their housing may have contained more rooms. Here is a description of a German peasant's dwelling, as recounted in the mid-nineteenth century:

> Wherever you go you find relatively small houses, composed of a single family room with a small side chamber and a small kitchen. You climb up stone steps to a tiny entryway, straight back from which is the kitchen and on one or both sides living space; above is a garret for storage... Inside such a dwelling there invariably lives a family of numerous offspring. Sometimes several generations are on hand, sometimes as well several unrelated families. Especially common in these rooms are lateral relatives, who also have children. The household's few beds, always very dirty and sometimes thick and sweltering, are found both in the main room and the dark, fetid side chamber, so that normally 2-3 people, even of different sexes, sleep in the same bed (cited in Shorter, 1977).

Contemporary observers of these various places and times attributed all manner of social maladies and deviations to the crowded quarters people occupied. Physicians commonly ascribed the poor health of the urban lower classes to the practice of several families living in one-room apartments (Shorter, 1977). Crowding was seen as undermining law. Commenting on the lodging-houses in London in the 1850s, Henry Mayhew (1861; 1968) noted that most of their occupants were thieves, the inexpensive lodging attracting poor boys who learned how to pick pockets from the older men. Concerning these lodging-houses, Mayhew wrote: "At some of the busiest times, numbers sleep on the kitchen floor, all huddled together, men and women (when indecencies are common enough), and without bedding or anything but their scanty clothes to soften the hardness of the stone or brick floor.... More than 200 have been accommodated in this way in a large house" (1968:476).

Crowding, too, was said to take its toll on morality. The lodging-houses of London, according to Mayhew, were frequented by many juveniles, both male and female, as well as by adult men and women. In some of these places, he indicates, the occupants were "herd[ed] together promiscuously." "Boys," he says, "have boastfully carried on loud conversations, and from distant parts of the room, of their triumphs over the virtue of girls, and girls have laughed at and encouraged the recital. Three, four, five, six, and even more boys and girls have been packed, head and feet, into one small bed; some perhaps never met before. On such occasions any clothing seems often enough to be regarded as merely an encumbrance" (1968:477).

In referring to nineteenth century rural Germany, Shorter (1977) comes to a similar conclusion on the effects of household crowding on male-female relations. "If," he states (1977:40), "cramped housing took away the married couple's opportunity for intimacy, it also brought the unmarried into close physical contact--with the opposite results. So bad had the overfilling of domestic space become, reported the provincial government of Wiirzburg in 1839, that 'the hired hand and the farmer's son sleep often in the same room, and in the same bed, as the farmer's daughter and the maid. The result was illegitimacy."

Compared to continental Europe, some historians contend, the British and, later, the American colonists were well-off, having a measure of privacy unknown in France, Germany, Switzerland, and Scandinavia (Shorter, 1977). Until sometime in the nineteenth century, the vast bulk of the population on the continent, except for a small elite, continued to live in mostly one-room dwellings, with undifferentiated or no specialized spaces. By the seventeenth and eighteenth centuries, the British were moving toward more internally-segregated living quarters (Hoskins, 1963). Domestic living space came to be partitioned by function, potentially creating enclaves within the household for domestic intimacy.

American colonists, perhaps reflecting their English heritage, soon followed suit, building ever larger homes with specialized rooms. Flaherty (1972) points out that in Massachusetts the average rural dwelling increased from four rooms in the late seventeenth century to six rooms a century later. Increasingly, solid walls replaced temporary partitions, such as blankets hung to subdivide a room. This was especially critical in the development of private sleeping quarters and had important ramifications, according to social historians, for the emotional and sexual lives of Americans (Flaherty, 1972; Shorter, 1977).

While all of this attests to a long history of domestic crowding, at least in Western societies, the historical evidence tells us little about how people actually felt. Although this may merely reflect a void in the historical record, it could be the result of circumstances in times past. A sense of being crowded requires, after all, a standard of comparison. Subjective crowding is relative, dependent on a comparison of one situation with another. If, historically, most social situations were objectively crowded ones, it is unlikely people would have felt crowded. This is particularly true of domestic living space. If nearly everyone lived in similarly cramped quarters, there simply was no basis for comparison.

The development of larger dwellings with specialized interior rooms created a fundamental condition whereby comparisons could be made. Separate dwellings divided one family from another, and specialized rooms divided individual family members from each other. Individuals could thus evaluate their living circumstances relative to others. The development of specialized rooms was equally important for an individual's felt sense of privacy, for they enabled people to be alone or a couple by themselves in carrying out some activity. With the advent of functionally specialized rooms, individuals were no longer under the constant scrutiny of others present.

These developments, Mumford indicates (1961:382-385), started with the rich. It involved separating the kitchen from the scullery, removing entertaining to a salon, and moving meals to a dining room. Ladies would receive guests in a drawing room rather than their bedchambers. Husbands would retire to a study, and both sexes would have private sleeping quarters, where they could independently pursue amorous adventures.

We do not mean to imply by this that people's behavior was or is architecturally determined. Winston Churchill once remarked: "We shape our buildings; afterward our building shape us," a rather bold assertion of architectural determinism to which we do not subscribe. In all probability, the historical shift to larger dwelling units and divided interiors came about with changing economic and social conditions. The availability of land and growing affluence were necessary pre-conditions to the development of separate family dwellings. The division of domestic living space reflected in specialized rooms no doubt were an outgrowth of fundamental changes in people's values, especially of an increased value placed on the notion of privacy. All we are suggesting is that once separate dwellings with specialized interiors were in place, people were more apt to have a sense of feeling crowded and that their privacy had been invaded. Our reading of the historical record would suggest that these subjective states are relatively recent phenomena, dating at the earliest to the seventeenth century and in most places to the eighteenth or even the nineteenth century. This we think is important to note because, unlike early theoretical formulations dealing with crowding, most contemporary conceptualizations emphasize the importance of perceived crowding and a felt lack of privacy, as we shall see later in the chapter.

We turn now to a discussion of the theoretical perspectives on crowding, noting the various stances taken by different theorists and researchers. Along the way, we will review empirical literature bearing on the consequences of crowding, paying particular attention to two large-scale studies which our investigation, in a general way, replicates and extends. We make no pretense that our review of the research literature is exhaustive. There are literally hundreds of crowding studies dealing with both humans and lower animals. Even a book-length manuscript is inadequate to treat these in any exhaustive fashion. We have tried, however, to review what we judge to be some of the more representative and well-executed studies that have grown out of the various research traditions, and to discuss some of the more provocative of the research findings.

Early Theorizing

While historically crowding, as indicated above, was not confined to urban areas, the city has occupied the central focus and commanded the greatest attention of most observers. For early sociological theory, rural areas and rurality merely served as a reference point, a basis for comparison. The central problematic for early theorists was to characterize and explain the transformation of society as populations grew ever larger and became ever more concentrated in locales we now call cities. The organization of rural communities was taken for granted, not seen as being in need of explanation. Rural communities represented the traditional, the point of departure for modernizing, urban societies whose understanding theorists sought.

At the core of the problematic was the issue of how societies are socially integrated. First systematized by Tonnies' (1855-1936), two ideal types of society were suggested, the *Gemeinschaft* and the *Gesellschaft*. These, for Tonnies, were based on two essential types of human will, the former deriving from natural will and the latter from rational will. All interaction, according to Tonnies, is an expression of acts of will, and *Gemeinschaft* and *Gesellschaft* constitute two fundamentally different types of societies and forms of social integration. While these are pure types and no actual society exactly corresponds to them, traditional society tends to be *Gemeinschaftliche* and modern society *Gesellschaftliche*. Social relationships in a *Gemeinschaft*-type society are personal, based on fellowship, kinship, and neighborliness. Life revolves around the family and village, governed by folkways, mores, and religion. In contrast, relations in a *Gesellschaft* sort of society tend to be impersonal, character- ized by exchange and rational calculations. Cities dominate, social relationships are contractual, and social control takes the form of law, rather than being based on custom and religion. These distinctions would reverberate in the formulations of all modern societal typologies, all taking Tonnies' conceptualization as a point of departure (Martindale, 1960).

This was clearly the case with Durkheim's (1855-1917) analysis of social solidarity, which he saw as the essential property of society. Solidarity, to Durkheim, took two primary forms, mechanical and organic. Societies in which social solidarity is mechanical are those dominated by a collective consciousness, held together by friendliness, neighborliness, and kinship. A collective consciousness imposes values as imperative ideals, levying repressive sanctions in the event of deviation in order to express an outraged collective sentiment. Organic solidarity, on the other hand, pertains to social integration in societies characterized by specialization, a division of labor, and an interdependence between its component groups and institutions. Law is restitutive rather than repressive, its intent being to restore the social system to a workable state and not simply to vent rage as deviations from prevailing norms occur. Only in societies characterized by organic solidarity is anomie likely to occur. Anomie--the counterpart to social solidarity--is a state of confusion and "normlessness," a state of decay in collective sentiments and representations (Martindale, 1960).

These societal depictions, just as with Tonnies, were meant to represent ideal types, not actual societies. They were formulations to which actual societies could be compared, for the comparative method to Durkheim was the only method suitable to the study of social phenomena. Ideal types further serve as benchmarks against which changes in society can be assessed.

Unlike Tonnies, Durkheim was not content to simply formulate ideal types and categorize societies. He went beyond this and sought to explain how societies evolve, to find how societies change from one type of solidarity to another. One key to societal change, and one that is important to us here, concerned population growth. As populations grow in size, more complex societies develop, including the establishment of cities. With population growth comes a more intricate division of labor. For Durkheim (1893, 1947), the division of labor was in direct ratio with the volume and density of society, bringing about a condensation of society and a new form of interdependence among its parts. With increasing volume and density, Durkheim argued, even the conceptions of "space" will change, for those conceptions are based on the territory occupied by a society.

Simmel (1858 - 1918), a contemporary of Tonnies and Durkheim, took a different tack. Rather than viewing population density as an impersonal source of change, he considered density from the point of view of the individual. Simmel's main interest in the study of social phenomena steadfastly had to do with the reciprocal relations between human elements (Timasheff, 1963). To understand reciprocal relations requires an analysis of psychic interaction. In his classic piece "The Metropolis and Mental Life," Simmel (1905) saw cities as conglomerates where individuals were constantly making contact with others. Daily life involved vast quantities of interpersonal contacts at close distances. So much so, Simmel suggested, that in cities there was the ever-present potential of "overloading" one's nervous system. Having too many people within an individual's sensory range could lead to overstimulation. To avoid this, he observed, urbanites develop coping mechanisms, the principal adaptation being "social withdrawal." This involves the segmentalization of human relationships, resulting in many of the urbanite's contacts being highly superficial and utilitarian in character. Contacts tend to be impersonal or anonymous and of a highly transitory nature.

Many of the ideas of these early theorists were to crystallize in the writings of Wirth, a member of the so-called Chicago School, which had a tremendous impact on the development and course of urban sociology. Wirth's essay "Urbanism as a Way of Life" was to become a classic in urban sociology, having a long-term impact on observers of the urban scene and how they viewed the city.

In that essay, Wirth (1938) delineated what he saw as three principal characteristics of the city: a large-sized population, densely concentrated, and made up of a heterogeneous population. From these distinctive characteristics, he deduced the outlines of the urban way of life. Number, density, and heterogeneity, he contended, create a form of social organization in which primary groups are inevitably replaced by secondary contacts. Dissimilar to relations in primary groups (e.g., family, friendships), these secondary contacts are impersonal, segmented, superficial, transitory, and sometimes predatory. The city dweller, as a consequence, becomes anonymous, isolated, relativistic, rational, and secular. The only means by which an individual can function in urban society, Wirth argued, is to combine with others to organize ever larger, and usually impersonal, social entities. He concludes (1938:22): "Personal disorganization, mental breakdown, suicide, delinquency, crime, corruption, and disorder might be expected under these circumstances to be more prevalent in the urban than in the rural community." In the city, Wirth suggests, the family is notably weakened and its significance substantially diminished.

These early theoretical formulations on urban society and city life, as we shall see momentarily, have had an enormous impact on how crowding has been viewed and how investigators from different disciplines have approached its study.

The Research Traditions

Crowding studies do not form a unitary body of literature. Although we can see a common thread of concern in various theorists' perspectives on urban life and the organization of urban society, these perspectives devolved over time into two distinct sociological approaches to the study of crowding. The one approach, consistent with the more macro-orientation of Tonnies and Durkheim, is ecological in nature. Its basic strategy has been to correlate various population measures to different manifestations of social pathology, such as crime, mental illness, mortality, etc. The second approach, its theoretical impetus stemming from Simmel, is more social psychological and its orientation to crowding less macro. Studies in this tradition rely on reports from individuals and eschew the aggregate statistics used in ecological analyses.

Complementing these traditions, another line of crowding research has grown out of the discipline of psychology. Psychological research typically has focused on small groups in situations where the dimensions of crowding can be experimentally manipulated or in field studies where crowding can be easily observed. A fourth strand of research derives from animal studies, which often have produced very dramatic results that have served to stimulate hypotheses about how crowding may affect human behavior.

To place the present study in context, we review each of these traditions and examine some empirical studies and their results associated with the four approaches. We begin with the studies of lower animals.

Animal Studies

One approach to crowding not in the sociological tradition has been most informative to it, nonetheless, in raising significant research issues. This is the study of lower animals. This section, in fact, might well be subtitled "Of Mice, Other Animals, and Men," with due apologies to John Steinbeck. Researcher interested in animal behavior have studied a wide variety of animals under dense conditions, and several have not been loath to generalize their ethological findings to the behavior of humans, enumerating what consequences crowding may have for them. A number of the findings conjure up Malthusian nightmares. During the 1960s, a time of urban turmoil and widespread rioting, a number of books popularized the animal research, suggesting that the innate qualities of humans are not compatible with modern urban life. Appearing under such titles as *The Naked Ape, The Human Zoo,* and *The Territorial Imperative,* a few of the books became best-sellers.

Theoretically, much of the animal research has been informed by Selye's General Adaptation Syndrome (1950, 1952). Selye described a common pattern of response among lower animals when they are subjected to non-specific stress, which density presumably could bring about. The pattern or syndrome involves three stages: an alarm reaction, a stage of resistance, and, finally, one of exhaustion. Each stage is signaled by varying physiological changes. In the initial phase, the adrenal cortex increases in size and adrenal secretions become elevated. The thymus, spleen, and lympthatic structures shrink. White blood cells become more numerous. Bleeding ulcers appear. Metabolic changes occur, resulting in a loss in body weight. This is followed by a stage of resistance in which the animal mobilizes its defense mechanisms, reversing the responses of the alarm reaction and returning to a state of normal equilibrium. Should the stress continue or increase, a stage of exhaustion sets in. The animal suffers lowered resistance due to the stress. Disease occurs and, eventually, the animal dies. An organism's ability to withstand sustained stress, according to Seyle, is finite.

Homeostatic theory also has guided animal studies and been used to interpret their results. As set forth by Christian (1965, 1971), this theory, rather parsimoniously, suggests the following. Assuming high density is stressful, as stress increases, adrenal activity will increase. As adrenal activity becomes elevated, physical malfunctions will increase, including reproductive malfunctions and death. Thus, the size of the population is reduced, returning it to a state of equilibrium.

How do the results from animal studies accord with these theoretical notions? Numerous investigations have documented that there are, indeed, endrocrine responses when animals are in highly dense situations (Christian, 1965; Louch, 1956; Eechaute et al., 1962; Varon, 1966). Increases in adrenal size and activity have been observed among mice, rats, and monkeys, among others. As animal populations grow, reproductive failure increases. There is increased infant mortality, elevated levels of intrauterine mortality, inhibited physical and sexual maturation, irregular estrus cycles among females, and reductions in the fertility of males.

Deviant and aberrant behavior are frequent observations among animals in high density populations. In what is perhaps the best known series of animal experiments, Calhoun (1962) placed domesticated Norwegian rats in an enclosure, provided adequate food for all, and allowed the population to grow. The enclosure contained four pens, each with its own food and water supply. Groups of the same size and sex composition were placed in each pen, which had interconnecting ramps permitting the rats to traverse from one to another. One of the striking developments in several of the experiments was what Calhoun called a "behavioral sink." This was where a disproportionate number of the animals would take up residence in one of the pens, leaving other pens under-populated. As much as three-quarters of the population would assemble in only one pen during periods of feeding.

Over an interval of 16 months, several pathologies emerged. Among the females, many were unable to carry their pregnancy to full term. Even if they did, others did not survive the delivery of their litters. An even greater number failed to provide maternal care, putting their offspring at risk and increasing infant mortality to as high as 96 percent. Among the males, normal behavior patterns were disturbed. Sexual deviation (homosexuality, pansexual behavior, and frantic heterosexual behavior) abounded. They engaged in the cannibalism of the young. Some were frequently overactive, while others were pathologically withdrawn. Only a small number of individuals remained normal.

Few studies, especially those on free-roaming animals, report behavioral changes as dramatic as these. Yet, under high density conditions, across species there do seem to be some fairly common patterns. These have been summarized by Freedman (1975:23), who indicates that when density increases:

1. At a certain point the population declines sharply.
2. There is greatly increased infant mortality caused primarily by inadequate nest building and the care of the young by females.
3. There is increased aggressiveness and a breakdown in normal social behavior.
4. Some animals become recluses and no longer engage in any social behavior.
5. The strongest animals survive and are able to breed, raise young, and in general live a normal life.
6. Adrenal activity is increased and male gonadal activity somewhat decreased by exposure to larger numbers of other animals.

What is at the root of these regularities among lower animals is still in question, however. The widely drawn conclusion is that these are the direct result of density and that they are innate responses, which may very well have their counterparts in human reactions to crowding. But this is cast in doubt on several scores.

First, there are the animal studies themselves. It is not clear from many of the reports whether it is density per se or the actual size of the population that may trigger the aberrant responses. A number of researchers contend, as Freedman (1975) does, that the size of an animal population plays the more important role. Certainly, in free-roaming populations, increases in size are likely to put a strain on food supplies, which in turn could bring about many of the same outcomes. There is also the possibility, raised by Lloyd (1975), that it is neither density nor population size that is responsible, but that the aberrant responses are due to stress induced by social pressure.

This raises a second critical point. Much of the research literature on lower animals conveys the impression that such animals are non-social when, in fact, many are highly social in nature. Many animal studies leave one with the idea that all reactions are innate and unmediated by other factors. This is a false impression. One little noted, but consistent, finding in this body of literature is that the responses to density (or population size or stress) depend on the animal's status in a rank hierarchy, with dominant individuals being unaffected. Subordinates or those lowest in rank display the most severe reactions (Christian, 1971; Lloyd, 1975; Freedman, 1975).

Although many of the findings on lower animals are in accord with homeostatic theory and the general adaptation syndrome, they do not account for all of the patterns observed among lower animals. There is some evidence, for example, that high density does not necessarily increase the susceptibility to disease. It may depend on the type of disease or even the strain of the animal. To account for all of the observed patterns, Freedman (1975) argues, problems in the social interaction among animals must be recognized. As he (1975:35) puts it:

> When there is another animal in the cage or the backyard or the prairie, he must be dealt with. When there are ten others, they must be dealt with. The more there are, the more frequent and intense the social interactions.

Elsewhere, Freedman (1975:40) writes:

> Crowding, or simply the presence of a large number of other animals, acts primarily as an intensifier of the social interaction. When there are sufficient resources, this results in increased stimulation, excitement, and general activity level. It will accordingly produce an increase in adrenal activity but will not produce an increase in emotionality or a decrease in health. However, the presence of a large number of other animals will intensify the competition for any scarce resource, whether it be food, space, or anything else.

Does this mean the animal studies have no relevance to human crowding? There are two answers to this question: yes and no. Just as other species, humans have a biological system subject to the laws of biology. While human culture is a unique and highly complex adaptation to our environment, it does not remove us entirely from being subject to biological and physiological processes. The issue is not whether humans are different than other animals but it is a problem of assessing if there are any commonalities across species. In doing so, we must proceed with caution and avoid overly-simplistic extrapolations, as the popularizers of ethological research have done. As Freedman (1975:41) concludes: "Even if every other animal behaved in a particular way, this would not justify drawing the firm conclusion that humans behave the same way." If nothing else, the ethological literature provides us with valuable insights about behavioral possibilities and suggests hypotheses concerning behavioral patterns we might observe among humans. This we will find to be the case in our later discussions on sexual relations, reproductive behavior, and health.

The Ecological Approach

Within sociology, the ecological perspective has a venerable history, dating in particular from the founding of the Chicago School and the work of Park and Wirth. Ecology is concerned with the activities of collectivities, usually communities, within some spatial setting. It may deal with the interrelationships between cities or communities as they are distributed through space, or it may have to do with the internal structure and dynamics within a particular community. In the latter sense, ecology is concerned with the interplay between the spatial and patterns of human relationships (Gist and Fava, 1971). Ecology does not deal with individuals as individuals; it is concerned with groups or categories of people who have some common defining characteristic, such as race, income, or marital status. These population characteristics may have consequences for how people behave and interact with one another.

An important element within any ecological system is population. For the ecologically-inclined crowding researcher, however, it is not the size of a population per se that is of interest. Rather, the central point of interest is in how dense or how concentrated the population is. The reason for this is simple: large cities may have low density, as it is possible for small communities to have high density. If the unit of analysis is some spatial area, such as a census tract, its density may be a more crucial variable affecting behavior than the absolute size of the population.

Within the ecological framework, pathology is any phenomenon that reduces the adaptivity or survival potential of the community (Choldin, 1978). It is in this context that ecologists ask such questions as: Does high density housing adversely affect the health of workers, influencing the sustenance activities of the community as a whole? Does high density living increase crime, which may be expensive and disruptive to the community? Does high density affect mental health or produce high levels of delinquency, two other possible costs to a community's ability to adapt and survive?

In examining the connection between density and social pathology, those using the ecological approach have looked at a breadth of outcomes which could be detrimental to communities. These include: the death rate, infant mortality, perinatal mortality, accidental deaths, rate of suicide, tuberculosis, venereal disease rates, rate of mental hospitalization, birth rate, illegitimate birth rate, juvenile delinquency, imprisonment rate, various crime rates, public welfare, hospital admissions, and the divorce rate. Typically, these are aggregated into rates for neighborhoods or some other areal unit (Choldin, 1978).

Early ecological studies were typically correlational, often reporting moderate relationships between measures of population density and one or more of the above pathologies. For example, Faris and Dunham (1939), in what is now considered a classic piece of ecological research, used such an analysis in examining the distribution and incidence of mental and nervous disorders in Chicago. In general, their findings revealed that the incidence of schizophrenia, alcoholic psychoses, and drug addiction was much higher in the slum area, the most densely populated section of the city, and tended to decline from the city center to the peripheral areas. Patterns of suicide, crime rates, and illegitimacy showed similar variations.

The early documentation of a link between population density and different forms of social pathology has not gone without challenge. While it is sometimes permissible to make inferences about individual behavior from aggregate data (Firebaugh, 1978; Hammond, 1973; Hanushek, Jackson, and Kain, 1974), in practice it is difficult to know whether all necessary conditions have been met to make such inferences, the result being the commission of the ecological fallacy. Furthermore, the conclusion that density was harmful to human well-being was based on simple correlational techniques which did not separate the effects of other factors. While the area of cities with the most pathology were dense and crowded, they were also the areas with the most poverty and heterogeneous populations, such as recent migrants. It was not until the 1960s that multivariate analysis came into use and researchers had the ability to extricate the independent effect of density from those of poverty and minority status (Choldin, 1978).

In using these multivariate techniques, the results of more contemporary studies have been highly inconsistent. A number of investigators, for instance, report finding no relationship between density and mortality, at least when other confounding factors are controlled (Newsom, 1973; Choldin and Roncek, 1976). In one study an unexpected negative relationship concerning mortality is observed (Winsborough, 1965), while another notes a significant positive relationship, net of the influence of socioeconomic status (Schmitt, 1966). A similar mixture of results pertains to juvenile delinquency, crime rates, and infant mortality (Choldin, 1978). After controlling for social structural factors, the one consistent result reported in the literature is a positive relationship between density and rates of mental illness, as measured by admissions to mental hospitals. In using cities as the unit of analysis, however, most studies find no relationship between density levels and the incidence of pathology (Choldin, 1978), leading some to question what is the proper unit of analysis in determining areal density.

As Choldin (1978) points out, most ecological studies have used intraurban density measures, but they have been deficient in relying on overly large units of analysis. The use of census tracts and even larger subareas within a city may obscure the actual influence spatial factors may have on the generation of pathology. Within a given census tract, there may be a mixture of housing types, such as apartments and single-family dwellings. There may be considerable variation in the age and racial composition of the population. Household composition can vary greatly. Cities may be even more unsuitable as the unit of analysis, although they are appealing to ecological researchers because they approximate whole communities. Many cities, however, contain within their official boundaries large tracts of undeveloped land. Any gross density measures will underestimate the effective density of the built-up part of the city. Since cities vary in the amount of undeveloped land they claim, city-to-city comparisons can be misleading.

One of the most thorough ecological assessments of the density-pathology relationship relies on Chicago as a natural laboratory, the site of early ecological research. Galle and his associates (1972, 1979) examined five manifestations of pathology across 74 community areas: mortality, fertility, the rate of juvenile delinquency, the public assistance rate, and mental hospital admissions. They decomposed ground-level density into two dimensions. The one they call "structural press" (e.g. housing units per structure, residential units per square mile) and the other "interpersonal press" (e.g. persons per room, rooms per housing unit). While their 1972 study was cross-sectional in design, their

1979 analysis looked at data for four different time periods (1940, 1950, 1960, 1970).

The overall results of the two studies were quite similar. In their own words, they state: "our analyses of aggregate data from Chicago show that (a) there are very likely some effects of crowding; (b) collinearity between crowding and socioeconomic status and race is so strong at the aggregate level that it is impossible to separate the crowding effects from the social-structural effects, and so one cannot determine with these types of data how important crowding is as a variable; and (c) the problem of collinearity probably is a major reason why other investigators using aggregate data have come up with inconsistent results" (Gove and Hughes, 1983: 37-38). Elsewhere, they suggest: "After all, it is fairly reasonable that poor people, who cannot afford better housing arrangements, are much more likely to be found living in highly crowded conditions. This ... may appear to be trivially obvious to many, but the strength of this finding over alternatives--density as a major cause of pathological behavior or social structure as a major cause--needs to be stressed.... The best we can say at this point is that much more information is needed, information that can be gained only from data more suitable for answering those kinds of questions" (Galle and Gove, 1979:25, 27).

It is precisely this impasse in concluding anything about the density-pathology issue that led researchers to take a different approach to the question, resulting in other traditions of inquiry as to how crowding affects human behavior. Psychology was one discipline to take up this challenge.

The Psychological Tradition

Psychology, of course, focuses on the individual, in the main centering on intrapsychic phenomena and behavioral predispositions. However, much of the psychological research on crowding has incorporated various behavioral measures into their design, in particular looking at the effects of density on interaction patterns and task performance.

Many of the initial psychological studies of crowding were experimental in nature. They involved putting a given number of volunteer subjects into a small or large room (or sometimes groups of different sizes in the same amount of space) and then measuring some outcome. Often the outcomes of interest were physiological responses, engaging in affiliative behaviors (e.g., subjects looking at each other or positive head nodding), mood states, and task abilities (Baum and Epstein, 1978). Two general conclusions emerged from this research: (1) people in cramped spaces expressed a sense of discomfort and otherwise evinced negative mood states and (2) they performed less well in completing complex tasks, but there was no association between density and performance ability involving simple tasks. Many studies, however, failed to find that density--in the objective sense of that term--had any harmful effects (Freedman, 1975).

A major advantage of the laboratory experiment is the ability to manipulate or control the variables of interest--in this instance, the number of people in a finite amount of space. What was overlooked in early experiments were possible intervening processes which had not been controlled and could mediate any crowding effect. Later experiments took such mediating factors into account and began to make a clear distinction between crowding as a physical variable and crowding as an emotional response (Stokols, 1972). The weight of the evidence showed that, as a physical variable, crowding had few, if any, effects (Freedman, 1975). Even the consequences of feeling crowded, it generally was concluded, were highly conditional or situational. Among other things, the impact of crowding depended upon the individual's coping abilities, prior history with crowding, the relationship with others in the group (friends or strangers), the attributions made to the situation by the subject, and the amount of control he or she had over the situation (Baum and Epstein, 1978).

One of the striking features of laboratory experiments is their artificiality, consisting of contrived settings far removed from the "real world." Virtually all experiments are short-term and the subjects are free to terminate their participation at any time. All of these features mitigate against being able to produce the crowding effects that may characterize real-life situations, and even to generalize to them should any such effects be found. It was perhaps for this reason that environmental psychologists increasingly turned to naturalistic settings in carrying out crowding research.

A wide variety of settings have been explored. Field studies have been conducted in such settings as dormitories, housing projects, naval vessels, train stations, stores, offshore oil-drilling platforms, and prisons (Aiello, Epstein, and Karling, 1975; McCarthy and Saegert, 1979; Dean, Pugh, and Gunderson, 1975; MacKintosh, West, and Saegert, 1975; Langer and Saegert, 1977; and Cox, Paulus, McCain, and Schkade, 1979). Generally, the field studies have yielded results indicating that crowding can have adverse effects. It has been found, for example, that crowding in dormitories and housing projects produces negative affect and social withdrawal (Aiello et al., 1975; Valins and Baum, 1973). There are increased illness complaints on crowded naval ships (Dean et al., 1975). In congested stores and train stations, cognitive functioning is disrupted (Langer and Saegert, 1977; MacKintosh et al., 1975). Crowding in prisons can increase physiological signs of stress and elevate blood pressure levels (Cox et al., 1979; D'Arti, 1975). Residential crowding leads to arousal, feelings of discomfort, and a state of stress (Jain, 1987).

Since the external validity of laboratory research is in question, the *in vivo* character of field studies represents a distinct advantage. They, at least, deal with people in natural settings. Still, as Baldassare (1979) points out, field studies have their disadvantages as well. When people know they are being observed, they may alter their behavior in some ways. There is, too, a question as to their generalizability inasmuch as most field studies deal with only one or two settings. Most critically, though, many such studies are not as naturalistic as they are represented to be. It is often impossible to observe "normal" people in their everyday settings and, as a result, most field studies are concerned with populations that have unusual characteristics (e.g., college students, criminals, mental patients, and individuals in unusual occupational circumstances, such as sailors and oil-rig workers). In short, such studies may be too unrepresentative to yield valid and generalizable data.

Psychological research, however, has contributed significantly to our understanding of crowding as a cognitive process. A common thread running through this body of investigation, both the experiments and the field studies, is that people react to their environments, and the responses people have to their physical surroundings are often complex in nature.

The shortcomings, as well as the contributions, of psychological research alert us to the need to examine individuals in a representative range of natural settings, such as their residence, and to take into account, conceptually and methodologically, the reactions people have to their structural circumstances. This is precisely what research cast in a social psychological vein has done.

The Social Psychological Approach

Drawing on Simmel's contention (1905) that dense circumstances lead to an "overloading" of an individual's nervous system, the social psychological approach--like the psychological tradition--takes the individual as the primary unit of analysis. However, in contradistinction to this latter tradition, which is most interested in the intrapsychic outcomes of crowding, the social psychological approach looks at intrapsychic phenomena as being intervening mechanisms in how structural features of an environment can affect one's behavior. What psychology looks at as central dependent variables, social psychology views as intermediate steps in a causal chain, with behavioral outcomes constituting the end point of that chain.

Many of the studies using the social psychological approach date from the 1970s, although earlier ones can be found that would qualify as a part of this research tradition (Riemer, 1945; Loring, 1956). In large measure, it would seem, social psychological studies were a reaction to the deficiencies of ecological research and reflect the direction the discipline of sociology was then taking. A major concern among sociologists centered around the problem posed by the ecological fallacy and a lack of consensus among ecological researchers as to how areal density should be measured. Regardless of the motivation, the result was that researchers increasingly turned to the household as a more proximate context of crowding, and they increasingly eschewed the examination of aggregate data, relying instead on self-reports made by individuals.

Implicitly or explicitly, social psychological studies of household crowding using individual reports are largely based on a stress model. This model posits that the effects of crowding are mediated by psychological stress or some closely related phenomenon, such as felt demands (Booth, 1976; Gove and Hughes, 1983). Theoretically, congested conditions are viewed as creating the necessity to interact with others present. As the sources and frequency of interaction multiply, stress or the expressed demands on an individual intensifies. As stress escalates, it becomes manifested in a person's behavior and possible aberrant responses to others present. It is assumed (there being some documentation for the assumption -- cf. Sherrod and Cohen, 1979) that while coping behaviors will alleviate stress in the short-term, sustained stressful conditions ultimately will result in some form of pathological reaction. Because the household is a place where people spend a great deal of time and a place to which they habitually return, the household may constitute a source of chronic stress. From a social psychological point of view, crowded households are the most proximate cause of any observed pathological behaviors.

As the case with investigators working out of the other research traditions, social psychological researchers have examined a wide range of potential pathological outcomes, including mental illness and strain, disturbances in marital relations, physical illness, breakdowns in parent-child relationships, conflict inside and outside the home, and problems associated with sex and reproduction.

While most of the social psychologically-oriented research has been conducted in Europe and North America, a few such studies have been carried out elsewhere. For example, Marsella and associates (1970) investigated the effect of dwelling density on the mental health of a small sample of Filipino men (N = 99). Examining a broad array of mental-health measures, they found three indicators to be associated with overcrowded household conditions. A study in Singapore (N = 121 families) also observed a positive relationship between household crowding and "worrying" and stress (Hassen, 1977a, b). This was compounded when the housing unit was shared with non-family members and when the unit was located on higher floors, both of which had negative effects on emotional well-being. In this study, overcrowding was also noted to weaken the control parents had over their children and to adversely affect the academic performance of children. Overcrowding, Hassen concluded (1977b), created the conditions whereby juveniles were more likely to engage in delinquent behaviors. Both of these studies, it should be noted, were based on small samples and they additionally suffer from a lack of controls, which potentially could cause the observed outcomes.

However, a Hong Kong study, with a much larger sample size, came to the same conclusion with regard to the parent-child relationship and the effect that dwelling density has on the supervision of children (Mitchell, 1971). High-density housing, Mitchell found, encourages children to leave the household, reducing the parents' knowledge of and control they have over their children. Although housing conditions had no apparent effect on husband-wife interaction, they were related to some less severe manifestations of emotional strain, worrying and being unhappy, and they discouraged interaction with neighbors and friends. One of the strongest effects Mitchell found was in the amount of stress people felt when there was a doubling-up arrangement among non-related households and when the dwelling unit was situated on an upper floor in a multistory building. The combination of these two conditions, Mitchell concluded, was particularly deleterious to the emotional health of individuals.

Somewhat similar conclusions were reached in an investigation of Parisian households (Chombart de Lauwe, 1961). In crowded dwellings, "tensions" were noted between mothers and children and parents reported more frequent child misbehavior, implying that overcrowding may result in less parental supervision. Having too little floor space per person was also associated with family discord.

This last conclusion is echoed in an Italian study, where it was found that both the number of persons per room and square meters per couple were associated with a higher frequency of quarreling (Gasparini, 1973). The more husband-wife quarrels increased, the more inadequate they viewed their dwelling, suggesting a subjective component in how crowding may affect family behavior. In common with some of the former investigations, Gasparini found crowding to have an effect on children, in this case having to do with how nervous they felt and how well the children performed in school.

A study by Baldassare (1979) enjoys the distinction of being based on national surveys. It draws on the Quality of Life Survey and several cycles of the continuous national survey conducted by the National Opinion Research Center, using persons per room as its central crowding measure (part of the analysis deals with neighborhood density). Among other things, Baldassare reports that household crowding is associated with housing dissatisfaction, the desire to move, an index of poor marital relations, and lower overall satisfaction with family life. In general, though, Baldassare views these findings very tentatively and as providing limited support for the crowding-pathology hypothesis. It is his contention that various social and personal adjustments serve to reduce the adverse effects of crowding, with some subgroups being less able to reduce the effects than others. The most vulnerable persons, he suggests, are ones of middle to older age, in poor health, having few economic resources, and suffering from psychological problems.

Baldassare is properly tentative about the findings from these national surveys. Because the surveys were not specifically designed to examine the issue of crowding effects, many of the measures relied on are far from optimal, especially those used as dependent variables. Many of them are simply single-item indicators. In trying to assess the impact of subjective crowding, which was found to be unrelated to most of the potential outcomes inspected, the surveys each contained only one item. In the one case, the item asked about the shortage of rooms, and in the other survey the reference was to a shortage of space within rooms. As we will see momentarily, other investigations are based on more highly sophisticated measures tapping both independent and dependent variables.

Two other large-scale studies of relevance here are ones that were specifically designed to investigate the effects of household crowding. Both were conducted in North America, the one in Toronto and the other in Chicago (Booth, 1976; Gove and Hughes, 1983), and both are informed by the social psychological stress model mentioned earlier. Inasmuch as each of these studies serves as a major point of reference for the present study, a bit of background is in order. Specific findings from the two studies will be discussed later in the relevant chapters.

The Toronto investigation involved a sample of 552 wives and 344 husbands drawn from 13 of the more densely populated census tracts in the city. The stratified multiple-stage probability sample was designed to yield a sample in which the number of people exceeded the total number of rooms in their dwellings. Close to half of the sample (48 percent) lived in situations where the number of family members exceeded the number of rooms (Booth, 1976).

Conceptually, the study distinguished between four different dimensions of crowding: objective household congestion, subjective household crowding, and objective and subjective neighborhood crowding. Elaborate procedures were undertaken to develop reliable measures of these four dimensions. In response to the deficiencies of many studies preceding it, the analyses of the Toronto study incorporated systematic controls for sex, age, education, ethnic origin, and the husband's occupation. Specific tests were made to determine whether a series of stressors intensified the effect of crowding.

As a departure from many prior investigations, multiple dependent variables were examined as potential manifestations of pathology. These included: aspects of family relations, adult health, sexual relations and reproduction, child health and development, community life, and aggressive political activity. Altogether, 344 relationships were analyzed, of which 14 percent (48) were statistically significant. Of the latter, 33 of the 48 pertained to the impact of household crowding, the remainder having to do with neighborhood crowding. Most of the significant relationships concerning household crowding (21 of the 33) involved the inhabitants' perceptions of their conditions and not their objective circumstances.

Among the study's general findings were the following (Booth, 1976:103):

1. In general, objectively crowded household and neighborhood conditions have no adverse effect on the adult inhabitants.
2. Objective household crowding has small adverse effects on child health and physical and intellectual development.
3. When adverse effects are found, they are small but persist regard less of the housing type (high rise, row house, single family, and so on).
4. Where crowding has adverse effects, they are generally caused by congested household conditions and not compressed neighborhood conditions.
5. The feeling of being crowded is not always related to actual conditions. Some feel crowded who are not, by external standards, and others, living in very compressed conditions, often do not feel crowded.
6. Crowded conditions occasionally have greater adverse effects when people are already under stress due to low income or other problems.
7. Childhood experience with crowding sometimes facilitates adult adaptation to current crowded conditions.

As Booth (1976:103), the principal investigator, put it: "We ... find congested conditions are not particularly stressful." He (1976:104) further concludes that: "The minute effects of crowding revealed in our analysis indicate that we have a great deal of flexibility in housing people in dense environments. We can continue to house people in densely populated areas without fear that it will result in significant personal disorganization and decrements in the health of the inhabitants."

This is a conclusion diametrically opposed to that arrived at in the Chicago study. The Chicago study was conducted contemporaneously with the Toronto project, involving interviews with 25 people in each of the 80 selected census tracts within the city limits. The tracts were chosen to minimize collinearity between socioeconomic status, race, and crowding. This resulted in the selection of four different types of tracts: (1) those with low levels of socioeconomic status and low levels of crowding, (2) lower socioeconomic tracts with high levels of crowding, (3) tracts with high socioeconomic status and low crowding, and (4) those with high socioeconomic status and high levels of crowding. In all, 2035 men and women were interviewed, 22 percent of whom lived alone (Gove and Hughes, 1983).

As in the Toronto study, a distinction was made between objective and subjective crowding, the latter involving two scales designed to capture the experience of feeling crowded. Persons per room serves as the objective indicator of crowding. Reflective of the notion that crowding manifests itself in an overload of disruptive social demands and intrusions into one's privacy, the scales of subjective crowding concern felt demands and a lack of privacy. Felt demands and a lack of privacy are viewed as intervening between the objective situation and the reactions to crowding, as manifested in certain psychological and social outcomes (Gove and Hughes, 1983).

The Chicago study also examined a broad range of possible outcomes that might be interpreted as pathological in character. These included: physical and psychological withdrawal, ineffectual planning behavior, the impact on mental health, social relations of various sorts, child care, physical illness, and some aspects of sex and reproduction.

On the basis of their analysis, Gove and Hughes (1983:223) conclude:

> We found that for the overall sample the effects of crowding were very strongly related to a number of direct responses to crowding, ranging from physical withdrawal from the home to psychological withdrawal in the home (where the person consciously ignored others), to a lack of planning, and to feeling physically and psychologically drained. Crowding was also found to be strongly related to poor mental health, to having poor social relationships in the home, to a number of aspects of poor child care, to an inability to adopt the sick role, and to being dissatisfied with one's home. Crowding had some effects on reducing the frequency of sexual intercourse, was related to some extent to the ineffective use of birth control, and was probably related to having a miscarriage or abortion.... The effects of crowding as measured by persons per room tended to be largely explained or interpreted by the experience of excessive demands and lack of privacy--particularly with regard to poor mental health, poor social relationships in the home, and poor physical health, all areas where the effects of crowding tend to be

particularly strong.... Our analysis showed (with the exception of social relations outside the home) that the experience of crowding, on the average, independently explained almost as much variance in the dependent variable as was independently explained by the combined effects of the six control variables (sex, ethnicity, marital status, education, family income, and age). In short, our analysis showed crowding in the home to be a variable of significant substantive importance.

There ensued what for academics was a lively debate (Gove and Hughes, 1980a, b; Booth, Johnson, and Edwards, 1980a, b). The questions raised, charges and counter-charges made, centered around several issues. Among the points of contention were issues of conceptualization, sampling problems, questions of measurement, problems of analysis, and, most crucially, matters of interpretation. For details, the reader is referred to the exchange between the respective research teams.

Booth and associates and Gove and associates, in spite of their differences, do agree on a few things: (1) it is important to distinguish between, and adequately measure, objective and subjective crowding; and (2) the size of the crowding effects observed in the two studies are very comparable. This latter point of consensus, in our view, is most troublesome, for if the magnitude of effects are quite similar, how can one come to such diametrically opposed conclusions about the consequences of crowding? Unfortunately, we have neither a theoretical rationale nor any statistical guidelines for accepting whether an observed effect is strong, modest, or weak. At bottom, these are matters of interpretation, which may be influenced by our training, experience, or preconceptions.

It is noteworthy, nevertheless, that both studies found statistically significant relationships between crowding, whether as objectively or subjectively measured, and the various outcomes examined. We say this because there is one major and fundamental difficulty in interpreting the results of prior studies, let alone being able to apply them to other settings. And this goes to the crux of the issue raised in this debate about the problem of adequately sampling a population in order to detect the impact of crowding. Currently, European and North American densities, and especially the level of household crowding, are relatively low by world standards. Persons per room in North America is 0.5 (Gove and Hughes, 1983), hardly what most people would consider very crowded conditions. The level of household crowding is somewhat higher in Europe, hovering in the range of 0.6 to 0.8, depending on the specific country (United Nations, 1985). Again, these are hardly what we would think to be highly crowded circumstances. To be able to detect any crowding effects in these situations is rather remarkable, but it makes it more understandable why there may be disagreement about the strength of the impact that crowding has.

A more adequate test of the crowding-pathology hypothesis requires a setting where crowding is more intense and a setting that is more typical of the housing situation of most people around the world. That is to be found in Asia, where the levels of household crowding reach three to four times the levels prevailing in Europe and North America. This issue of sample adequacy served as a major impetus for undertaking the present study and was a prime consideration in the selection of Bangkok as a research site.

The Bangkok Study

Guided by the stress model, which is at the core of the social psychological approach to crowding, we have sought to extend, and elaborate on, the Toronto and Chicago studies. The stress model, as indicated in our introduction, suggests the following two hypotheses:

H1:   Ceteris paribus, the higher the level of household crowding, the greater the amount of stress experienced.

H2: The greater the amount of stress experienced, the higher the incidence of adverse outcomes.

This constitutes, of course, a highly restricted model, for there are numerous known and theoretically relevant effects that influence each of the model's components. Socioeconomic level, for example, is one of the more powerful predictors affecting a host of social phenomena, not the least of which is housing. People with less education and income are notoriously disadvantaged in housing markets, being disproportionately restricted to more cramped dwellings and housing with fewer amenities (lower liveability). Such subgroups also are characterized by larger family size, which contributes to objective crowding and is likely to affect the perception of crowding. Likewise, socioeconomic status generally is inversely related to physical health (Cockerman, 1986). Not only do lower status individuals have shorter life spans but they tend to contract infectious diseases more frequently, perhaps due in part to their more congested living circumstances. Compounding this, they are likely to have less accessibility to adequate health care facilities or the means to afford such. Indirectly if not directly, socioeconomic status also is likely to influence the individual's ability to manage their home environment. With fewer available resources, lower socioeconomic persons are less apt to have the education or financial means for coping with the problems in a dense home situation. This may be further accentuated by large family size. Young children are often noisy and disruptive, and their activities are frequently unpredictable, adding to the difficulties of adjusting to congested settings (Rodin and Baum, 1978; Sherrod and Cohen, 1979; Baldassare, 1979).

A lack of statistical control for socioeconomic effects has been one of the major deficiencies of crowding investigations conducted outside of North America, and it is something we routinely take into account in all of our later analyses, in addition to introducing numerous other controls in order to isolate the unique impact household crowding may have.

While prior studies have not found a very high correlation between objective measures of crowding and subjective crowding (Booth, 1976), it is reasonable, with some qualifications, to expect a positive relationship between them. It is highly improbable that a setting will be viewed as crowded unless there is some degree of objective crowding present. Part of the imperfect correlation between objective and subjective crowding may be due to variations in space demands (Booth, 1976). Small children do not require the same amount of space as adults; nor do married couples have the same requirements as two unrelated adults. Furthermore, room needs are not likely to be proportional to the number of people added. Whereas a three-room dwelling may meet the needs of a couple with no children, it does not follow that nine rooms would be required if they had four children (the number of rooms needed to hold constant the number of persons per room). Thus, we can expect a positive association between objective crowding and the perception of crowding, albeit an imperfect one. We would anticipate, moreover, that objective levels of crowding will negatively influence a dwelling's liveability. This is to say, highly congested homes are likely to be seen as less desirable places to live and less preferable places in which to rear children. As a result, perceived crowding may be affected indirectly (through dwelling liveability or housing satisfaction) as well as directly.

To provide continuity with prior research, we adapt measures of subjective crowding from the Toronto and Chicago studies. Subjective crowding is anticipated to relate positively to stress. The higher the level of perceived crowding, the higher the level of stress experienced. Virtually every social psychological study suggests this or some closely related phenomenon to be a crucial linkage in explaining pathological behaviors (Altman, 1975; Booth, 1976; Desor, 1972; Gove, et al., 1979; Levi and Anderson, 1975; Milgram, 1970; Stokols, 1972). Most studies, however, have left stress unmeasured, the Toronto and Chicago studies being exceptions to the rule. As discussed in the next chapter, we attempt to directly measure stress in two different ways. We further hypothesize another direct relationship that is likely to affect stress levels. As

Baldassare (1981) has shown, people do vary in their abilities to adjust to high density in primary environments, those who are relatively powerless being less able to cope with and manipulate that environment. We expect that some individuals will exercise less household control, thus further elevating their stress levels and accentuating the crowding effects.

The general model suggests, at the same time, a direct and positive relationship between felt stress and disturbed family relations. Past research has emphasized the crucial importance of an optimal level of stimuli in order for persons to engage in effective behavior. Any excess stimuli tend to produce problematic behaviors (Altman, 1975; Desor, 1972; Booth, 1976; Gove and Hughes, 1983; Welford, 1974). While all social situations entail some degree of stress, our anticipation was that it would reach particularly high levels under congested conditions. In the home environment, for example, contact between persons is inevitable, interaction is difficult to avoid, and one's activities are easily observable. Because of the relative intimacy involved in family life, evaluations of one's behavior on the part of others are likely to be a more continuous part of one's daily round of activities. Hence, insofar as elevated stress levels are likely to interfere with the "normal" course of interaction, higher levels of conflict between family members would be expected. In particular, such conflict would be manifested between husband and wife, between parents and children, and, perhaps to a lesser extent, between the primary family and other members of the household (an older generation, other relatives, or unrelated occupants). Across all categories in highly crowded conditions, qualitative assessments of relations are expected to be poorer, arguments more frequent, feelings of affect lower, physically aggressive behavior more prevalent, and child care less effectual.

In addition to the focus on family relations, stress-related, psychological problems and physical disorders are treated as dependent variables. As numerous studies have documented (Cockerman, 1986), stress is a significant impetus in physiological change. In particular, stress can lead to the development of hypertension, peptic ulcers, muscular pain, compulsive vomiting, asthma, migraine headaches, and reports of angina (Moss, 1973).

Finally, as was done in the Toronto and Chicago research, we look at the potential effects crowding may have on the sexual relations between husbands and wives, and examine its impact on several aspects of their reproductive behavior.

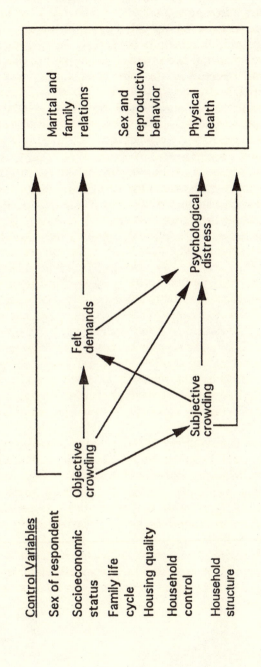

Figure 2.1 Causal Ordering of Theoretical Variables

The full model, including all hypothesized direct relationships, is diagrammatically shown in Figure 2.1.

In addition to the relationships suggested in Figure 2.1, there is ample reason to expect that some interaction effects may be observed. Prior crowding studies have found, or alluded to, the multiplicative effects of gender and household structure. Where it is appropriate, we test for these effects in our analyses.

Before we proceed to those analyses, there are several methodological and measurement issues to be considered. Because of the profoundly different cultural context of Thailand as compared to North America, it was plain at the outset that, despite our desire to replicate and extend past research, it would not do to merely translate previously used interview items. The process of developing valid and reliable indicators, even though we had numerous North American examples to draw on, was far more complicated than that. It involved many fits and starts, advances and subsequent retreats. We detail these in the next chapter.

3

A Research Odyssey:
Methodological Considerations

Every research project, as Hillery (1982:xi) points out, is in reality an odyssey. Although one may have a definite destination, getting there usually involves the unexpected. It often involves many twists and turns, fits and starts. A project has a natural history, not necessarily proceeding "as it might or as it should, or even as it could, but as it did." Such is our case. Much of this had to do with methodological issues.

The primary objective of this study was to test the aforementioned model of crowding effects, a model derived mainly from the findings of prior studies conducted in North America. As we have mentioned, one of the fundamental difficulties in interpreting and extrapolating these findings to other societies stems from the fact that household crowding in North America is atypically low by world standards. For this reason we chose an Asian city, Bangkok, that more closely typifies the housing situation existing elsewhere in the world.

Bangkok is a striking example of a primate city. Its population, as recently as 1960 numbering 1.8 million, now exceeds six million people. As the center of commerce, finance, manufacturing, and trade, Bangkok dominates the entire economic fabric of the country, as indeed it dominates in nearly every sphere of Thai culture--whether it be political, religious, or educational. Bangkok's primacy is illustrated by the fact that its population is more than 50 times as large as Thailand's second largest city (Sternstein, 1984). Over 60 percent of the national urban population of Thailand resides in Bangkok (Fuller, 1990a). Most importantly, for our purposes, families in Bangkok experience, in an objective sense, a high level of household crowding. The average number of persons per room is 2.1 versus 0.5 persons per room found in North America. According to the most recent available data, household crowding in Bangkok exceeds that of Hong Kong, a city commonly characterized as the most crowded in the world (United Nations, 1985).

Doing research in a country other than one's own is fraught with difficulties one does not normally encounter. Clearly, one of the first issues that must be confronted is the relevance of one's hypotheses and whether there are cultural equivalents of one's conceptualization of a research problem. There was the initial question, in short, as to whether Asians and Westerners react to crowding in a similar manner. While, on the one hand, Bangkok seemed to be an ideal research site because of its high level of household crowding, there is the contention that Asians are indifferent to, or actually prefer, crowded living conditions (Loo and Ong, 1984). Does the concept of crowding have any meaning to Thais? Is the notion of privacy, so highly valued by Westerners, relevant? Furthermore, it was not clear at the outset, even should these concepts have relevance, exactly how this might be manifested in the behavior of household members. What sorts of behavior do Thais find irritating or to violate some family norm? Obviously, a creative strategy was required.

To develop meaningful measures of the relevant concepts, we used focus group interviews, a qualitative research technique relatively uncommon in sociological research. This was a crucial preparatory step in designing a survey interview schedule we administered at a later date.

The Focus Group Interviews

Focus group interviews, as the name suggests, involve group discussions focused on a particular topic of interest. Focus group interviews have several typical characteristics. The groups are assembled for the purpose of conducting a group discussion on a particular topic, or a closely related set of topics. The groups generally are fairly small (e.g., 6 to 8 persons), and ideally they are comprised of individuals who do not know each other. The members of any given group are relatively homogeneous in terms of characteristics that the researcher believes are important with respect to the topics to be discussed. A moderator usually follows a discussion guide prepared by the researcher, in order to focus the discussion on the topics of interest. In the best of circumstances, the moderator stimulates a genuine discussion among the members of the group, rather than simply sequentially questioning the individual members of the group (Morgan, 1988; Krueger, 1989).

Because of our interest in household crowding, we recruited individuals for the focus groups primarily from lower income, more crowded households. We felt we could probe such issues as privacy, family conflict, and felt demands more easily with individuals living in relatively high levels of household crowding. Although the actual level of household crowding was allowed to vary, all focus group members were recruited from Bangkok slums and lower-class flats. There were usually eight members for each group, and a detailed discussion guide was prepared for the native Thai moderators.

Of particular importance was our decision concerning the ways in which group members should be "homogeneous." The topics of interest we wished to explore included the central concepts from our theoretical model, such as subjective crowding, lack of privacy, norms about family interaction, family conflict, and felt demands. We anticipated that men and women might have different needs for privacy, different reactions to crowding, or different levels of felt demands; that perceptions of crowding and problems associated with crowding could vary by level of household crowding; and that issues of crowding and privacy might weigh more heavily on members of extended families than on persons living in the context of a nuclear family. Thus, gender, level of household crowding (high or low), and household type (nuclear or extended) became the defining characteristics for the focus groups. These three dichotomies defined eight types of focus groups. One focus group interview was conducted with each type of group.

Since ethnic Chinese comprise about 10 percent of Bangkok's population, two additional focus groups were formed involving only those with a Chinese background. The one group was comprised of men, the other of women. This enabled us to explore whether there were significant differences that might be necessary to take into account in selecting a representative sample, constructing the survey instrument, and in the subsequent analyses of the survey data. There has been a great deal of discussion concerning ethnic differences in the reaction to crowding (Hall, 1969), and Gove and Hughes (1983) have presented some evidence that, in American society, blacks are more reactive to crowding than are whites, with Hispanics being the least reactive. But we discovered, in the analysis of the focus group discussions, there were few meaningful distinctions between the ethnic Chinese volunteers and native Thai group members. In terms of the discussions about the crowding experience, the reactions to that experience, and their family relations, there were only minor differences between the two groups.

The interviews proved to be invaluable in suggesting the relevancy of the concepts in our theoretical model. A major concern at the outset of the project was the meaning of crowding in the Thai context. Thais have a history of crowding, even in rural areas, and appear to be a very placid people in the face of all sorts of travails. Despite high objective levels of crowding, could it be that Thai don't feel crowded? Or, even if they feel crowded, could there be some cultural norm that would prevent its expression? The focus group discussions quickly dispelled these questions. Consider these excerpts:

Moderator: "Do you think a parents' personal room is a necessary one?"

Prasert: "It's necessary indeed, if we can afford one."

Michao: "I think every family would like that. To have parents' own room would make lives easier, more comfortable."

* * * * *

Soomrouy: "Sometimes I think that with the children growing up ... very soon we'll have the problem of sleeping space. We can't have them sleep together when they are grown up. Each must have a separate sleeping space. It's certainly going to be crowded..."

* * * * *

Somsak: "Our own kids also grow up. Now, there seems to be a problem of crowdedness. The children grow up like big trees, and big trees can't stay in a small house."

* * * * *

Moderator: "When the kids grow up, how does this become a problem for the family?"

Manas: "Living space problem is first. The bedroom is too small for grown up children. Suppose you have four kids, the bedroom is alright when they are under 10, but once they grow over that age, they need more rooms. The ideal number of children should be two, but you just can't always strictly control that and more come. Then, we have problem when they grow up, particularly the toilet. We have only one toilet, toilet-jam every morning."

* * * * *

Supatra: "In my house, there are 15 people. But if you ask about personal room, we have one, but the privacy is a rather relative matter. We don't have a total privacy in a house with these many people. When I want to be alone, I must go into my room and lock the door. And I mean lock it!"

While it appears that Thais are relatively well adjusted to a level of crowding that would be intolerable for most North Americans, it is clear from the accounts above that Thais are not content with high levels of household crowding and feel that the high level of crowding often experienced reduces their privacy. We found clear evidence of attempts to reduce the level of crowding and increase privacy. Although these efforts are often constrained by various circumstances, people in small dwelling units frequently subdivide their floor space, sometimes in the vertical dimension, in order to reduce crowding and increase privacy.

The Thai notion of modesty requires that a married couple have at least some measure of privacy for sexual relations. Also, there is strong feeling that teenage daughters require a high degree of privacy for sleeping, dressing, and applying make-up. In order to enhance the sense of privacy, rooms are often partitioned so that individuals, couples, or other subfamily groups can have some measure of privacy. Partitions often consist of wood, furniture, or blankets. Even mosquito netting can serve the dual purpose of preserving privacy while protecting sleepers from mosquito bites, a persistent problem in a tropical climate.

In slum households, it is not uncommon to find that lofts have been constructed to provide additional sleeping space. These lofts, suspended about one meter from the ceiling, are regarded as somewhat unpleasant because one can neither stand nor sit on them, and they tend to be rather stuffy. Nevertheless, by increasing the amount of sleeping space, these lofts maximize the use of space and reduce the number of people who have to sleep on the floor.

During waking hours, there is usually a fairly high level of activity and noise in households, particularly in those households with some type of economic activity. The noise, activity, and constant conversation may be more welcome to most Thais than it would to most Americans. It is said that if a Thai is alone, that person is lonely, and the assumption is it is therefore good to join the individual and strike up a conversation.

Although high activity levels and noise may not be bothersome to most Thais, several focus group participants mentioned that they would sometimes leave the household in order to relax. One focus group participant mentioned that he would sometimes go out and ride the bus simply to relax. Buses in Bangkok are often extremely crowded, sometimes having standing room only.

From the focus groups we found evidence that a high level of crowding may contribute to conflict in Thai households. In spite of an initial impression of Thais as being placid and unperturbed, it was not uncommon for the focus group participants to mention arguments and physical violence as occurring between household members. Specifically, there were numerous reports of arguments and of family members hitting or kicking each other, or hurling objects at each other. There were even reports of stabbings. Since most of our focus group participants were from relatively crowded households, these reports of conflict are consistent with the hypothesis that high levels of household crowding lead to conflict among family members.

With respect to felt demands, it was generally the case that wives, rather than husbands, tended to feel that more demands were placed on them by other family members. Husbands were not exempt from demands of other family members, but they seemed to be shielded from the demands of their spouses and children to a greater extent than was true of their wives. Moreover, in extended families, it was evident that to be a son-in-law or daughter-in-law is a disadvantaged position. It is a position that appears to be very stressful precisely because the individual has little control over what takes place in the household.

Focus group interviews, of course, are not amenable to the verification of research hypotheses. But in this case, they were very valuable in establishing the cultural relevance of our notions of crowding and some of the effects it might have. The interviews were of value in another way, and this concerns the construction of the survey instrument we would later use.

Meaning is embedded in language, and the specific questions to be asked and the precise wording of the interview schedule was of critical importance in being able to elicit the information we sought. As in English, in Thai a given word may have more than one meaning, and in other cases there may be different words to refer to the same phenomena. The problem of meaning is further compounded by the fact that there are differences in the vocabularies and the use of words by people of varying educational attainment and social class. Many of the people who were likely to be a part of our survey sample, we knew, would have relatively low levels of formal education. While we did not want to simply take a questionnaire that had previously been used in crowding research, translate it, and go into the field, we did want to replicate, at least in a rough sense, previous studies of household crowding. The focus group interviews helped to bridge the gap between the language of the researchers and the street language of Bangkok.

Translation of specific questionnaire items to be used in the subsequent survey required a great deal of clarification of the nuances of meaning in both the Thai and English versions. Through a series of back-translations, not only the Thai version but also the English version of the questionnaire evolved, at times in a painfully slow fashion.

In constructing the questionnaire, we borrowed or modified many items used in earlier crowding studies (Booth, 1976; Gove and Hughes, 1983) relying heavily on the experience gained from the focus groups. Many specific items were rephrased to make them more understandable to our respondents. A major problem was that many of the English items were too abstract. By listening to the way the focus group participants talked, it was plain that the Thai focus group members used simpler local language. We tried to reformulate the questionnaire items into language that would be readily understandable to the average Bangkokian. (The majority of people in Bangkok are literate, but the modal level of formal education is about four years.)

Some changes were made in specific words simply to include words that would be more commonly used by our respondents. Sometimes the Thai word that would be the most obvious choice as a translation of the English was deemed to be too abstract, too formal, too restricted to well-educated people or to even have a different connotation in Thai than in English. For example, the most obvious translation for "proud" (in the phrase "felt proud because someone complimented you on something you had done," which was an item from a proposed scale) was felt to be more appropriate for the feeling one gets from a major accomplishment, e.g., raising three healthy children. Since we wanted to include minor triumphs, a different Thai word was used, and the phrase was back-translated into English as "felt good because someone complimented you on something you had done." Conceivably, a good translator could have made the same choices, but we feel that the Thai co-PIs, who translated the survey instrument, were sensitized to issues of word choice and made more aware of the common idiom as a result of having been intimately involved in the focus group interviews, and that they therefore made more appropriate decisions in the translation process. The focus group interviews thus helped us learn the "natural vocabulary," or colloquial expression, of Bangkokians, a major benefit of focus group research (Morgan, 1988).

As another case in point, one item in a scale called "psychological distress" asks "How often have you felt that people are trying to pick quarrels or start arguments with you"? This item was borrowed from a previous survey, but we were able to use a phrase (*haa ruang*) that came directly from a focus group interview; the phrase roughly translates, "looking for a subject to complain about." There were many other such instances where a specific phrase from a focus group served as a more appropriate translation.

Besides sensitizing us to the issue of word choice, the focus groups also taught us to make the questions simple and concrete. A number of revisions were made to make the questions more specific, and closer to the phrases used by our focus group participants. As examples, some of the items we changed were: (1) From: "Even members of a family need to get away from each other now and then." To: "In this house, I have almost no time alone." (2) From: "Home is a place where people get in each other's way." To: "In my home, people get in each other's way." All of these may seem to be very minor alterations. The non-equivalency in some other languages, notably including the Thai language, make changes such as these--subtleties to Westerners--the difference between intelligibility and non-intelligibility. Not only the vocabulary but the structure of a language is crucial to the determination of meaning.

Other revisions used specific examples mentioned by focus group participants. For instance, we changed: "At home, do you have a place which you consider to be your own?" to "At home, do you have a place where you can get away from the children?" The reason for the change is that we learned, first of all, that no one has such a place in most households and that, in addition, when asked if other household members ever moved their possessions, several focus group participants indicated that only the children, not other adults, disturbed their things. Another question ("Do you ever go into another room to get away from other members of the family?") was included because several focus group participants mentioned it in response to a question that asked "Do you have a personal space?" (or words to that effect). This item is used in our scale measuring physical withdrawal. A similar example of a change made to reflect the wording of the focus group participants is: "Do you often feel it is impossible to finish things that you have set out to do?" This was changed to "Is there often so much going on about you that it is impossible to finish things that you have set out to do?" This item is part of a scale measuring "inability to finish tasks."

In addition to guiding the revision of existing items, the focus group interviews provided the raw material to construct many new questionnaire items, particularly items dealing with family conflict. In the focus group interviews, some time was spent discussing what husbands and wives quarrel about. Knowledge of the kinds of things that spouses argue about aided us in constructing a series of items that comprise what we call the "marital arguments" scale. For instance, many focus group participants mentioned quarrels about irritating habits, spending too much money, talking to members of the opposite sex, drinking alcohol, gambling, household chores, and disciplining the children. These complaints provided very concrete issues, ones which we were fairly confident would be relevant to the survey respondents.

In a question about physical conflict between spouses, we included probes for slapping, hitting, and kicking, because all of these actions were mentioned in the focus groups. Similarly, an item on physical discipline of children included a probe to determine if the respondent disciplined their child(ren) with their hand, their foot, or a piece of wood, again because all of these actions were mentioned in the focus groups. Several items comprising an "irritability" scale, originally devised for a North American study, are based on examples mentioned in the focus group interviews. On a more positive note, the focus group interviews also provided examples of ways in which parents are supportive of children, examples that became part of a scale measuring supportive behavior toward children.

Even such apparently straight-forward terms as "room" and "bedroom" needed to be clarified, based on the focus group experience. We learned, for example, that different kinds of rooms may be used as bedrooms and that many households subdivide their space in various ways, e.g., by hanging blankets or using furniture as a room divider. This prompted us to ask in the questionnaire about room partitions and to keep a record both of the number of rooms as constructed and the number of rooms formed by partitions. This resulted in an objective measure of household crowding not previously used in crowding research.

In some cases, the experiences relayed to us by the focus group interviews led us to keep items from previous studies of crowding, because these items were obviously relevant in Bangkok. In other cases, we omitted items that we might have included (e.g., children getting into trouble with the police) because there was no mention of such events in the focus groups. Some items simply seemed to have no relevance and, in the interest of brevity, were dropped.

The focus group interviews further produced hypotheses to be tested during the analysis of the survey data. As mentioned, to be a son-in-law or a daughter-in-law in the household appeared to be a disadvantaged position, an extremely stressful position precisely because the individual has little control over what takes place in the house hold. This led us in the analysis of the survey data to examine whether, in fact, sons- and daughters-in-law are more responsive to household crowding than are other household members. The idea that household members in different positions respond differently to crowding is not entirely new (Baldassare, 1979, 1981). But these particular subgroups have not been singled out before, perhaps because it is relatively rare to find sons- and daughters-in-law in American households.

The focus groups added weight, moreover, to the notion that the degree of household control has an important impact on how individuals respond to crowding. Although this is a variable previously identified as affecting the felt experience of crowding, it has never been adequately measured. Based on the focus group interviews, we were prompted to devise a scale measuring household control, trying to more directly get at one's sense of control.

Another hypothesis emerging from the group interviews concerns how household members attempt to re-establish privacy when it is threatened. Focus group participants were asked what they needed to do to have privacy for sexual relations. Several participants indicated that this is much less of a problem when the children are very young, less than three years old. Older children, they suggested, stay up later at night and are more aware of what is going on. Therefore, in looking at the effects of crowding on reproductive behavior, including the frequency of sexual intercourse, the focus group interviews suggested that it is necessary to examine the effect of the age of the children.

The focus group interviews, in sum, provided us with a rich source of information about family interaction, family conflict, manifestations of stress, and perceptions of crowding in the context of Bangkok. They further proved to be highly valuable and, in various ways, contributed substantially to the development of the survey questionnaire. The result, we believe, is that we have been able to measure the theoretically important variables with greater validity and reliability, and our experience leads us to believe that focus group interviews can profitably be used whenever researchers attempt to conduct empirical research in a new cultural context.

The Survey

Our ultimate intention, of course, was to rigorously test a rather large number of hypotheses concerning the effects of crowding. To do so required reports from individuals about their living circumstances, information concerning their family relations, and data on their well-being. With this in mind, a representative sample of Bangkokians was sought. Since a principal focus of the study had to do with family relations, all men and women who were part of the sample were married and residing with his or her spouse. This focus also required that eligible respondents have at least one child living at home. A further requirement was that the wife in the sample household be no more than 45 years of age. Since stress has a central theoretical role in our.model and since migration can be a stressful experience, recent migrants (living in Bangkok less than one year) were excluded.

Bangkok is divided administratively into 24 districts, which are comprised of 150 subdistricts. Three of these districts were omitted from the sampling frame because of their low population densities. Out of the more than six million people in Bangkok, the omitted districts had a combined population of only 167,113, according to 1980 census data. The density of the three districts was uncharacteristically low. The average density was 313 persons per square kilometer, compared to 4690 per square kilometer, or 12,148 persons per square mile, for the remaining 21 districts. The National Statistical Office, Bangkok, generously provided assistance in selecting the sample. Initially, the districts were arranged by population density in order to implicitly impose stratification by population density. Using probability-proportional-to-size (pps) sampling, the National Statistical Office selected 45 subdistricts. As the next step, again using pps sampling, three blocks from each subdistrict were selected. Detailed maps showing each housing unit in the sample blocks were used to randomly select households to be interviewed. In carrying forth this plan, interviews were conducted in 2017 households. The response rate was 87 percent. A total of 1399 wives and 618 husbands were interviewed. The unequal number of husbands and wives presumably reflects the greater availability of the latter and is characteristic of household surveys in the U.S. as well (Gove and Hughes, 1979:133).

The interview instrument itself was the product of a lengthy process. At the outset of the project, our desire was to replicate, at least in a general way, two of the better conducted crowding studies using individual data, notably one conducted in Toronto (Booth, 1976) and one in Chicago (Gove and Hughes, 1983). As a starting point, an extensive review was made of the measures and interview items used in these studies. Considering cultural differences and the average levels of formal education in the respective societies, various items and scales were rejected, while others were retained. Many of the latter, however, were modified on the basis of the focus group interviews, as we have indicated. In addition, many new items and scales--in particular one having to do with household control--were devised. Even these underwent modification following a pretest of the interview schedule. Through a series of back-translations, alternating between English and Thai versions, needed alterations became apparent. Also, part of the process of training the 21 Thai interviewers involved a pretest of the interview schedule. A debriefing of the interviewers, as well as an analysis of the pretest data, suggested further revisions. The resulting interview schedule is contained in Appendix A.

By design, all of the sample households included a married couple with at least one child. In recent decades, government policy has sought to reduce population growth and, in fact, Thai family size has declined substantially (Knodel, Chamratrithirong, and Debavalaya, 1987). In our sample, the average couple had 2.1 children. Some couples had as many as seventeen children but they were a distinct minority; only 10 percent of the sample had more than three children. The average household size was 5.5. The majority of these households, 72 percent, were comprised of nuclear families. However, extended families of various types are common in Bangkok, comprising 28 percent of the total households. Fully 25 percent of the sample households were three-generation families. Ten percent of the households consisted of not just one but two or three married couples and their offspring.

As in most developing countries, men have more education than women, but the gap is not as large in Thailand as in some other countries.

For men and women alike, the modal level of educational attainment is four years of education (34 percent of the men and 44 percent of the women have exactly four years of education). In recent years, six years of education has become much more common. In spite of this low modal level of education, a substantial minority of both men and women have some post-secondary education: 22 percent of the men and 15 percent of the women. Other characteristics of the sample are shown in Table 3.1.

As to the representativeness of the sample, several comparisons indicate a close parallel to known characteristics of Bangkok as a whole. Not only are there close parallels in terms of household size, the family composition of the household, and the levels of formal education but there is a close approximation between the sample and the Bangkok population with respect to other demographic characteristics. As the figures for age in Table 3.1 indicate, there is general correspondence between the males and females in the sample and the married population of Bangkok, with a slight under-representation of people over 40 years old. Sample eligibility for women, it will be recalled, was restricted to 45 years or less.

A more important issue concerns the sample's representativeness with respect to socioeconomic status. The Bangkok census, unfortunately, does not report data on either individual or household income, which would permit us to make direct comparisons with our sample. The census, though, does include questions about a variety of household and family possessions, which we can consider as an indirect or surrogate indicator of socioeconomic status. As may be seen in that portion of Table 3.1 showing the percentage distribution of durable appliances and vehicles, there is general comparability between the sample and the Bangkok population as a whole, although with respect to some specific possessions there is an over-representation (e.g., motorcycles) and in others an under-representation (e.g., radios). Some of this disparity may reflect the growing affluence of Bangkokians, as most of the more expensive possessions are over-represented in the sample. (There is an eight year difference in the census report and when the sample was selected.)

Another means of assessing the representativeness, as well as the adequacy, of the sample concerns our central focus, just how much crowding there is. Part of the controversy surrounding studies conducted in North America has had to do with the samples on which their findings are based (Gove and Hughes, 1980a; Booth, Johnson, and Edwards, 1980a; Gove and Hughes, 1980b; Booth, Johnson, and Edwards, 1980b). In regard to the Toronto study (Booth, 1976), Gove and Hughes allege that it is based on "a very atypical sample and one that was very homogeneous in both crowding and social characteristics. As a consequence of this homogeneity, one would expect little variation on most variables and

Table 3.1 Bangkok and Sample Characteristics

HOUSEHOLD SIZE

	Sample		Census	
	Number	Percent	Percent (1-10 +)	Percent (3-10 +)
1 person	----	0.0	5.8	----
2 persons	----	0.0	10.9	----
3 persons	307	15.2	14.5	17.3
4 persons	491	24.3	16.9	20.3
5 persons	450	22.3	15.4	18.5
6 persons	281	13.9	12.2	14.7
7 persons	163	8.1	8.7	10.4
8 persons	106	5.3	6.0	7.2
9 persons	75	3.7	3.7	4.4
10 or more	144	7.0	6.0	7.2
Total percent		100.0	100.0	100.0
Total sample	2017		901,871	752,104
Mean size		5.5	5.1	5.6

FAMILY COMPOSITION

	Sample		Census	
Number	Percent	Percent	Percent (all)	(male)
Unrelated individuals	----	0.0	8.0	6.3
Nuclear	1451	71.9	70.4	74.9
Three generation	360	17.8	17.9	15.6
Bi-nuclear	65	3.2	2.7	2.3
Three generation, bi-nuclear	141	7.0	1.1	0.9
Total	2017	100.0	100.0	100.0

(continues)

Table 3.1 *(continued)*

EDUCATION OF RESPONDENT

Years Completed	Number	Percent
0-3	147	7.3
4	823	40.3
5-7	313	15.5
8-12	417	20.7
13-15	316	15.6
16	1	0.0
Total	2017	100.0

Median education = 5.2 years
Median education of husband = 6.7
Median education of wife = 3.9

AGE BY SEX

	Sample				Census	
Age in years	Male		Female		Male	Female
	Number	Percent	Number	Percent	Percent	Percent
Less than 20	----	0.0	24	1.7	----	4.3
20-24	24	3.9	175	12.5	8.4	15.7
25-29	82	13.2	314	22.5	17.8	21.4
30-34	139	22.5	339	24.2	18.9	18.3
35-39	162	26.2	316	22.6	16.8	15.6
40-44	106	17.1	190	13.6	15.8	14.0
45-49	53	8.6	40	2.9	12.6	10.7
50 or more	53	8.6	----	----	9.8	----
Total	619	100.0	1398	100.0	100.0	100.0

(continues)

Table 3.1 *(continued)*

INCOME

	Number	Percent
Below 2000 Baht	77	3.8
2000-2999 Baht	199	9.9
3000-3999 Baht	373	18.6
4000-4999 Baht	302	15.1
5000-5999 Baht	267	13.3
6000-7999 Baht	253	12.6
8000-9999 Baht	127	6.3
10,000-13,999 Baht	218	10.9
14,000-19,999 Baht	67	3.3
20,000 Baht or more	119	5.9
Total	2002	100.0

Median = 4688 Baht

DURABLE APPLIANCES OWNED BY HOUSEHOLD

	Sample		Census	
	Number	Percent	Number	Percent
Air conditioner	206	10.3	83,168	9.6
Automobile	325	16.2	165,475	19.0
Telephone	466	23.1	194,711	22.4
Motorcycle	495	24.5	104,775	12.0
Bicycle	617	30.6	170,114	19.6
Refrigerator	1460	72.4	529,960	61.0
Radio	1530	75.9	825,599	95.0
Television	1885	93.6	695,674	80.1
Fan	1981	98.2	782,722	90.1

Note: Percents may not add to 100.0 due to rounding error.

(continues)

Table 3.1 *(continued)*

PERSONS PER ROOM (PPR)

Value	Number	Percent
PPR < 1	172	8.5
PPR = 1	274	13.6
1 < PPR < 2	711	35.3
PPR = 2	214	10.6
2 < PPR < 3	186	9.2
PPR = 3	186	9.2
3 < PPR < 4	28	1.4
PPR = 4	126	6.2
PPR > 4	120	5.9
Total	2017	100.0

TYPE OF HOUSING

	Number	Percent
High density slum	115	5.7
Low density slum	291	14.4
Flat	129	6.4
Suburban subdivision	135	6.7
Mixed commercial	634	31.4
Concrete shop house	410	20.3
Wooden shop house	200	9.9
Townhouse, apartment	30	1.5
Other	72	3.6
Total	2016	100.0

that the relationships found would be very modest" (1983:42). But the Chicago study is not based on a representative sample either. The data for that study came from 80 selected census tracts within the city limits (Gove and Hughes, 1983). Although Gove and Hughes note that considerable attention was given to "a representative selection of tracts in terms of the types of housing units," they elsewhere caution "one should not generalize the specific values found to any population other than the specific census tracts selected" (1979:133).

Average household size in Bangkok is quite similar to that of the sample. For Bangkok as a whole, average household size is 5.1 persons versus 5.5 for our sample. The former figure is somewhat lower because it includes nonfamily households, which we would expect to be smaller. Our sample, of course, includes only families. Moreover, the percent of Bangkok family households that are nuclear, as opposed to being vertically or horizontally extended, is also quite similar to that found in the sample, 75 percent versus 72 percent (National Statistical Office, 1983). These comparisons suggest the sample is quite representative of family households in Bangkok.

More to the point of the sample's adequacy, the figures in Table 3.1 concerning household size indicate that a broad range is represented. Given the requirements for sample eligibility, the smallest household size is three. But as may be seen, there is representation of households considerably larger than this. In the highest category shown in the table, 10 or more persons per household, there are some households that contain as many as 15-20 people. While these are households of considerably greater magnitude than one would find in Europe or North America, the range itself indicates adequate variation and anything but a homogeneous sample. It is important to note, in addition, that the vast majority of Bangkok households, as is the case with all of the sample households, are comprised of families. In all of Bangkok, only eight percent are nonfamily households. Unlike in the industrialized world, it is very rare for an individual to live alone; only about one percent of the population does so. This is in sharp contrast to the United States, where over nine percent of the population lives alone and more than 20 percent of all households are occupied by only one individual (Statistical Abstract of the United States, 1988).

In regard to objective household crowding, here, too, there is considerable sample variation. There was at least one person per room in over 90 percent of the households, at least two persons in over 40 percent, at least three in over 20 percent, and at least four in over 10 percent of the households. Although it was rare, some sample households had 0.5 or fewer persons per room, and fully 22 percent had no more than one person per room. Overall, this yields an average number of persons per room of 2.1, with a standard deviation of 1.3. Estimating from the 1980 census, the mean number of persons per bedroom in all of Bangkok was 2.07. In terms of area, the average number of persons per 100 square meters was 12.25. To have the same level of household crowding in the United States, a 1500 square foot home would have 17 people living there.

This, it might be mentioned, seems to be quite typical for Asian cities. Hong Kong, as we have noted, is often identified as one of the most crowded cities in the world. Bangkok's level of crowding, however, is very comparable to that of Hong Kong. The population density in Hong Kong is 13,097 persons per square mile (1986), compared to 9,280 in Bangkok (1987). Considering only the most densely settled parts of each city, Hong Kong Island, with a population of 2.1 million, had a density of 73,815 persons per square mile, while the five most densely populated districts in Bangkok had a combined population of 1.3 million, with a density of 70,880 per square mile. More to the point, the level of household crowding in the two cities is similar, the average persons per room in Hong Kong being 1.9, according to the most recent data available (United Nations, 1985). If anything, Bangkok today may be somewhat more crowded than Hong Kong due to the latter city's growing affluence in recent years, enabling more people to find less crowded accommodations.

Crowding and Culture

Edward Hall, in his classic book *The Hidden Dimension* (1969), first pointed out the different ways peoples of various cultures use space and the varying distances involved when individuals of different cultures interact with one another. This has led a number of crowding researchers to suggest that the reactions to crowding may be conditioned by the cultural context (Booth, 1976; Gove and Hughes, 1983), some people being more reactive than others. Even within a given culture, there is variation in the intensity of an individual's reaction, several investigators have concluded (Baldassare, 1981; Booth, 1976; Gove and Hughes, 1983), depending on ethnicity, gender, the actual composition of the household, and a person's hierarchical position in the dwelling unit.

In choosing Bangkok as a research site, we were consciously seeking a locale that was very different than those where most crowding research has been carried out. One possible interpretation of the mixed findings of earlier studies and their equivocal conclusions is that some of the investigations, at least, have used samples of populations where the level of household crowding was so low, and the range of crowding so truncated, it would be difficult to detect any crowding effects. Even when such effects have been observed, the relationships noted are selective and modest (cf. Booth, 1976), intimating that crowding has very little to do with social disorganization and lowered well-being. By sampling a population where household crowding is three to four times that in Europe and North America, our initial thought was that crowding effects might be more easily detectable. It would allow us, furthermore, to examine if there is a "tipping point" in the effect of crowding. That is, it would permit an examination of whether at some point on a scale of objective crowding, pathological effects greatly increase and become more highly pronounced. In our case, this would be a point where decrements in family relations and individual well-being drastically increase. All of this suggests that in Bangkok, with its obvious high levels of household crowding, we might expect to find especially strong crowding effects.

Contrary to this hypothesis, though, there are several cultural features that could result in finding modest crowding effects, or perhaps none at all. Many investigators have made the point that, in a general sense, humans are highly adaptable, accommodating their behavior to a great diversity of circumstances (Baldassare, 1979; Booth, 1976; Gove and Hughes, 1983). If this is true, it could easily account for the selective and modest crowding effects noted in the research literature.

With particular regard to Thailand and Bangkok, additional features may mitigate finding any strong effects. First, even in rural areas, where land is relatively abundant, similar levels of persons per room are found. Most Thais (83%) still live in rural areas, and many Bangkokians are first- or second-generation migrants from rural areas. This history of crowding may make it easier for Thais to accommodate to high levels of crowding. Second, the tropical climate allows household members to be out-of-doors many hours every day, during all seasons of the year. Living space is not confined to the housing unit itself, but expands to adjacent communal areas. Moreover, in Bangkok, those who work outside the home often work longer hours than the typical American and may have a time-consuming commute to work. This means that some household members are absent during most of their waking hours. Hence, the effective level of crowding might be lower than indicated by a simple "head count." Third, Thai normative structure stresses the avoidance of interpersonal conflict and encourages the maintenance of harmonious relations, thus moderating any potential effects of crowding. Finally, Thais appear to value social interaction more than Americans do, while placing less value on privacy. Where an American may wonder whether it is appropriate to disturb someone who is alone, Thais assume that a person who is alone is lonely and will welcome a conversation. For many Thais, high levels of household crowding may simply provide protection from loneliness and offer many opportunities for social interactions. Our examination of this issue of culture appears in the final chapter.

Major Scales and Measures

There are several measures and scales common to the analyses to follow, and it seems appropriate to introduce them at this point. Consistent with the research model, throughout subsequent chapters we will be discussing three major components of that model: objective household crowding, subjective crowding, and psychological stress. These can be measured in various ways.

The most frequently used measure of objective crowding is the ratio of persons per room, simply calculated by finding how many residents there are and dividing by the number of rooms in the dwelling. This measure has the advantage of not only being simple but culture-free, being easily applied in a variety of cultural settings. Its obvious disadvantage is that the ratio of persons per room fails to take into account that not all rooms are of equal size, and it does not consider that residents are in the household in different numbers for varying lengths of time during the day and night. For these reasons, we will have occasion to draw on other measures of objective crowding, particularly in our discussion of the linkage between objective and subjective crowding.

Measuring subjective crowding is a more complicated matter, as is always the case where we attempt to tap into subjective states. As a perceptual phenomenon, subjective crowding has been conceptualized in two basic, but interrelated, ways. Representing one approach, Stokols (1978) suggests that the experience of being crowded grows out of a mismatch between the space one desires and the space that is available. When this mismatch occurs, stimulus overload takes place. The assumption is that people are cognitively aware, and there is an optimal level of stimuli for them to act competently and effectively. Compressed space, however, tends to increase stimuli beyond this optimal level and the result is an overload of a person's nervous system (Desor, 1972), hence the feeling of being crowded. To be sure, people may use a variety of mechanisms to cope with the stimuli or to cognitively shut them out. But sustained compressed spatial conditions overtax a person's ability to process the stimuli (Milgram, 1970). As a result, one becomes tense and irritability is escalated.

While acknowledging the role of stimulus overload in the experience of crowding, Altman (1975, 1976), among others, contends that privacy is central to understanding the effects of crowding. Invasions of privacy occur when one is exposed to more contact with others than a person desires. The lack of privacy involves unwanted interaction. As Chapin (1951: 165) puts it: "Intrusions on the fulfillment of personal desires need to be shut off in order to avoid the internal tensions that are built up from the frustrations, resentments, and continual multiple contacts with others." In Goffman's (1959) terms, privacy involves the back-region," which is necessary to sustain interaction and public conduct. Thus, it is not simply the sheer amount of stimuli that is important, but the experience of crowding involves the regulation of the amount of interaction to which one is exposed. This approach to crowding is more social in character, for every society has a highly institutionalized set of rules concerning interaction, when it is and when it is not acceptable to remove one's self from unwanted interaction. Cultures provide guidelines as to what are appropriate responses to those demands.

Conceptually, neither approach to dealing with the experience of crowding is clearly superior. In our view, they should be considered as complementary ways of thinking about the crowding experience, and we treat them as such. In the analyses to follow, two scales are used to tap the experience of being crowded. The one scale is called "perceived crowding" and the other "lack of privacy." The first is an adaptation from the Toronto study (Booth, 1976) and the lack of privacy scale derives from the Chicago survey (Gove and Hughes, 1983).

Perceived crowding is a four-item scale based on agree–disagree statements. The scale items consist of: (a) At home, there are too many people around; (b) In this house, I have almost no time alone; (c) In my home, people get in each other's way; (d) At home, I don't have enough room to do things conveniently. The items are very similar to those used in the Toronto subjective crowding scale, but they have been subjected to some modification. They are scaled so that a higher score indicates that the respondent feels more crowded. The alpha coefficient for this scale is .80.

The lack of privacy scale, tapping the other dimension of subjectively felt crowding, is a five-item scale, two of which were used in the Chicago study. It is comprised of the following: (a) At home, do you have as much privacy as you want; (b) At home, if you want to relax or work quietly at some task without interruption, do others leave you alone; (c) At home, if you want to talk quietly to someone in the family (e.g. husband/wife) without others listening to your conversation, are you able to do that; (d) At home, does it seem as if you can never be by yourself; (e) At home, if you want to be alone, is there someplace you can go to be alone? A higher score indicates the respondent more acutely feels that privacy is lacking. The alpha for the scale is .70.

Although perceived crowding and lack of privacy are designed to measure the total experience of crowding, they differ in that perceived crowding is primarily perceptual in nature, while lack of privacy refers to social interaction. The items that comprise the perceived crowding scale refer principally to whether the person perceives that his or her home is crowded, e.g., there are too many people around and there is not enough room to do things conveniently. The items in the lack of privacy scale, on the other hand, refer more directly to interaction among household members, e.g., whether there are interruptions when the respondent is trying to work quietly or have a discussion with a specific household member. The two scales are correlated with each other (.32) but, as determined by factor analysis, each scale comprises a separate and single factor. These scales, as well as all others in our analyses, are based on the unweighted sum of the component items.

Virtually every model of crowding effects, as well as numerous empirical studies, suggest that psychological stress or some closely related phenomenon is a crucial linkage in explaining how crowding leads to pathological behaviors (Altman, 1975; Booth, 1976; Desor, 1972; Levi and Anderson, 1975; Milgram, 1970; Stokols, 1972). As with subjective crowding, psychological stress refers to a feeling-state, which is difficult to conceptualize and measure. It is one of those concepts that is intuitively meaningful, but is variously defined and measured in the psychological and mental health literature. However, how stress is manifested, it is generally agreed, is multi-faceted. For this reason, we measured stress in two principal ways, one having to do with the notion of distress and the other a measure of the demands placed on an individual.

As Mirowsky and Ross (1989) point out, psychological distress takes two major forms: depression ("feeling sad, demoralized, lonely, hopeless, worthless, wishing you were dead, having trouble sleeping, crying, feeling everything is an effort, and being unable to get along") and anxiety ("being tense, restless, worried, irritable, and afraid"). Depression and anxiety are not clearly distinct forms of psychological distress, but instead are closely intertwined (Mirowsky and Ross, 1989; Dohrenwend et al., 1980). Tapping the broader concept of felt stress, our measure of psychological distress is a scale comprised of ten items that reflect various symptoms, including several aspects of anxiety and depression.

In the first six items of the distress scale, respondents were asked to indicate how often they had certain feelings during the previous few weeks. The possible responses were: often, sometimes, rarely, or never. The feelings were: (1) Anxious about something or someone, (2) That people are trying to pick quarrels or start arguments with you, (3) So depressed that it interferes with your family activities, (4) That personal worries were getting you down physically, that is, making you physically ill, (5) Moody, and (6) Felt you were confused, frustrated, and under a lot of pressure. The remaining four items were phrased in a somewhat different manner, but had the same response categories, except for the last question. These last four items were: (7) Are you ever bothered by nervousness, i.e., by being irritable, fidgety, or tense? (8) Do you ever feel that nothing ever turns out for you the way you want it to? (9) Do you have trouble concentrating or keeping your mind on what you are doing?, and (10) Are you the worrying type—you know, a worrier? (yes, no). The scale has a high degree of reliability, an alpha coefficient of .84, and is scored so that a high score indicates greater psychological distress.

Gove and Hughes (1983) contend that part of the crowding experience entails a perception of the demands made of an individual, and it does seem logical that people in congested circumstances are more likely to perceive there is more social pressure created by those around them. To us, however, the causal sequence of potential crowding effects is somewhat more complicated. We view felt demands as being the result of feeling crowded, reflecting the stressfulness of that experience. As such, felt demands intervenes between subjective crowding and possible decrements in the social relations of household members. While we depart from Gove and Hughes in the conceptualization of the process, we were able to successfully translate their scale of felt demands into Thai, with only slight modifications.

The scale is comprised of four items: (1) Does it seem as if others are always making demands on you, (2) At home, does it seem as if you almost never have any peace and quiet, (3) At home, does it seem as if you always are having to do something for someone else, and (4) When you try to do something at home, are you almost always interrupted? The scale has a reliability of .68, identical to that in the Chicago study. The higher the score, the greater the perceived demands.

Other measures and scales peculiar to a given analysis will be introduced as we discuss various dependent variables designed to tell us something about the outcomes of crowding.

The Mode of Analysis

In order to sort out the unique effects of the crowding variables, multiple regression is used throughout the analyses. We report standardized betas because unstandardized b's are impossible to interpret without knowing the metric for each variable. In particular, unstandardized b's provide no information on the relative effects of the independent variables, while standardized betas do yield this information on their effects within a given population (Hargens, 1976).

The relationships between household crowding and the various dependent variables are examined in several stages. First, the zero-order relationships between crowding and the dependent variables are examined. Second, the relationships between objective crowding and the dependent variables, controlling for relevant background variables, are inspected. As the next step, we look at the relationships between the dependent variables and both objective and subjective crowding, controlling for relevant background variables. Finally, an examination is made of the relationships between objective and subjective crowding and the dependent variables, controlling for relevant intervening variables, as well as the background variables.

In some analyses, we are particularly interested in knowing whether there are any differences between women and men in terms of the effects of household crowding. One approach to this would be to run all analyses separately for wives and husbands. Another avenue is to combine all respondents and use interaction terms to determine whether there are differences between wives and husbands. For the sake of economy, we present the analyses in which women and men are combined and interaction terms are examined.

4

The Feeling of Being Crowded

"I used to think of wanting to be by myself... but I know I can't do it... it's impossible." Focus Group Participant

An unresolved issue in crowding research has to do with why people feel crowded. Logic and common sense tell us that the more people there are in a finite amount of space, the more likely they are to feel a sense of being confined or crowded. Indeed, our research model explicitly posits a linkage between objective crowding and a subjective response to congested circumstances.

Only three studies of which we are aware have looked closely at this issue, and all of them are studies conducted in North America. Consistently they report a positive relationship between the two crowding dimensions, as we would anticipate. Curiously, though, the correlations between the two dimensions are far lower than we might expect and, generally, we might characterize them as moderate relationships.

Background

Baldassare, for example, in analyzing data from two existing datasets (the ISR Quality of Life Study and the NORC Continuous National Survey), reports a correlation of .24 between persons per room, the most commonly used objective indicator, and an ISR item regarding a shortage of space within rooms--the latter taken to be a measure of perceived crowding (1979). A somewhat higher correlation (.34) existed between persons per room and a NORC item concerning the perceived lack of a sufficient number of rooms within the household. Given the magnitude of these relationships, other factors plainly contribute to the perception of spatial inadequacies. In fact, Baldassare notes that persons per room explains only 6 percent and 12 percent of the variance in the two respective crowding items. The addition of five control variables with persons per room in a regression equation raised the explained variance to 7 and 16 percent, respectively. Much of the additional explained variance, Baldassare reports, is attributable to a family life cycle variable reflecting the presence of children in the household.

In their Chicago study, Gove and his associates (1979; 1980b: 868) assert that "persons per room [is] strongly related to the subjective experience of crowding...," but nowhere do they report a zero-order correlation between the objective measure and their two scales of subjective crowding, a scale of excessive social demands and one tapping the perceived lack of privacy. But elsewhere they report on the relationships between the scales and persons per room combined with six control variables. Gove et al. (1979: 65) point out that persons per room along with the six control variables explain slightly more than 14 percent of the variance in the lack of privacy scale. Explained variance in the felt demands scale is somewhat higher, 15.5 percent. Although this suggests a somewhat stronger relationship between objective and subjective crowding than does Baldassare's analysis, the amount of variance explained by objective crowding indicates that the experience of being crowded is largely unaccounted for by the objective circumstances, at least as measured by persons per room.

In a similar vein, findings from the Toronto crowding study suggest that objective crowding alone accounts for only a small proportion of the subjective sense of being spatially confined (Booth and Edwards, 1976). While a correlation of .51 was observed between persons per room and a three-item scale of objective household crowding, the scale itself was only modestly associated with a subjective household crowding scale. For females and males, respectively, the zero-order correlations were .12 and .19. In a regression, using a subjective crowding scale as the dependent variable, the investigators included several independent variables: objective crowding, social and ethnicity measures, the Langner Index of Psychophysiological Disorder, and four measures of powerlessness. Altogether, these variables explained from 10 to 18 percent of the variance in subjective crowding, depending on the gender of the respondent. The greatest contribution to explained variance was the Langner scale, accounting for half of the explained variance. Objective crowding explained approximately 20 percent of the explained variance. Booth and Edwards conclude that while subjective crowding is little related to objective crowding, the experience of being crowded is also more than the mere reflection of generalized anxiety or psychological problems, or the result of social and ethnic differences.

This leaves us with conundrum. If the association between objectively crowded households and the subjective experience of crowding is not a strong one, and the variation in perceived crowding is only partly afunction of the objective circumstances, what accounts for why people feel crowded? The logical question is: How can this be?

Three possibilities come to mind. First, there have been a limited number of objective crowding measures used to examine the relationship with subjective crowding. All three studies mentioned used the persons per room measure. Only the Toronto study went beyond this in creating a new objective crowding indicator, what is called in that study a rooms deficit measure. This raises the possibility that the proper measure of objective crowding has not been inspected. It may well be that there is an objective indicator superior to the persons per room measure and the rooms deficit indicator.

Prior studies have assumed that the relationship between objective and subjective crowding is a linear one, and it may be necessary to go beyond the simple zero-order correlations and test whether the relationship is curvilinear or if there is either a threshold effect or a ceiling effect. By a threshold effect, we mean a point beyond which objective crowding greatly accentuates its perception. A ceiling effect, in contrast, would be a point beyond which increases in objective crowding have little additional effect on subjective crowding. If the actual relationship between objective and subjective crowding involves a threshold or a ceiling, or is curvilinear, the simple zero-order correlations examined in earlier studies might well be weak simply because the functional form of the relationship previously has been misspecified. It also may be critical to look at whether there are certain circumstances under which objective and subjective crowding are more highly related.

Another possibility as to why people feel crowded concerns the effects other potential exogenous variables have on the basic relationship between objective and subjective crowding. This is predicated on the idea that much of the impact of subjective crowding—and hence the modest relationships noted in prior studies—is actually due to various coexisting circumstances.

The Analysis

To test these various possibilities, we first created seven different indicators of objective crowding. The simplest of these, the most widely used crowding measure, is the ratio of persons per room. An elaboration of this measure is the total persons per room. The construction of this indicator is based on our observation that what constitutes a room in Bangkok can be highly variable. Especially in the slums, it is a common practice to partition a room in order to create a larger number of smaller living areas. Total persons per room is thus based on the total number of residents divided by the number of rooms in the dwelling, including all rooms formed by partitions. A related, but distinct, measure concerns the ratio of permanent residents per 100 square meters in the dwelling unit, the latter based on respondent reports. The resulting ratio is multiplied by 100. This measure also explicitly recognizes that rooms can be variable, in this case varying by size.

A more complicated indicator of objective crowding, a rooms deficit measure, is one deriving from the Toronto study (Booth, 1976). This is an indicator that assumes that not all household members require the same number of rooms. Adults and children, for example, do not necessarily have the same space needs. Moreover, as the size of a household increases, the addition of each single individual does not proportionally increase the need for space. To construct the rooms deficit measure, several steps are required. First, the number of rooms in the dwelling is regressed on the number of people in the household along with information on household composition. To be more specific, the number of rooms is regressed on (1) the number of pre-school age children in the household, (2) the number of school age children in the household, (3) the number of adults in the household, (4) the number of married couples in the household, and (5) whether the household has members from two or three generations. This yields the predicted number of rooms needed for a household of a given size and composition. By subtracting the actual number of rooms from the predicted number of rooms, one obtains the rooms deficit score, which may have either a positive or negative value. Insofar as people may judge how crowded they are or how deficient their households are by comparison to what is typical for their particular culture, this measure has the advantage of norming crowding to a given culture.

Two other deficiency measures were created. These are constructed in the same way as the rooms deficit indicator, but they rely on the total number of rooms, which includes partitioned areas, and the area in square meters. These alternate measures are called total rooms deficit and area deficit. As before, the actual number of rooms or area is subtracted from a predicted score, based on regression. Like the original rooms deficit measure, the values derived in both cases can be either positive or negative.

The final objective crowding measure is another ratio variable, others per room, which is somewhat akin to the persons per room indicator. Rather than relying on the reported number of residents, however, others per room uses in its numerator the number of people other than the respondent who are in the household when the respondent is at home and awake. This information is taken from the time-budget detailing the week day immediately prior to the interview, indicating who was in the dwelling and for how long they were there (see Appendix A). While persons per room reflects the number of persons who reside in the dwelling unit, others per room reflects the potential for interaction between the respondent and other members of the household. Others per room differs from persons per room in that both the respondent and other household members may be away from home for varying periods of time during the day. This measure has the advantage of being more sensitive to the temporal dimension of crowding, as it explicitly takes into account that not all household members are at home all of the time.

As the dependent variable, subjective crowding is measured by the two scales described in Chapter 3, the one having to do with perceived crowding and the other concerning a lack of privacy.

Perceived crowding and lack of privacy, it will be recalled, differ in that perceived crowding is primarily perceptual in nature, while lack of privacy refers to social interaction. In other words, the items that comprise the perceived crowding scale refer principally to whether the person perceives that his or her home is crowded, e.g., there are too many people around and there is not enough room to do things conveniently. The items in the lack of privacy scale refer more directly to interaction among household members, e.g., whether there are interruptions when the respondent is trying to work quietly or have a discussion with a specific household member.

To examine whether the effects of objective crowding might be associated with other exogenous factors, six potentially explanatory variables are considered.

The first of these pertains to the amount of exposure a person has to the actual experience of objective crowding. Even if there are a large number of persons present in a relatively confined space, if the amount of time spent in the household is comparatively brief, the experience may not be defined as a crowded one. Information bearing on this is taken from the aforementioned time-budget indicating the total number of hours the respondent is home and awake. Hereafter, we refer to this measure as hours home.

Subjective crowding also may be accentuated by the sheer number of people present while one is in the household. A variable to reflect this, called others, consists of the sum of the number of others present during the time (by hours) the respondent was awake at home. This variable, as mentioned, is the numerator of others per room, and it gives us some indication of the potential sensory overload a person might experience.

The social relationship between those who share a residence could, in addition, potentially affect the experience of crowding. We constructed two variables to tap household composition. Since three-generation families are fairly common in Bangkok (25 percent of the sample households), one of the measures concerns whether the family is nuclear or multi-generational. The second composition measure is an indicator of those situations where the household is shared by two or more married couples and their children.

Control for household composition and the construction of the scale on household control discussed below were prompted by several exchanges in the focus group discussions where the subject of in-laws was brought up. In one male group, for instance, the following conversation took place.

Moderator: "How do you find staying with the in-laws?"

Chaowalit: "We must stay. If not, we won't make it."

Petch: "I feel somewhat uncomfortable."

Somchai: "Moderately uncomfortable, I feel."

Chokchai: "We must consider them.... kind of cannot do what we please.... For example, I don't dare bring friends to come to the house to have a drink.... sometimes my wife told me to go drink outside, and I would feel like losing face with friends.... I once told my father-in-law that I wanted for just one time to drink with my friends.... he didn't say "yes," he only nodded. I felt somewhat reluctant.... It's hard to say. It's their house."

Wanchai: "In my house, I think I have freedom to have my friends to come to drink."

Chokchai: "I don't have that kind of freedom.... I can't even raise my voice when arguing with my wife. I must consider her father."

Somporn: "Sometimes I can't even kick my own wife (laugh).... We must consider other people."

Chaowalit: "Let me tell you.... in my house when the father-in-law is drunk.... he will be shooting his mouth about anything, everything... and me, an outsider (in-law)... I dare not mingle.... I must go away in this case.... you know the house is not mine."

When several individuals of different ages and gender share a residence, a status hierarchy tends to develop, with some members of the household having greater control over the home environment than others (Baldassare, 1981). Under objectively congested circumstances, we would expect that those who have less control will feel more crowded, given their relative inability to manipulate the household environment. Household control is a three-item scale we devised based on responses to the following: (a) When I want to move a piece of furniture in the all-purpose room, I can go ahead and move it without asking if others agree; (b) If I want to invite a friend to visit my house and be entertained, I can go ahead and invite him without asking if others agree; (c) If one of my relatives comes to visit from up-country, I feel free to invite him to stay here for several days; I don't have to ask others if they agree. The higher the score, the more household control the respondent perceives himself or herself to have.

There is, finally, some reason to believe that males and females do not react in the same way to objectively crowded conditions. This has been found to be the case both in crowding experiments and in studies using individual-level survey data (Freedman, 1975; Gove and Hughes, 1983; Booth, 1976). Perhaps due to their greater attentiveness to others, women are thought to be generally more reactive to crowding. Based on these findings, gender of respondent is included in some of the analyses.

Objective and Subjective Crowding: How Are They Related?

Consistent with prior research, the zero-order correlations between the seven objective crowding measures and the scales of subjective crowding are in the moderate range (Table 4.1). For perceived crowding, the correlations range from a low of .17 for the objective measure total rooms deficit to a high of .20 for persons per 100 square meters, with a median of .18. With regard to the lack of privacy scale, the lowest zero-order correlation is with area deficit (.12), the highest involving the original rooms deficit measure (.23), with a median of .22. On the face of it, the range in these correlations would suggest that no single objective indicator is clearly superior, particularly with respect to perceived crowding. More importantly, even under circumstances of high household crowding--such as in Bangkok--the findings indicate that there is not a strong association between objective and subjective crowding.

One reason this may be so, as we have suggested, may have to do with the nature or shape of the relationship between objective and subjective crowding. Prior investigations have proceeded on the assumption, left untested, that there is a linear relationship between the two dimensions: as households become increasingly congested, people feel more crowded. It is possible, of course, for the relationship to take other forms. Two possibilities are of particular interest. At the lower end of the continuum, increases in the level of objective crowding may have little effect, as crowding remains a minor annoyance. At the higher end of the continuum, however, increases in crowding may have a marked effect. Alternatively, the effect of objective crowding may be reversed. Crowding may have a muted effect, or may lose its effect altogether, at the higher end of the crowding continuum. The former pattern might be called a threshold effect, the latter a ceiling effect. Either type of effect might occur gradually or abruptly. These four non-linear relationships are shown in Figure 4.1.

The curvilinear pattern (Figure 4.1a, b) can be investigated by using both objective crowding and the square of objective crowding to predict subjective crowding. The linear term is expected to have a positive sign. If the squared term is significant, its sign indicates whether the effect is a threshold effect or a ceiling effect; a positive sign indicates a threshold effect, a negative sign a ceiling effect.

The "bent line" pattern (Figure 4.1c, d) can be investigated by using an interaction term. To do this, we created the interaction term by dichotomizing objective crowding at its median and multiplying this dichotomy (coded 0, 1) by the continuous objective crowding measure. Both the continuous objective crowding measure and the interaction term are then used to predict subjective crowding. Again, the linear term is expected to have a positive sign. If the interaction term is significant, a positive sign means that the effect of objective crowding on subjective crowding is greater for higher levels of objective crowding, while a negative effect means the opposite. The value of the interaction term is 0 for cases falling below the median on the objective crowding measure and is equal to the objective crowding measure for cases above the median. Thus, the coefficient for the interaction term indicates the direction and magnitude of any change in the slope of the line above the median.

The results for the three different models (linear, curvilinear, interaction) are contained in Tables 4.2 and 4.3.

As the findings in those tables show, all of the models are statistically significant, although none of them explains more than a small amount of the variance in either perceived crowding (Table 4.2) or a perceived lack of privacy (Table 4.3). While the differences in the coefficients tend to be rather modest, in the majority of the cases, the curvilinear form is superior in describing the relationship between objective and subjective crowding. This holds for the indicators persons per room, persons per total rooms, persons per 100 square meters, and others per room. For the curvilinear models, objective crowding explains 2.8 to 4.7 percent of the variance in perceived crowding and 2.0 to 6.8 percent of the variance in perceived lack of privacy, depending on the specific measure of objective crowding.

In the linear models and curvilinear models, the linear term is significant and positive, i.e., those who are objectively more crowded, feel more crowded. In the interaction, or threshold, models, the linear term is significant only when a deficit measure is used; in those cases, the linear term is again positive.

Table 4.1 Zero-order Correlations of Objective and Subjective Crowding Measures

	1	2	3	4	5	6	7	8	9
1. Persons per room	1.00								
2. Total persons per room	.924	1.00							
3. Persons per 100 square meters	.546	.562	1.00						
4. Others per room	.789	.742	.408	1.00					
5. Rooms deficit	.787	.736	.499	.572	1.00				
6. Total rooms deficit	.756	.779	.507	.545	.964	1.00			
7. Area deficit	.315	.291	.491	.232	.457	.431	1.00		
8. Perceived crowding	.178	.185	.198	.184	.171	.167	.187	1.00	
9. Lack of privacy	.218	.216	.176	.220	.227	.210	.120	.315	1.00
Mean	2.067	1.948	12.252	14.800	1.495	1.431	110.021	6.423	2.374
Standard Deviation	1.333	1.223	11.794	12.565	.000	.000	.000	2.430	1.970

72

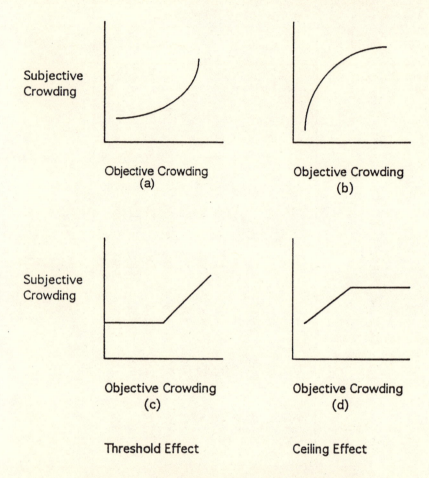

Subjective
Crowding

Objective Crowding
(a)

Objective Crowding
(b)

Subjective
Crowding

Objective Crowding
(c)

Objective Crowding
(d)

Threshold Effect

Ceiling Effect

Figure 4.1. Four Potential Nonlinear Relationships
Between Objective and Subjective Crowding

Table 4.2 Effect of Objective Crowding on Perceived Crowding for
Three Different Models, Unstandardized Regression
Coefficients: All Respondents

Measure	Linear	Curvilinear	Threshold
Persons per room			
b1	.325[a]	.675[a]	-.140
b2	----	-.050[a]	.367[a]
R2	.032[a]	.038[a]	.037[a]
N	(2015)	(2015)	(2015)
Persons per total rooms			
b1	.367[a]	.749[a]	-.175
b2	----	-.055[a]	.421[a]
R2	.034[a]	.042[a]	.041[a]
N	(2000)	(2000)	(2000)
Persons per 100 square m			
b1	.041[a]	.080[a]	.030
b2	----	-.001[a]	.010
R2	.039[a]	.047[a]	.039[a]
N	(2008)	(2008)	(2008)
Rooms deficit			
b1	.277[a]	.285[a]	.281[a]
b2	----	.015	-.009
R2	.029[a]	.029[a]	.029[a]
N	(2015)	(2015)	(2015)
Total rooms deficit			
b1	.283[a]	.291[a]	.274[a]
b2	----	.022	.018
R2	.028[a]	.028[a]	.028[a]
N	(2000)	(2000)	(2000)

(continues)

Table 4.2 (*continued*)

Measure	Linear	Curvilinear	Threshold
Area deficit			
b1	.004[a]	.007[a]	.002[b]
b2	----	-.00001[a]	.012[a]
R2	.035[a]	.046[a]	.055[a]
N	(2008)	(2008)	(2008)
Others per room			
b1	.036[a]	.063[a]	.018
b2	----	-.00004[a]	.015
R2	.034[a]	.043[a]	.034[a]
N	(2013)	(2013)	(2013)

[a]p<.05; [b]p<.01; [c]p<.001
b1=linear effect   b2 = curvilinear or interaction effect
Note: There are no control variables.

Table 4.3 Effect of Objective Crowding on
Lack of Privacy for Three Different Models, Unstandardized
Regression Coefficients: All Respondents

Measure	Linear	Curvilinear	Threshold
Persons per room			
b1	.322[a]	.782[a]	.011
b2	----	-.066[a]	.247[b]
R2	.048[a]	.065[a]	.051[a]
N	(2017)	(2017)	(2017)
Persons per total rooms			
b1	.348[a]	.772[a]	.066
b2	----	-.062[a]	.219[b]
R2	.047[a]	.061[a]	.049[a]
N	(2002)	(2002)	(2002)
Persons per 100 square m			
b1	.029[a]	.063[a]	-.002
b2	----	-.001[a]	.028
R2	.031[a]	.040[a]	.032[a]
N	(2010)	(2010)	(2010)
Rooms deficit			
b1	.299[a]	.305[a]	.237[a]
b2	----	.014	.136
R2	.051[a]	.052[a]	.052[a]
N	(2017)	(2017)	(2017)
Total rooms deficit			
b1	.290[a]	.300[a]	.202[a]
b2	----	.027	.190
R2	.044[a]	.046[a]	.046[a]
N	(2002)	(2002)	(2002)

(continues)

Table 4.3 *(continued)*

Measure	Linear	Curvilinear	Threshold
Area deficit			
b1	.002[a]	.004[a]	.001[c]
b2	----	.00004[a]	.006[a]
R2	.014[a]	.020[a]	.022[a]
N	(2010)	(2010)	(2010)
Others per room			
b1	.034[a]	.066[a]	.002
b2	----	.00004[a]	.028
R2	.048[a]	.068[a]	.051[a]
N	(2015)	(2015)	(2015)

[a]p<.05; [b]p<.01; [c]p<.001
b1=linear effect b2 = curvilinear or interaction effect
Note: There are no control variables.

In the curvilinear models, the squared term has a significant negative effect on both perceived crowding and perceived lack of privacy in the models involving persons per room, persons per total rooms, persons per 100 square meters, and others per room. The negative sign indicates a ceiling effect. The curvilinear term has no effect in the models involving the rooms deficit measures. Overall, this set of findings would suggest that the relationship between objective and subjective crowding is not a linear relationship as previous researchers have presumed and, therefore, the strength of the relationship is muted, at least in part, because of a ceiling effect. This ceiling effect is most clearly shown in Figure 4.2.

Results from the interaction, or threshold, model underscore the complexity of the pattern. Analyses involving persons per room and persons per total rooms suggest that increasing levels of objective crowding have little impact on subjective crowding among those cases below the median level of objective crowding, but objective crowding does have a significant impact on subjective crowding among cases above the median. Results of the analyses concerning the rooms deficit

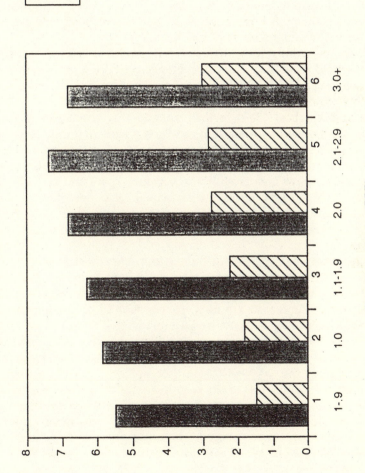

Figure 4.2 Subjective Crowding by PPR

measures, however, suggest that increasing levels of objective crowding has an effect throughout the continuum.

Subgroup Differences in Feeling Crowded

It is possible, of course, that crowding may have an especially strong effect for certain subgroups, but not for others. In order to examine this possibility, the sample was dichotomized in several ways and the analyses reported in Tables 4.2 and 4.3 were replicated for each group.

Specifically, the sample was dichotomized according to gender, whether the respondent has a high or low level of household control, and, for three-generation households, whether the respondent's parents or parents-in-law are members of the household.

Men and women may differ in the degree to which they are reactive to household crowding. Gove and Hughes (1983:15), for example, argue that women are more attentive to the needs of others and, consequently, are likely to be more reactive to crowding. Baldassare (1979, 1981) and Gove and Hughes (1983) further contend that reactions to crowding maybe conditioned by the extent to which a particular individual is able to exert power in the context of the household. More powerful household members are able to minimize the negative effects of household crowding, because they have greater ability to organize space and activities in the home.   Our focus group discussions also suggested that, in three-generation households, adults who live with their parents-in-law feel behaviorally constrained, relative to others who live with their own parents.

The results, summarized in Table 4.4, provide little consistent support for the hypotheses that women, people with low household control, and adults who live in their parents-in-laws' home are more reactive to objective crowding than are men, people with high household control, and adults who live in their own parents' home.

Comparing men and women, objective crowding, as expected, has a greater impact on perceived crowding for women than for men, but objective crowding has a greater impact on lack of privacy for men than for women. Contrasting adults who live with their own parents versus their in-laws, objective crowding, as we would expect, has a greater impact on the lack of privacy for those living with in-laws than for those living with their own parents, but objective crowding, contrary to prediction, has a greater impact on perceived crowding for those living with their parents than for those residing with in-laws. In the contrast between those with low versus high household control, objective crowding, as expected, has a greater impact on lack of privacy for those with low household control, but objective crowding has about the same

Table 4.4 Explained Variance for Perceived Crowding and Perceived Lack of Privacy, Using Seven Measures of Objective Crowding and Three Different Models: Summary Results for Various Subgroups

Group and Dependent Variable	N	R² based on persons per room			Mean R² for all seven measures			Number of times R² for group exceeded R² for comparison group by .01 or more		
		Linear	Curvi-linear	Inter-action	Linear	Curvi-linear	Inter-action	Linear	Curvi-linear	Inter-action
Perceived Crowding										
Husbands	611	.029	.033	.029	.031	.037	.035	0	0	0
Wives	1389	.033	.041	.042	.035	.041	.040	1	2	3
With parents	289	.035	.063	.055	.041	.062	.056	3	3	5
With in-laws	166	.030	.083	.037	.031	.061	.042	1	3	1
High control	1709	.030	.036	.035	.034	.040	.039	2	2	2
Low control	291	.044	.057	.047	.033	.039	.035	2	2	2

(continues)

Table 4.4 *(continued)*

Group and Dependent Variable	N	R² based on persons per room			Mean R² for all seven measures			Number of times R² for group exceeded R² for comparison group by .01 or more		
		Linear	Curvi-linear	Inter-action	Linear	Curvi-linear	Inter action	Linear	Curvi-linear	Inter-action
Lack of Privacy										
Husbands	612	.065	.079	.069	.049	.058	.054	4	4	4
Wives	1390	.041	.060	.044	.037	.047	.039	1	1	1
With parents	289	.013	.054	.031	.013	.030	.023	0	0	0
With in-laws	167	.039	.070	.043	.036	.060	.039	5	6	4
High control	1710	.047	.065	.052	.042	.052	.045	1	1	1
Low control	292	.059	.077	.060	.047	.059	.050	3	3	2

effect on perceived crowding regardless of whether the respondent has low or high household control. What few differences there are tend to be small. For the contrast between men and women and that between high and low household control, the difference in R-squared is usually not more than 1.0 percent. In the contrast between adults living with parents versus in-laws, the difference usually is at least 1.0 percent, but is rarely more than 3.0 percent.

Other Influences

The findings relevant to determining the effects of other exogenous variables on subjective crowding are contained in Table 4.5. Since the various objective indicators relate similarly to the two dimensions of subjective crowding, the analysis is confined to using only persons per room and others per room. All four models shown in Table 4.5 are statistically significant, although the predictors explain substantially more of the variance in the lack of privacy than they do with respect to perceived crowding. They explain about 19 percent of the variance in the latter variable, in contrast to explaining about nine percent of the variance in perceived crowding.

Other than objective crowding, the most consistent predictors of perceived crowding and perceived lack of privacy are household control and housing satisfaction (Table 4.5). Interestingly, household control is positively related to perceived crowding, but negatively related to the lack of privacy. That is, controlling for the objective level of crowding, individuals with more household control perceive more crowding, but individuals with less household control report a greater lack of privacy, i.e., experience more interruptions in their daily activities. Housing satisfaction, on the other hand, is negatively related in a consistent way to both dimensions of subjective crowding. The less satisfied people are with their residences, the more crowded they feel. Neighborhood crowding is positively associated with perceived crowding, but it is not statistically significantly related to a lack of privacy.

The number of others present and the number of hours the individual is home are fairly consistent predictors of perceived crowding and a lack of privacy. Others present is positively related to both measures of subjective crowding. If there are more people present, the respondent feels more crowded. However, the number of hours at home, it will be noted, is negatively related to perceived crowding and a perceived lack of privacy. This may suggest that there is a perceptual contrast effect which occurs when one spends a great deal of time outside the household (and presumably in less crowded circumstances). It could well be that the scale items concerning subjective crowding have a different meaning to

**Table 4.5 Standardized Regression Coefficients for the Effects of
Objective Crowding and Other Exogenous Variables on
Subjective Crowding, with Controls**

	Perceived Crowding	Lack of Privacy	Perceived Crowding	Lack of Privacy
Persons per room	.284[a]	.317[a]	-----	-----
Persons per room squared	-.174[b]	-.220[a]	-----	-----
Other persons per room	-----	-----	.268[a]	.304[a]
Other persons per room squared	-----	-----	-.161[a]	-.187[a]
Sex of respondent	-.005	.034	-.000	.038
Number of couples	.020	-.020	.041	.000
Number of generations	.043	.010	.047	.015
Hours home	-.071[c]	-.037	-.112[a]	-.081[b]
Others home	.163[a]	.101[a]	.101[b]	.028
Household control	.106[a]	-.175[a]	.105[a]	-.175[a]
Housing satisfaction	-.077[b]	-.253[a]	-.082[a]	-.255[a]
Neighborhood crowding	.080[a]	.038	.081[a]	.038
Want to get out of house but can't	.011	.033	.012	.035
R-squared	.091[a]	.187[a]	.090[a]	.190[a]

[a]$p < .001$; [b]$p < .01$; [c]$p < ,05$

those who spend most of their waking hours outside of the household than for individuals who are at home most of the time. Alternatively, the number of hours spent at home may be in part a response to the perception of crowding; those who feel more crowded at home may arrange to be at home less. One of the more telling anecdotes about the crowding experience to come from the focus group research concerns a male participant, who indicated that when he felt too crowded at home, he went for a bus ride. Bangkok buses, at most times of the day, are standing-room-only and, at peak hours, have people clinging to their sides. It would appear that the anonymity of a crowded bus obviates, at least in part, the perception of crowding and a felt lack of privacy that one may experience in the context of the household. Another, and not incompatible, explanation of these negative correlations is that there may be a satiation effect among those who stay in the household long hours; after some point in time they simply may become inured to the household congestion.

The results also show that, controlling for the objective level of crowding, women are no more likely to feel crowded than are men, people who live with another married couple are no more likely to feel crowded than are members of one-couple households, and persons from three-generation households are no more likely to feel crowded than are those from two-generation households. It thus appears that the feeling of being crowded in not conditional on these three variables and that they do not suppress the overall effect of objective crowding on a subjective sense of crowding.

Conclusions

While there is undoubtedly a dynamism to the perception of space (Hall, 1969), we find, as others before us, that the relationship between objective and subjective crowding is a modest one. We have closely examined the nature of that relationship in an attempt to ascertain why it is not a stronger one. Contrary to the assumptions of prior investigations, we find that the relationship between objective and subjective crowding is not a linear one. The feeling of being crowded does not increase over the entire range of objective crowding. Instead, the results suggest that there is a ceiling effect. Those people living in the most extreme of congested circumstances feel no more crowded than individuals residing in households somewhat lower on the scale of residential crowding. The level of perceived crowding appears to peak when the number of persons per room is about 2.5, and the level actually declines to a minor degree thereafter. Thus, in part, the strength of the objective crowding-subjective crowding relationship is reduced by a ceiling effect.

The findings indicate that this holds almost regardless of which objective crowding measure is used. Past studies have relied heavily--most of them solely--on the persons per room measure, which has the virtue of being easily computed and applied in a variety of cultural settings. However, persons per room is an exceedingly oversimplified indicator, and it fails to empirically tap some of the theoretically important dimensions of the crowding experience. It fails, for example, to take into account that not all rooms are of equal size; it does not consider that residents are in the household in different numbers and for varying lengths of time during the day and night. It was for this reason that we created several new objective indicators of household crowding to test the premise that one or more might be a superior measure of objective crowding and, therefore, a stronger predictor of feeling crowded. As the analysis shows, this is not the case, as most of the objective measures are similarly correlated to subjective crowding. This would rather emphatically suggest that the modest relationship between the two types of crowding is not an artifact of measurement, and that the explanation of its modest nature lies elsewhere.

This suggests the possibility that the relationship may be stronger under certain specified conditions. Specifically, that objective and subjective crowding might be more highly related among women, those living with their in-laws, and among people with low household control. But as we have seen, the results are mixed and even when the expected patterns emerge, the differences tend to be rather small. If there are particular conditions under which the objective-subjective crowding relationship is stronger, we have failed to tap them.

The findings suggest, in sum, that while objective crowding may be a necessary condition, it is not sufficient to explain why people feel crowded. Why they feel crowded is largely a consequence of household circumstances and individual reactions to those circumstances. For example, as our analysis shows, the degree of household control has a significant and persistent effect on subjective crowding.

The situational nature of feeling crowded is highlighted by the results pertaining to the presence of others. While the presence of others elevates a subjective sense of crowding, as one would anticipate, so does spending less time at home than elsewhere. This may be due to three possibilities, which require further exploration. Feeling crowded, although one is in the household less time, could stem from a contrast effect between the home and other settings, or it could be that the subjective experience of crowding is the impetus to spend fewer hours in the household. Unfortunately, our data do not address these points. Alternatively, as we have suggested, it could well be that those who spend long hours in the household simply become inured to its congestion. Given the evidence for a ceiling effect and the non-linearity of the objective-subjective crowding relationship, we are inclined to accept this latter explanation. If this is the case, it would help explain why other crowding researchers (Booth, Johnson, and Edwards, 1980a,b) have found the adverse effects of subjective crowding to be unexpectedly selective and the relationships to various aberrant behaviors relatively modest in strength.

We should add, however, that these various explanations are not mutually exclusive, and that all three may have some viability. It seems reasonable that people will perceive, and perhaps react to, their primary environment differently than they do their secondary environment. The tropical climate of Thailand allows virtually year-round access to the out-of-doors and permits a high degree of spatial mobility. This creates the possibility for daily contrasts between the two environments. It further constitutes a circumstance for those who feel crowded in their primary environment to readily escape it. As Baldassare has argued (1978), having rational capacities, people learn over time how to deal with sensory overload that may come about because of crowding and engage in a strategy of what he terms "specialized withdrawal" in order to reduce the overload. Because of their household responsibilities, such as mothers with young children, some individuals may find it more difficult, and perhaps impossible, to escape the primary environment. It would be these individuals, we might suspect, who are most apt to be inured to household congestion. As an old Thai saying indicates: "A tight space is okay; a tight heart is more difficult."

To say objective crowding is a necessary but not sufficient condition to feeling crowded and to suggest that there is a relatively modest relationship between objective and subjective crowding should not lead us to conclude that neither of them has any consequences for how people behave. On the contrary, objective crowding plainly has something to do with how individuals perceive a situation. And, as our theoretical model suggests, it is that perception which will trigger a chain of reactions, some perhaps being of an adverse nature. It is to these potential reactions, or crowding outcomes, that we now turn. Because of the ceiling effect noted, we use the natural log of the objective and subjective crowding measures in examining their potential effects.

5
Crowding and Psychological Well-Being

If Stokols (1976) is correct in asserting people will be more reactant to the primary environment, one of the major outcomes of household crowding may have to do with an individual's psychological state and sense of well-being. Because of the social norms governing family life, particularly the expectation of harmonious relations, people may find it difficult to cope when their immediate environment is seen as being deficient, whether it be in terms of needed space or the ability to have some privacy. Rather than any immediate behavioral response, the first manifestations of a breakdown in coping mechanisms may be a psychological reaction or, for that matter, several psychological reactions. Since the home is a place to which one habitually returns, the perception of its deficiency can act as a chronic stressor, thereby intensifying any psychological reactions.

Currently, the causal connections between crowded dwellings and psychological reactions are poorly understood and open to speculation. Our theoretical model would suggest that objective crowding operates through the perception of such and a felt lack of privacy, resulting in elevated stress, which in turn may lead to other psychological costs. This, we think, specifies a plausible sequence of effects. There are two bodies of research literature that provide us with some clues as to what may be involved in the process and how psychological costs are incurred. One body of research has its origins in psychology; the other deals with life events and their consequences.

The psychological literature bears mainly on the connection between subjective crowding and stress, and how the former elevates the latter. Basically, what this body of psychological research suggests is that stress results from two distinguishable sources of interpersonal disturbances attendant to crowded conditions. One type of disturbance concerns distractions or unwanted social inputs. The other source of disturbance has to do with the interruption of activities, or interference (Sundstrom, 1975).

In crowded situations, distractions may be unavoidable, as they would not be in less congested circumstances. Unwanted conversations, uninvited nonverbal behaviors associated with intimacy, and even the noise created by others present possibly raise the level of stress a person experiences. Besides intrusions, crowded households may enhance the probability of interferences with a person's activities (Stokols, 1972). For example, if two people are conversing, or working on a task, other people present may make noise, attempt to redirect the conversation or activity, jostle the interactants, or otherwise create distractions that elevate stress.

This is essentially the reasoning of the stimulus overload approach to crowding and its effects. Theoretically, it traces from Simmel's (1905/1969) characterization of urban life as a situation where people have overabundant daily contacts at close distances. As more and more people come within an individual's sensory range, the nervous system becomes "overloaded." To compensate, urbanites, Simmel observed, develop coping strategies, the principal one being "social withdrawal." Social withdrawal is an attempt to limit social interaction or avoid it altogether. Wirth (1938) later elaborated on these ideas in his depiction of urbanism as a way of life, suggesting that there might be a counterpart to social withdrawal which is purely psychological in nature. Even in the presence of others, one may cope with the overabundance of stimuli by psychologically withdrawing.

Limited evidence, and mostly indirect evidence, does suggest such an overload adaptation. Desor's work (1972) is frequently cited, where she had subjects place figures in scaled-down rooms until they thought the space was too crowded. The subjects varied the density of the figures with different room designs, suggesting the importance of how a situation is perceived. Moreover, the subjects increased the number of figures within a space as the number of partitions increased, the partitions serving as barriers to visual stimuli. (It will be recalled that most of our focus group participants were recruited from slum areas, where partitions of various sorts were commonplace fixtures in households.) Field experiments also have reported deficits in task performance because of overstimulation in dense shopping environments (Saegert, Mackintosh, and West, 1975), and observations of urban pedestrians indicate that as city size increases, people walk faster, perhaps to minimize the amount of stimulation they encounter (Bornstein and Bornstein, 1976).

In counterpoint, some argue that the concept of stimulus overload has little usefulness in understanding proxemic patterns. Evans and Eichelman (1976) contend that the actual reception of stimuli has nothing to do with how humans respond. What is important is what the stimuli cognitively represent, and we are likely to respond differently in the presence of strangers than we do amidst people with whom we have an intimate relationship. Choldin (1978), too, takes the position that, as rational beings, humans learn to cope by using a strategy of "specialized withdrawal." As he puts it: "when confronted with high densities, individuals learn to conserve energies by attending to more rewarding encounters and avoiding neutral or potentially harmful interactions. Those having rational capacities can thus learn over time to avoid the experience of cognitive fatigue or social overload" (1978:42). Choldin would expect withdrawal to be more likely in encounters of a secondary nature (with strangers, neighbors, meeting new people) than ones that are primary in character (friends and family).

Since our focus is on the family, this would imply that we are not likely to find any crowding effects within the context of the household, the most primary of all environments. There is another possibility, however. Rather than social withdrawal, to which Choldin alludes, we might observe another type of specialized withdrawal that takes the form of psychological withdrawal. Even if there are no behavioral reactions to crowded conditions in a primary environment, it may be possible, at least as a short-term and intermittent coping strategy, for an individual to simply ignore the demands of others present or to pretend he or she did not hear the cues for interaction initiated by others.

Research literature on life events provides us with additional insight on how the experience of crowding can have consequences for psychological well-being. This body of research basically addresses the linkage between stress and various pathologies. What this research documents is a stress-pathology linkage, showing a positive relationship between life events and chronic strains and a multiplicity of physical and psychological outcomes (Kessler, Price, and Wortman, 1985). These outcomes include: illness susceptibility (Holmes and Masuda, 1974), general health status (LaRocco, House, and French, 1980), psychiatric impairment (Myers, Lindenthal, and Pepper, 1971), and general mental health (Dohrenwend and Dohrenwend, 1981).

The fundamental reasoning in life events research is that events represent change in the life course, which creates a disequilibrium imposing a need for readjustment. Disequilibrium makes a person vulnerable to stress and its consequences, which become evident during the period of readjustment (Kessler, Price, and Wortman, 1985). A great deal of this research focuses on such life events as job loss, death of a spouse, divorce, and rape. Exposure to such events elevates stress and sets off a process of adaptation. The effects of the event may be mediated by the social support an individual has and by various coping strategies, both of which may serve as buffers and act to reduce the deleterious effects of stress. As far as psychopathology specifically is concerned, Thoits (1983) has concluded that the most stress-provoking aspects of life events are their undesirability, magnitude, time clustering, and uncontrollability.

Although our concern here is not with life events as operationalized in this body of research, it appears reasonable to view one's housing and the fact of being crowded on a day-to-day basis as a source of chronic stress that may have psychological consequences. As has been rather persuasively shown in general community surveys, chronic stresses are more strongly related to nonspecific distress than life events themselves (Pearlin, Lieberman, Meneghan, and Mullen, 1981). We would expect, then, that people in crowded circumstances will manifest lower degrees of psychological well-being than those who reside in less congested housing.

Some Prior Studies

Studies dealing with household crowding and well-being have been comparatively sparse and their findings have been rather equivocal. What few studies we have had, though, have been geographically dispersed. Three come from Asia, including the cities of Manila, Hong Kong, and Singapore.

After factor-analyzing a large array of mental health measures, Marsella and associates (1970) found three of the factors to be associated with crowded housing conditions among Filipino men. Two of the factors, however, were also related to socioeconomic status, which was not controlled for in their analysis. Between this lack of statistical control and the small sample size (N = 99), the study is suggestive but does not furnish very strong support of a relationship between crowding and mental well-being.

One of the findings from Mitchell's (1971) survey of Hong Kong was a strong relationship between crowding and general unhappiness. Individuals in crowded households also tended to worry more. Both of these relationships were reduced when income was introduced as a control variable, although they still applied to the poor. Two indexes of more serious psychopathology, Mitchell found, were unrelated to overcrowding. However, both indexes--one an indicator of emotional illness and the other a measure of hostility--were positively related to floor of residence, suggesting some association between housing and individual well-being.

The Singapore study was based on data collected from 121 families residing in high-rise public housing, all of whom were of similar socioeconomic status. Crowding, Hassen (1977a, b) observed, was related to worrying and to stress. The emotional health of individuals was worst among those living on higher floor levels and where the dwelling was shared by persons who were not family members.

Data from New York provide stronger support for the crowding--well-being hypothesis. In collecting information from individuals who had applied to a mental-health program, Kahn and Perlin (1967) noted a strong relationship between hospitalization and the persons per room in the interviewee's residence. The rate of hospitalization increased significantly when the ratio was more than one-half of a person. When persons per room exceeded 1.0, the rate of hospitalization was almost four times that of individuals in the lowest crowding category. Crowding, they also found, was positively related to a prolonged duration of mental symptoms. Unfortunately, socioeconomic status was not controlled. It is worth noting that close to 78 percent of the Bangkok sample reside in situations where there is more than one person per room.

In general, these studies have been plagued by a lack of control for theoretically important factors, small and non-random samples, and sometimes both deficiencies, in addition to questionable measures of mental health. Perhaps the most convincing evidence we have of a connection between crowding and psychological well-being comes from the Chicago study, where an attempt was made to overcome these methodological problems (Gove and Hughes, 1983). Gove and Hughes, in that study, found that mental health is adversely affected by both objective (persons per room) and subjective crowding, although somewhat more strongly so by the latter than the former. They constructed or adopted eight different scales, trying to tap different dimensions of well-being. The scales concerned psychiatric symptoms, positive affect, a combination of the former called a mental-health balance scale, nervous breakdown, happiness, self-esteem, normlessness, and manifest irritation. Gove and Hughes point out that the crowding variables, on average, independently account for 37 percent of the total explained variation, with six control variables and collinearity accounting for the remainder.

While many of the studies dealing with crowding and psychological well-being have been poorly designed, they, along with conversations in our focus groups, gave us ample reason to anticipate there may be some fairly strong relationships between overcrowding and various psychological symptoms of disturbance. Witness these accounts and exchanges, suggesting an attempt to withdraw from the immediate situation--either physically or mentally:

Moderator: "Where do you go to be by yourself?"
Soomrouy: "In the house... making a long face. So no one dares to come near me. If not, I would come down from the flat and stay down until I feel better."

Sukit: "I feel I am my own self more when I'm outside.... doing my buying-selling.... I'm more myself out there.... when I'm home.... it's all different.... if not my wife, it would be my kids to come up with something.... something to bother me."

Moderator: "What do you do, then, when bothered?"

Sukit: "I just act like I didn't hear anything."

Rattanaporn: "Worse thing we do now is just refrain from talking to each other."

Prasert: "But if in bad mood, I'd rather be far, far away from my wife."

Petch: "I think it is because we have a lot of children in the house.... my children, my wife. When I want to have some time for myself, I send my children away.... then it will be my sister who comes to us for money... Oh! I had to give it to her just to buy me some peace.... then there will be my children having a problem outside of the house and I would hear my mother screaming at the top of her voice. My wife will be talking something more, which sooner or later will have to relate to me as the father of the children.... you know. It's like there is no time to be alone because there are so many living with us."

Despite the gentle demeanor and compliant nature of Thais, exchanges such as this led us to expect that men and women living in crowded households would exhibit more psychological symptoms and have lower levels of psychological well-being.

The Analysis

Psychological well-being is widely acknowledged to be a multidimensional concept (Bryant and Veroff, 1984). We, a accordingly, incorporated nine different measures of psychological well-being in the survey in order to capture some of the breadth of this concept. Seven of these are multiple-item scales. All of the indicators are inverse indicators of psychological well-being.

An important inverse indicator of psychological well-being is psychological distress. Psychological distress, as Mirowsky and Ross (1989:21) point out, has two major forms: depression ("feeling sad, demoralized, lonely, hopeless, worthless, wishing you were dead, having trouble sleeping, crying, feeling everything is an effort, and being unable to get going") and anxiety ("being tense, restless, worried, irritable, and afraid").

As Mirowsky and Ross (1989) and Dohrenwend et al. (1980) argue, depression and anxiety are not clearly distinct forms of psychological distress, but instead are closely intertwined. Our first scale, which we call "psychological distress," is a broad scale comprised of ten items that reflect many of the aspects of psychological distress referred to by Mirowsky and Ross. The items for this scale and all other scales can be found in Appendix B.

The second scale, called "unhappiness," comprised of three items reflects how unhappy the respondent is. The third measure, "irritability," is formed by six items indicating how often the respondent becomes irritated, abusive, or violent. The fourth scale, "psychological withdrawal," consists of three items pertaining to how often the respondent behaves so as to deliberately minimize interaction with other household members.

"Distraction", "loneliness" and "lethargy", are scales based on three, four, and five items, respectively, that reflect the extent to which the respondent has difficulty focusing on and completing daily tasks, feels lonely, and is lethargic.

Besides these seven scales, two single items serve as additional indicators of psychological well-being. These are: (1) Have you ever felt that you were about to lose your mind (go crazy)? and (2) Have you ever seriously thought about committing suicide? Both items are coded 1 = never, 2 = ever.

Several of these scales are adaptations of scales used in the Chicago study. Our psychological distress scale, for example, is a modification of Gove and Hughes' psychiatric symptoms scale, itself a combination of items from the Langner scale (1962) and from Dohrenwend and Cranwell (1970). The reliability of our psychological distress scale is virtually identical to that reported by Gove and Hughes for their psychiatric symptoms scale (1983:60). Our irritability scale is a modification of Gove and Hughes' manifest irritation scale, and has a similar reliability (1983:61). The psychological withdrawal scale is a modification of Gove and Hughes' psychological withdrawal scale. While the reliability of this scale is lower than that of the other scales used, it is similar to the reliability of Gove and Hughes' scale, even though we included only three of their four items (1983:55).

One scale, "felt demands," is used as an intervening variable in the following analyses. Felt demands is based on four items indicating the extent to which the respondent feels that other household members make demands on him or her. The content of this scale, and its reliability, is identical to the felt demands scale used by Gove and Hughes (1983:54). It does, however, play a slightly different role in the model. Gove and Hughes introduce lack of privacy and felt demands simultaneously, while we elaborate the causal ordering by introducing these two variables sequentially.

To disentangle the effects of crowding, several control variables are used: socioeconomic status, household structure, stage in the family life cycle, and household control. Socioeconomic status is represented by family income and the respondent's education. Family income was ascertained by asking the respondent to indicate which of ten income categories best represented the family income (see Appendix B). Education refers to the number of years of formal education completed. Two aspects of household structure are included in the analyses: (1) whether the household has two or three generations and (2) the number of married couples in the household. Stage in the family life cycle is identified by counting the number of minor children the respondent has in each of three broad age groups: (1) pre-school age, (2) elementary school age, and (3) high school age.

In prior studies by Baldasarre (1979) and by Gove and Hughes (1983), household control ("power") was indexed by the person's position in the household, an indirect indicator of power. Here, we measure household control as a continuous variable rather than as a nominal variable. Specifically, household control is a three-item scale indicating the extent to which a respondent perceives that he or she has the authority to make decisions within the household without consulting others.

Inasmuch as gender differences in psychological well-being have been of enduring interest to social researchers (Bryant and Veroff, 1984), we use interaction terms to determine whether there are differences between husbands and wives. Interaction terms were formed for sex and persons per room, perceived crowding, lack of privacy, and felt demands (1 = husband, 0 = wife). If the sex-persons per room interaction term was found to have, say, a significant positive effect on psychological distress, this would mean that persons per room has a significantly greater effect on psychological distress for husbands than for wives.

To avoid high multicollinearity, particularly involving the interaction terms, we used a "two pass" strategy. Each interaction term was introduced singly at the appropriate stage of the analysis. After each endogenous term was entered, the corresponding sex interaction term was added and then dropped before adding the next variable. As one example, the sex-persons per room interaction term was introduced after persons per room was entered into the equation. Then, this interaction term was removed, and other terms (lack of privacy and felt demands) were added to the model. In the second pass, each stage of the regression analysis was repeated, adding at the appropriate stage each interaction that was significant in the first pass, and retaining these interaction terms in later stages, rather than dropping them out as had been done in the first pass. In practice, there was never more than one significant interaction term in the final equation for any given dependent variable, indicating that there were few cases in which a variable had a different effect for men and women.

Zero-Order Relationships

The zero-order correlations contained in Table 5.1 show that persons per room is modestly but significantly related to all nine measures of psychological well-being, and all of the correlations are in the expected direction. For example, people who live in households that have more persons per room tend to display more psychological distress (r = .13), are less happy (.13), more lethargic (.15), and lonelier (.16). The other correlations, it will be seen, are more modest than these.

Both measures of subjective crowding tend to be more strongly related to psychological well-being than is objective crowding. Both perceived crowding and lack of privacy are significantly correlated with the six indicators of psychological well-being. Lack of privacy tends to be more strongly correlated with psychological well-being than is perceived crowding. For perceived crowding, the highest correlation is .22, while the highest for lack of privacy is .32.

Multivariate Results

Turning to the multivariate analyses, we first examine the effects of objective crowding, controlling for background variables, then add the subjective measures of crowding, and finally include felt demands in the model.

Persons per room, as can be seen in Table 5.2, has a small but significant effect on psychological distress, unhappiness, lethargy, and on loneliness, with the control variables included in the model (Beta1). In each case the beta is about .07 or .08. However, persons per room has no effect on irritability, psychological withdrawal, the feeling that one may "lose one's mind", or whether the respondent has ever contemplated suicide. There are no sex differences in the effect persons per room has on psychological well-being.

Table 5.2 presents the total (nonspurious) effects, direct effects, and, by implication, the indirect effects of persons per room, lack of privacy, and felt demands on the measures of psychological well-being. The total effect of persons per room (after the control variables have been added) is found in the column labelled Beta1, the total effect of lack of privacy is in Beta2, and the total effect of felt demands is in Beta3. The direct effect

Table 5.1 Zero-order Correlations Among Crowding and Measures of Psychological Well-Being

	1	2	3	4	5	6	7	8	9	10	11	12	13
1.Persons per room	1.000												
2.Perceived crowding	.192c	1.000											
3.Lack of privacy	.266c	.337c	1.000										
4.Felt demands	.134c	.204c	.403c	1.000									
5.Psychological distress	.130c	.225c	.325c	.371c	1.000								
6.Unhappiness	.129c	.090c	.308c	.201c	.362c	1.000							
7.Irritability	.080c	.137c	.177c	.217c	.451c	.182c	1.000						
8.Psychological withdrawal	.079c	.177c	.187c	.329c	.387c	.132c	.272c	1.000					
9.Lethargy	.147c	.160b	.266c	.283c	.610c	.261c	.346c	.317c	1.000				
10.Distraction	.093c	.204c	.289c	.362c	.509c	.225c	.291c	.416c	.382c	1.000			
11.Loneliness	.156c	.150c	.324c	.357c	.656c	.343c	.348c	.399c	.522c	.497c	1.000		
12."Lose your mind"	.073b	.091c	.220c	.196c	.366c	.198c	.228c	.161c	.332c	.207c	.336c	1.000	
13."Contemplate Suicide"	.071b	.096c	.182c	.166c	.288c	.191c	.216c	.095b	.247c	.176c	.289c	.330b	1.000
Mean	.564	1.770	.603	3.643	11.086	8.590	5.354	4.021	5.436	4.359	4.149	1.155	1.093
Standard Deviation	.552	.472	.677	2.605	6.431	1.799	3.311	2.716	3.321	2.851	3.018	.362	.291

[a] p<.05; [b] p<.01; [c] p<.001

Note: The correlations are based on list-wise deletion of cases with missing data (N=1992).

The natural logs of persons per room, perceived crowding, and lack of privacy are used in this analysis.

**Table 5.2 Relationship Between Measures of Psychological
Well-Being and Objective and Subjective Crowding, with Controls:
Standardized Regression Coefficients**

	Beta1	Beta2	Beta3
Psychological distress (N=1989)			
Persons per room	.071[b]	.020	.016
Lack of privacy	----	.303[c]	.191[c]
Felt demands	----	----	.283[c]
R^2	.048[c]	.127[c]	.193[c]
Perceived Crowding	----	.209[c]	.149[c]
Unhappiness (N=1996)			
Persons per room	.073[b]	.028	.027
Lack of privacy	----	.269[c]	.239[c]
Felt demands	----	----	.076[b]
R^2	.051[c]	.113[c]	.117[c]
Perceived Crowding	----	.061[b]	.032
Irritability (N=1990)			
Persons per room	.048	.020	.018
Lack of privacy	----	.168[c]	.099[c]
Felt demands	----	----	.173[c]
R^2	.020[c]	.044[c]	.069[c]
Perceived Crowding	----	.172[c]	.136[c]
Sex-perceived crowding	----	-.279[b]	-.283[b]
Psychological withdrawal (N=1996)			
Persons per room	.009	-.022	-.027
Lack of privacy	----	.183[c]	.063[a]
Felt demands	----	----	.302[c]
R^2	.031[c]	.060[c]	.135[c]
Perceived Crowding	----	.157[c]	.100[c]
Lethargy (N=1991)			
Persons per room	.085[c]	.046	.043
Lack of privacy	----	.233[c]	.150[c]
Felt demands	----	----	.207[c]
R^2	.053[c]	.099[c]	.135[c]
Perceived Crowding	----	.131[c]	.085[c]
Distraction (N=1996)			
Persons per room	.037	-.010	.015
Lack of privacy	----	.279[c]	.162[c]
Felt demands	----	----	.293[c]
R^2	.027[c]	.093[c]	.164[c]
Perceived Crowding	----	.185[c]	.123[c]

(continues)

Table 5.2 *(continued)*

	Beta1	Beta2	Beta3
Loneliness (N=1996)			
Persons per room	.075[b]	.025	.020
Lack of privacy	----	.300[c]	.194[c]
Felt demands	----	----	.268[c]
R^2	.066[c]	.143[c]	.202[c]
Perceived Crowding	----	.118[c]	.057[b]
"Lose your mind" (N=1994)			
Persons per room	.020	-.014	-.016
Lack of privacy	----	.206[c]	.157[c]
Psychological distress	----	----	.123[c]
R^2	.023[c]	.059[c]	.071[c]
Perceived Crowding	----	.076[c]	.043
"Contemplate suicide" (N=1995)			
Persons per room	.031	.005	.004
Lack of privacy	----	.207[c]	.164[c]
Sex-lack of privacy	----	-.093[b]	-.090[b]
Felt demands	----	----	.105[c]
R^2	.019[c]	.047[c]	.056[c]
Perceived Crowding	----	.085[c]	.059[a]

[a]$p<.05$; [b]$p<.01$; [c]$p< .001$

Note: Controlling for sex of respondent, family income, education of the respondent, stage in family life cycle, household control, number of generations, and number of married couples in the household. The natural logs of persons per room, perceived crowding, and lack of privacy are used in this analysis.

of persons per room, after introducing lack of privacy, is found in Beta2, while the direct effect of persons per room, after introducing both lack of privacy and felt demands, is in Beta3. Similarly, the direct effect of lack of privacy, after introducing felt demands, is found in Beta3. Indirect effects (not shown) can be determined by subtracting the direct effects from total effects. For example, the total effect of lack of privacy on psychological distress is .303; the direct effect, after introducing felt demands is .191; and the indirect effect of lack of privacy on psychological demands is .112 (.303 - .191).

When subjective crowding is added to the model, objective crowding has no significant effect on any of the measures of psychological well-being (Beta2). In other words, the small effect of persons per room on four measures of psychological well-being disappears when lack of privacy is added to the model.

In regard to the effects of subjective crowding, we find that lack of privacy is significantly related to all nine measures of psychological well-being. People who feel that they lack privacy are more likely to experience psychological distress, be less happy, feel more irritable, withdraw psychologically, be lethargic and easily distracted, feel they are losing their minds, and are more likely to indicate that they have contemplated suicide. Perhaps surprisingly, but consistent with the hypothesis, people who feel that they lack privacy also feel lonelier. In this case, loneliness refers less to an objective state of isolation, and more to a psychological frame of mind. For example, two of the items comprising this scale are "no one cares about me" and "nothing is worthwhile anymore." People may be lonely even with lots of other people around.

All of these effects are in the hypothesized direction, and this model produces larger R-squares than did the previous model, sometimes dramatically larger. For example, with lack of privacy added to the model, the model explains 12.7 percent of the variance in distress and 11.3 percent of the variance in unhappiness, compared to 4.8 percent and 5.1 percent without lack of privacy in the model.

The sex-lack of privacy interaction term is found to have a significant effect on the contemplation of suicide. Among wives, those who feel they lack privacy are more likely to indicate that they have contemplated suicide; among husbands, this relationship is significantly weaker. A separate analysis for husbands indicates that for them lack of privacy has no significant effect on contemplating suicide.

The last stage of the analysis involves introducing felt demands as an intervening variable (Table 5.2, Beta3). The results of this last stage can be summarized fairly simply. First, felt demands has a significant effect on each measure of psychological well-being. People who feel that other household members make many demands on them are more likely to display psychological distress, be less happy, feel more irritable, engage in psychological withdrawal, report that they sometimes feel that they are losing their mind, indicate that they have contemplated suicide, and so forth. Second, felt demands partly mediates the effect of lack of privacy on psychological well-being. This can be seen in that the direct effect of lack of privacy is muted after the introduction of felt demands. However, lack of privacy, it will be noted, continues to exert a significant direct effect on all nine measures of psychological well-being, even after controlling for felt demands.

These findings are based on using lack of privacy as the indicator of subjective crowding. When the analyses are replicated using perceived crowding as the indicator of subjective crowding, the results are quite similar. Specifically, (a) with one exception, persons per room is not significant when perceived crowding is added to the equation; the exception is when unhappiness is the dependent variable; (b) perceived crowding has a significant effect on each measure of psychological well-being, before felt demands is added to the model; (c) the effect of perceived crowding becomes muted once felt demands is added to the model; (d) the effect of perceived crowding is usually weaker than the corresponding effect of lack of privacy; and (e) perceived crowding has a significant effect on seven measures of psychological well-being after felt demands is added to the model (distress, irritability, withdrawal, lethargy, distraction, loneliness, and contemplating suicide). Whether one uses the measure of subjective crowding from the Chicago study or the one from the Toronto study, the results are similar, but we can conclude that lack of privacy has a stronger and more consistent effect than does perceived crowding.

Gender Differences

In light of reports from prior crowding studies, we hypothesized that the effects of crowding on psychological well-being would be greater for women than for men. There is some--but very little--evidence in our data to support such a conclusion for Bangkok. Sex interaction terms for persons per room, lack of privacy, and felt demands were tested. None of the sex interaction terms for persons per room or felt demands was significant. Only one of the sex interaction terms for lack of privacy was significant. This interaction term, as noted above, indicated that women who lack privacy are more likely to report that they have contemplated suicide; a separate analysis shows no such effect on men. When perceived crowding is used as the indicator of subjective crowding, there is again only one significant sex interaction term, this time indicating that women who feel crowded are more likely to be irritable; a separate analysis shows no effect for men. In both cases, then, the empirical results are consistent with the expectations suggested by the literature. But these are only two cases out of thirty-six tests for interaction. At least as far as psychological well-being is concerned, in most of the comparisons, men and women respond in quite similar ways to both objective and subjective crowding.

Conclusions

Previous survey-based studies of the effects of household crowding on psychological well-being in developing countries have suffered from various defects that the present study has attempted to avoid. These defects include poor measures of psychological well-being, inadequate samples, and inadequate controls for socioeconomic status and other relevant variables.

One virtue of selecting Bangkok as the site for a study of the effects of household crowding is that not only is there a high average level of crowding, but the range and, more importantly, the dispersion in crowding are greater than is typically the case in the United States and other industrialized countries. Baldassare, for example, reports the standard deviations of persons per room for the two studies he utilized to be .33 and .31 (1979:72). The standard deviation in persons per room for our study (1.3) is larger. Furthermore, in the United States, over 90% of the households are confined to what, in Bangkok, is the lower end of the range, fewer than one person per room. In Bangkok, 22% of the households have no more than one person per room, while over 10% have four or more persons per room.

In the United States, finding cases above a "threshold," a point beyond which crowding begins to have detrimental effects on psychological well-being, is problematic. In Bangkok, where crowding frequently reaches the level of two, three, or even four persons per room, surpassing a threshold is not problematic. The converse problem, a "ceiling effect," where additional crowding has little incremental effect, may be more of a problem, as we detailed in the previous chapter. However, because of the variability in the degree of objective crowding, a "ceiling effect" cannot account for all of our results. Although the average level of household crowding is high in Bangkok, more than one-fifth of the households have no more than one person per room, a level of crowding that does not seem objectively large. Subjectively, the difference between .25 person per room and 1.0 person per room may be less than the difference between 1.0 person per room and 4.0 persons per room. Hence, one might argue that one would expect to find greater effects of crowding over the range of crowding found in Bangkok than in United States cities.

Our findings provide selective support, at best, for the notion that objective household crowding is detrimental to psychological well-being. Lack of privacy, in contrast, is strongly and consistently related to psychological well-being. The effect of perceived crowding is not quite as strong, but is quite consistent. Furthermore, felt demands has a consistent, and in most cases relatively strong, effect on psychological well-being. There is only limited evidence that women are more reactive to crowding than are men.

One possible concern in interpreting these findings has to do with the relationship between household crowding and socioeconomic status, making it difficult to separate the effects of these two variables. Gove and Hughes were particularly concerned about this problem in their study, and, rather than selecting a representative sample of Chicago, they deliberately selected a random sample in which the correlation between social class and crowding would be minimized (1983:48-49). We elected not to follow such a strategy, in part because of the practical difficulties of doing so in Bangkok, where the statistical baseline data are not as plentiful as in Chicago, and in part because of a reluctance to oversample unrepresentative areas (even if they could be found), e.g., low income blocks with low levels of household crowding, and high income blocks with high levels of household crowding.

The correlation between socioeconomic status and persons per room in the Bangkok sample is stronger than that found in the Chicago sample, but is remarkably similar to that reported in the Toronto study. In the present sample, the correlation between education and persons per room is -.25, compared to -.10 in Chicago (Gove and Hughes, 1983:49) and -.23 and -.19 in Toronto for husbands and wives, respectively (Booth and Edwards, 1976:314). In our sample, the correlation between income and persons per room is -.34, compared to -.15 in Chicago (1983:49); Booth and Edwards controlled for occupation rather than income. Hence, we do have more multicollinearity between socioeconomic status and household crowding than did Gove and Hughes, but the level of multicollinearity is acceptable. The tolerance scores for all independent variables for all regression models reported in Table 5.2 are well within acceptable limits (Montgomery and Peck, 1982:297-305). Using a representative, random sample does not hamper our ability to show that the subjective dimension of household crowding does indeed have important detrimental effects on psychological well-being.

How strong is the effect of subjective household crowding on psychological well-being? The standardized coefficients provide a quantified answer, of course, but they do not indicate if these effects are small, moderate, or large. One can better answer this question by comparing the effects of crowding to the effects of income. In Bangkok, perhaps even more than in the United States, the poor have few support systems enabling them to survive. Poverty creates constant stresses, which surely take their toll in terms of psychological well-being and otherwise (Srole, Langner, Michael, Opler, and Rennie, 1962; Dohrenwend, 1975; Kessler, 1982; Mirowsky and Ross, 1989). In fact, though, we find in every case that the effect of lack of privacy is greater than the effect of income. For example, in the final model, the effect of lack of privacy on psychological distress is .19, while the effect of family income is barely half as large (-.10). This suggests that household crowding indeed has profound effects on psychological well-being.

Despite the cultural differences, our empirical results in Bangkok are highly similar to those found in Chicago. Like us, Gove and Hughes found that the effect of persons per room on psychological well-being, controlling for background variables but not controlling for lack of privacy or felt demands, is modest, and that these effects disappear when controls for lack of privacy and felt demands are added. In a like vein, Gove and Hughes observed that both lack of privacy and felt demands have significant effects on psychological well-being, even when both of these variables, persons per room, and control variables are included in the model (1983:56,76).

Given the close correspondence between the results for Bangkok and those for Chicago, an intriguing issue is whether the effects of crowding in Bangkok are primarily a result of the high level of crowding or whether similar results might have been found in Bangkok, even if the level of crowding approximated that found in the United States.

We addressed this issue by restricting our analysis to those cases in our sample where there was no more than one person per room--this cut-off being an approximation of household congestion in the United States. Replicating Table 5.2 (N = 439), remarkably similar results obtain. The main difference is that within this narrow range of persons per room, objective crowding has no significant detrimental effect on any of the measures of psychological well-being. Lack of privacy, on the other hand, has a significant effect on each of the dependent measures, with the same caveat as before, namely, that lack of privacy increases the likelihood of contemplating suicide only for wives, but not husbands. As before, the effect of perceived crowding is weaker than the effect of lack of privacy. Perceived crowding has a significant effect on seven of the nine dependent measures. These results make it difficult to argue that Thais have become in any way habituated to high levels of household crowding. Significant deleterious effects prevail even within a relatively modest range of household crowding.

In sum, we find that objective household crowding--persons per room--has only weak and selective effects on psychological well-being, but the subjective experience of household crowding is a chronic stressor that has a strong and consistent detrimental effect on psychological well-being. These results pertain not simply to a single item or a single scale, but are documented by reference to a broad array of measures of psychological well-being. The effects are unmistakable for both men and women. At least in Bangkok, and possibly in other cities with comparable levels of household crowding, crowding constitutes a major threat to psychological well-being.

6

The Impact of Crowding on the Family

The family forms the core of the household. This is particularly true in Thailand, where it is a rarity for a single adult, either male or female, to live alone or separate from some family member. In suggesting that crowding has deleterious effects on social relations, crowding theory would lead us to expect that some of its most severe and adverse consequences would bear on the husband-wife relationship and the relations parents have with their children. We examine a range of these potential effects in this chapter.

Background: The Thai Family

To get married and to have a family are major goals for young Thais. Not only is the family highly valued but it constitutes a central social group around which the individual's life revolves. To a degree unknown in Western societies, many Thais live in family compounds or three-generation households.

Much of this stems from the agrarian nature of the Thai economy. Despite the inroads of modernization and industrialization, Thailand today remains largely agricultural. Over eighty percent of the population continues to reside in rural areas. Extended families provide a collective labor capacity needed for planting and harvesting. As the senior generation grows older and loses the capacity to work, extended families are further beneficial in providing care for the elders. Extended families constitute a form of social security for the elderly (Klausner, 1987).

In rural areas, family compounds remain fairly common. At the time of marriage, it is commonplace for the man to move in with his in-laws, at least for an initial period. The household at this stage of the life cycle is thus made up of young married daughters, their spouses, their children, and their parents. Later, a separate, but nearby, residence is set up. As one observer suggests, "The love of freedom among the Thais leads to the establishment of nuclear family systems ... which leads to the desire to set up their own home later on" (Wichiencharoen, 1972). Nevertheless, many tasks continue to be shared, especially in terms of food preparation and bringing produce to market.

In urban and industrialized Bangkok, nuclear families predominate. But one of the major factors contributing to household crowding is the de facto formation of extended families. Because of economic necessity, many families are unable to maintain a separate household, particularly in the early years of marriage. As in rural areas, a typical pattern involves newlyweds moving in with their parents, usually the wife's parents. Extended family formation is further reinforced by a sense of family obligation. With the rapid population growth that has taken place in Bangkok in the last two decades, a large portion of its residents are first-generation migrants from various rural areas around the country. Due to elaborate family relationships in the village of origin, people residing in Bangkok feel a sense of obligation to provide shelter to newcomers to the city. This sense of obligation sometimes goes beyond providing for kin. Strong friendship bonds between Bangkokians and people in their place of origin obligate them to sheltering those friends as they in turn migrate to the city (Fuller, 1990). In some instances, the obligation even entails providing for the kin of friends, not just the friends themselves.

Another type of extended family can be found in Bangkok. Rather than being vertically extended, comprised of three or more generations, this is one that is horizontally extended. It is usually made up of two or more married pairs and their children, where there is a kin bond between one of the spouses in each married pair. This could involve sisters and their immediate families, brothers with theirs, or, in some cases, a brother-sister combination. The household also may become horizontally extended by including unmarried siblings and cousins of the same generation. This is sometimes supplemented by the presence of nieces and nephews. These families of convenience are largely an outgrowth of economic necessity, and the household composition may be reconstituted when any of the members reach a point where they can afford their own dwelling.

Even though a nuclear family is the predominant family structure in Bangkok, such families are not "isolated" in the sense Parsons (1965) used that term to describe American society. There continues to be a strong sense of family ties and kin obligations. Urban Thais still consider themselves part of a larger network and feel they are part of an extended family of some kind. They seem to reflect the characteristics that Phillips (1965) earlier suggested were distinguishing attributes of the Thai peasant: in the interest of amity, there is a strong sense of love, obligation, and respect that derives from the simple fact of kinship.

Although family ties remain strong, large families are on the wane. Part of this undoubtedly can be attributed to the steady growth of urban areas. Part has to do with the industrialization process itself, where the economy is no longer family-based but relies on individual wage-earners. Child labor, unlike in a rural setting, has comparatively little value. The trend toward smaller families has been accelerated by a strenuous campaign on the part of the government and others to introduce effective contraception in order to reduce the fertility rate. Compared to many other developing nations, these efforts have been relatively successful. In the mid-1960s, the Total Fertility Rate was estimated to be 6.3 (Knodel, Chamratrithirong, and Debavalya, 1987). In the late 1960s, the fertility rate began to fall. By the mid-1970s, the Total Fertility Rate had dropped to about 4.9. The Thailand Demographic and Health Survey, conducted in 1987, reports a Total Fertility Rate of 2.11 for the country as a whole, having dropped from 2.36 during the period 1982-1986. Over that same interval, the Total Fertility Rate for Bangkok was 1.60. Even the national rate of 2.11 is below replacement level, estimated to be 2.25 (Chayovan, Kamnuansilpa, and Knodel, 1988). The average number of children in our sample households was slightly more than two, which is probably typical for more urbanized areas.

Marriage today is monogamous. This was not officially the case up until 1935, when the newly established People's Assembly enacted into law a proposed Marriage Bill that became a part of the Civil and Commercial Code. The Bill specified, for the first time, that all marriages were to be registered and only one wife could be legally registered. This, in effect, legally abolished the "old custom," declaring that all polygamous unions were henceforth illegal. As various historical accounts attest (Landon, 1939-1968), relatively few marriages were registered in the early days of the Marriage Law. However small, registration was a burden, involving a visit to a district office, with no discernible benefit from having an official declaration of one's marriage. In small communities, everyone knew the marital status of others and, early on, there were no penalties for the failure to register a marriage.

What proportion of the marriages, prior to 1935, were polygamous is unknown. If we take as our guide those societies where polygamy is considered the ideal form of marriage, it probably was a rather small proportion. In polygamous societies, it is usually only the men who are economically well-off who can afford to have more than one wife. As in any society, these men tend to be a small minority.

Today, registration is difficult to avoid. A house registration is required for any dealings with government agencies. Among other things, this concerns obtaining a birth certificate, entering a child into the public school system, buying a dwelling or land, and obtaining public health services. Only monogamous couples qualify for this registration. Informally, however, an unknown, but small minority of men maintain what are referred to as "mia noi" or minor wives, who do not have legal status. Generally, as a practical matter, legal and minor wives do not occupy the same household.

Unlike some Asian societies, mate selection in Thailand is by mutual choice, not a system of arranged marriage. As a saying goes: "To build a house, you must consider the person who is going to live in it. To build a bed, you must consider the person who will sleep in it."

This is not to say that parents play no role in the selection process, but that the parental role tends to be an indirect one. It may involve the recommendation of a "suitable person," the encouragement to pursue a particular relationship, or expressing approval or disapproval of a particular person. Dating among teenagers, in the American sense of that term, can be observed in Bangkok. Most dating, however, involves groups. But Thai parents remain uneasy about the dating process. During courtship, the rule still is to be chaperoned. Chaperonage enables the female to obtain the blessing of her parents and for the male to avoid creating a "bad name" for his future wife's family. Increasingly, at least in urban areas, chaperonage is by peers and not family members. Prior to an impending marriage, it is customary for the male or his parents to present to the female's parents so-called "milk money" or a brideprice. This may be in terms of cash or precious items, such as diamond rings, land, or objects made of gold.

Although some contend that the Thai marital relationship is an egalitarian one (Sangsingkeo, Leoprapai, and Sriburatham, 1988), there is opposing evidence. Thai culture emphasizes "macho" characteristics in males, and there is a clear double standard pertaining to sex, whether it be premarital or extramarital. Women bear the sole responsibility for household chores. On the other hand, most wives work, bringing valuable economic resources into the family. Particularly in lower income families, the wife's income may be more steady than the husband's. Furthermore, as Klausner (1977) points out, it is commonplace in Thai families for the wife to manage the family income. Husbands are expected to turn over all or the major part of their wages or salaries to their wives. There is also a matriarchal bias in Thai society. This is manifested linguistically by the ubiquitous compound words involving the term "mother." It can be seen in the pattern of sons-in-law residing, at least in an initial period following marriage, with the wife's parents.

Buddhism emphasizes responsibility and compassion as guiding principles, and Buddhism is a religion of action. It stresses the avoidance of extremes in all things. And so it is that harmony should reign in the family. Spouses should care for one another. Parents should love and protect their children. Children should respect their parents. It is within the family that one gains physical, psychological, social, and economic sustenance. But is it so? Particularly in crowded households, our theoretical model would suggest this prized harmony, care, and concern might be difficult to achieve. And it was plain from our focus group discussions that for these individuals achieving these values was especially elusive. This is blatantly illustrated in several of the group exchanges.

> Malee: "We don't have to show that we love anymore. If I do it, it would be so awkward."
>
> Chalerm: "I want a divorce, I want him to go. I only think of sewing. When he's drunk, he is very disgusting."
>
> Chamnian: "I'm not interested in seeing his face, but I am in his money."
>
> Lamjai: "I don't usually know where he goes, I don't care. My neighbor used to ask me how could I live with him not knowing what he does."
>
> * * * * *

> Michao: "Since we are getting older, we get calmer. As Sompong said, when we were young, still teenagers, we got hot temper. Now getting older, it's better to be calmer."
>
> Sukit: "What he just said is true. In my case, we also used to fight very often. But for the last few years, I felt that violence is no solution. The best solution is silence. Let her complain, let her do it whether she's right or wrong. I'd only keep quiet, and it works. Eventually she stops, tensions are eased. As a matter of fact, I sympathize with her somehow. She only stays home, not much activities, no varieties in life, monotonous. Of course, she is sure to have some frustrations, which she ought to let out. So just take that. Let her breathe out her frustrations, just like a radio station left turned on, don't pay attention."
>
> * * * * *

> Soomrouy: "I am with my husband very often, because he doesn't have to go to work. We have our own furniture business, so he stays around all the time. But when we are together alone in the house, we have nothing to say to one another. There have been hours we don't talk. It's just like that. There can be weeks that we stay in the flat together in the day time, cook and eat, after that he takes a nap, and I go

out and walk around. We really have nothing to say to each other."

Moderator: "How do you find this arrangement?"

Soomrouy: "Nice, quiet."

Nor was the elusive achievement of harmony, care, and concern necessarily confined to the marital relationship, as several focus group members attested to in discussing relations with their children:

Moderator: "What do you do when they get carried away with their playing?"

Attaporn: "I scream at them, and I often get physical with them too... I can't take a lot of that. As I said, I feel like I will have a nervous breakdown." (laughter)

Rattanaporn: "When it gets that way in my house, I will blow up... I'll hit and I scold. I don't do a lot of that now as my children are pretty much grown up. When they were younger, I remember I hit them almost every day. Even at that, they often got out of hand. The good thing was that the flat has the area downstairs. [Flats are constructed with an open area at ground level where children can play and people can congregate.] If we had to live all the time in the flat together, it could have been unbearable to live together in good health, both children and parents."

Moderator: "Why do you get so upset to hit them everyday?"

Rattanaporn: "They are both stubborn and disobedient, so I must hit them."

Moderator: "And what do they do?"

Rattanaporn: "They cry, of course." (laughter)

We now turn to an empirical examination of some of the marital and family outcomes that crowding might have, following a brief overview of some pertinent findings from previously conducted studies.

Prior Studies on Crowding and Family Relations

Selective support for the hypothesis that crowding adversely affects family relations has been reported in several studies. Based on a secondary analysis of two national surveys, Baldassare (1979) notes that crowding is fairly strongly related to decrements in marital relations, but that it has far less impact on the quality of parent-child relations. Specifically, as household congestion increases, husbands and wives both report having poorer marital relations and a lower degree of marital satisfaction. But crowding, Baldassare suggests, has far less of an impact on the quality of parent-child relations. Out of seven quality measures, he found only two to be related to household crowding. People in congested houses were less likely to say they enjoyed their children, and they reported less overall family satisfaction.

In a more elaborate analysis, using data from a sample of Toronto households, Booth and Edwards (1976) find modest effects between different crowding measures and various aspects of spousal relations. Among wives, subjective crowding was associated with the number of husband-wife arguments, threats to leave home, and a love decrement scale assessing the quality of the spousal relationship. Although perceived crowding had no effect on two dimensions of the parent-child relationship inspected (playing with children and striking children), the number of times parents hit their children was positively associated with objective household crowding. The crowding effects for husbands, however, were more selective, bearing on only one of the spousal relations measures and the dimension of the parent-child relationship involving the striking of children.

Like the Toronto study, Gove and Hughes' (1983) investigation of a sample of households in Chicago was specifically designed to examine the impact of household crowding on family relations. They observe an even broader array of crowding effects, involving both the objective and subjective dimensions of crowding. Their subjective measures of crowding, in particular, are consistently related to a lack of positive marital relations, the presence of negative relations, a low score on a marital relations balance scale, and not feeling close to one's spouse. Parents living in congested homes felt harassed by their children, were relieved when the children were outside the dwelling, showed less support for their children, and punished their offspring more frequently.

Two European studies provide additional support for the crowding hypothesis. In a study of Parisian households, Chombart de Lauwe (1961) looked at the effect of floor space per person, reporting that cramped space was associated with family discord in the form of tensions between mothers and their children and more frequent accounts of child misbehavior. An Italian study also notes evidence of family discord in crowded households (Gasparini, 1973). As measured by persons per room and square meters per couple, Gasparini concluded that crowding led to more frequent quarreling among husbands and wives. Crowding was also associated with increased reports concerning the nervousness of children and declines in the children's school performance.

Two Asian investigations are also pertinent, one being a survey on overcrowding in Hong Kong and the other a study of 121 families residing in high-rise flats in Singapore. In the Hong Kong study, Mitchell

(1971) found a strong connection between objective crowding and complaints about both a lack of space and an inadequate amount of privacy. He further suggests that high levels of crowding affects the communication between husband and wife and decreases their emotional happiness. Not unexpectedly, parents in crowded households were less likely to know where their children were, suggesting a weakening of parental control under crowded conditions. In general, the crowding effects observed were stronger where more than one family occupied a household and if they lived on a higher floor level of a residence. Overall, though, Mitchell does not find pervasive discord among crowded residences. In a similar vein, the Singapore study indicates an intensification of crowding effects when the housing unit is a shared one and when the unit is located on a higher floor level (Hassen, 1977a, b). Overcrowding, Hassen suggests, is related to both worrying and the amount of stress experienced. Like Mitchell, he found that people in crowded households supervised their children less, more frequently leading to delinquency on the part of the juveniles among them. As in the Italian study, children residing in crowded circumstances performed less well in school.

The Analysis

The Scales

To look at how crowding may affect the family, our analyses involve three scales dealing with the marital relationship and three scales bearing on parent-child relations. Later, we will look at how crowding affects relations between siblings and briefly examine its effect on violence.

One of the marital relations scales concerns the relative stability of the respondent's marriage. Thais speak of having a "hot heart," *jay rawn*. Roughly translated, it means being out of control or hot-headed. The focus group participants gave stark evidence that their marriages engendered a great deal of "hot heart."

Kannikar: "During the Buddhist lent, he does not drink. I think it's also because he has no money for it. He has not worked for three days. He has no money now. I remember before he left me seven years ago, he used to drink a lot, and I used to hate him. So one day I was cleaning the fish, the children were crying, the twins were only two years old. He walked in the house a little drunk and patted me on the head and walked pass me. I don't know what got to me. I threw the knife at him and it cut him in his stomach. He was taken to the hospital. I didn't even care to go with him. He was near death, but he did not tell the police who did it. After he got out of the hospital, I told him that he did not have to live here if he did not want to and I did not care for him anymore. Being married to him brought me a lot of hardship, and I wanted nothing to do with him. I also told his parents the same thing. After a while he got packed and went to live with his parents. It was his parents who came to visit me occasionally and told me that their son had changed a great deal, and they wanted me to take him back. After seven years and a lot of promises from him not to drink, I let him come back. He also told me the main reason to come back was to be with the children, and that was what he does now. I don't talk to him as a wife to a husband. Sometimes when he comes home with some money to give me, I will talk to him and be nice to him a little. I don't care at all what he does, where he goes, when he returns."

* * * * *

Moderator: "What do you do when you want to be alone with your husband?"

Kannikar: "I never want to be alone with him, nor talk to him. To tell you the truth, I never did want to be alone with him even before we were married. I hated him even before that. But my mother loved him a lot, and so she said to me to take him as a husband. I hated him like shit, I don't know how to sweet talk. I never did it with him."

* * * * *

Bang-on: "If he brings me money, I can sweet talk with him all day. Even if he scolds me, I won't get angry. When he does not give me money, I don't even want to look at his face."

Tima: "Seeing my husband is the start of the fight. When we meet, we always argue."

Kannikar: "My husband and I are the same, we get at each other every time we meet."

As these quotations suggest, harmonious marital relations were elusive for a number of the focus group participants, and they give some indication that several had unstable marriages. While many researchers lamentably use the term "marital instability" to denote divorce, it more appropriately designates a "shaky" intact marriage. It constitutes the negative pole of a continuum of marital cohesion (Booth, Johnson, White, and Edwards, 1984). Conceptualized in this manner, marital instability has two dimensions, a cognitive component and a behavioral component. The cognitive dimension has to do with what people think about their marriage, while the behavioral component concerns actions they have taken on the basis of these thoughts.

As one dependent variable in our analyses, we use a short form of a marital instability scale developed in the United States to investigate marital change over the life course (Booth, Johnson, and Edwards, 1983; Edwards, Johnson, and Booth, 1987). This scale has undergone extensive validation procedures in the United States and has been shown to have a high degree of reliability (.93). Using data from a panel study of life course changes in American marriages, the scale has been demonstrated to be predictive of subsequent divorce and permanent separation (Edwards, Johnson, and Booth, 1987). The abbreviated scale consists of four items, as shown in Appendix B. Using the Bangkok data, the scale relates, as it does in the United States, to two known correlates of divorce, family income and age at marriage. In each case, there is an inverse relationship. A higher score suggests a more unstable marriage.

A second scale we use taps the negative aspect of marital relations, namely a seven-item scale which we call "marital arguments." A higher score on this scale designates poor marital relations. The third scale, in contrast, is designed to measure positive affect or "marital companionship." This scale is not just the flip-side of the indicator of marital conflict, which the marital arguments scale is designed to measure. Indicators of negative relations alone may not be sufficient to detect potential crowding consequences. If people do adapt to household crowding or if they are able to cope with a highly congested situation, there still might be declines in the positive aspects of their relationships rather than merely increases in more unpleasant experiences. The higher the score on this four-item scale, the more frequently couples do things together and display positive affect toward each other.

If crowding has adverse consequences for the parent-child relationship, we would expect parents in congested households to be less supportive of their children, to feel more tension in this relationship, and to discipline their children more frequently. The scale items tapping these dimensions of the parent-child relationship are included in Appendix B. A higher scale score means, respectively, that the parent is more supportive, experiences greater tension, and disciplines the child(ren) more frequently.

As indicated in Chapter 3, two scales, felt demands and psychological distress, are used in the analyses as intervening measures of stress. Felt demands is a scale based on four items indicating the extent to which the respondent feels that other household members make many demands on him or her. This scale is adopted, with some modification, from the Chicago study (Gove and Hughes, 1983). In that survey, the scale was used as an indicator of subjective crowding, the idea being that those in objectively crowded circumstances would have more demands placed upon them because of the inescapability of the complex role obligations within the family. We are postulating a somewhat different, and more intricate, causal sequence. We think it is equally reasonable to view felt demands as being a result of one's perception of being crowded and an unrealized sense of privacy. Conceptually, we see felt demands as one consequence of stress, which theoretically has a central role in intervening between crowding (both objectively and subjectively measured) and pathological reactions. The higher the score, the more perceived demands the person reports.

The other stress measure concerns psychological distress. According to Mirowsky and Ross (1989) and Dohrenwend et al. (1980), depression and anxiety are not clearly distinct forms of psychological distress, but instead are closely intertwined. Tapping the broader concept of felt stress, our measure of psychological distress is a scale comprised of ten items that reflect various symptoms, including aspects of both anxiety and depression. A higher score indicates greater distress.

Clearly, marital relations may be affected by many factors other than household crowding and the intervening variables posited in our model. For example, the number and ages of a couple's children can affect the marital relationship. And, the presence of parents, parents-in-law, or married siblings in the same household may affect the quality of marital relations.

To separate these other effects, the analyses, as in the examination of psychological well-being, include controls for socioeconomic status, stage in the family life cycle, household structure, and household control. In addition, in looking at family relations, we introduce a control for housing satisfaction. The quality of one's housing and how satisfied or dissatisfied one is with it can easily confound the relationship between crowding and its possible outcomes; hence, the necessity to control for this factor. Quality of housing is measured subjectively by a variety of items. We created a scale called "housing satisfaction" based on 11 items that indicate the extent to which a respondent is satisfied with various specific aspects of his or her housing. As with the other scales, a listing of the scale items appears in Appendix B. A higher score on the housing satisfaction scale designates greater satisfaction.

Two of the prior North American studies suggest that women may be more reactive to crowding than are men (Gove and Hughes, 1983; Booth, 1976). Gove and Hughes (1983) contend that this is so because (1) women are more attentive to the needs of others and (2) women typically play a nurturant role, especially within the context of the household. Based on comparisons of the magnitude of regression coefficients, both the Chicago and the Toronto study find some support for this argument. This prompted us to look for possible interaction effects involving gender as it relates to marital and parent-child relations.

Marital Relations Results

The zero-order correlations involving objective household crowding show that persons per room is modestly, but significantly, related to each of the marital relations measures. As anticipated, higher levels of objective crowding are associated with greater marital instability and marital arguments. As also expected, a higher number of persons per room is associated with a lower score for companionship (Table 6.1).

Perceived crowding is significantly correlated with both marital instability and marital arguments. Lack of privacy, our other indicator of subjective crowding, is significantly related to all three measures of marital relations, and all of these correlations are in the expected direction.

Table 6.2 shows the relationships between marital relations and objective crowding, after introducing relevant controls. While persons per room is significantly correlated with all three measures of marital relations, these relationships disappear after controlling for the background variables (see Beta1 in Table 6.2). Depending on the specific dependent variable, family income, education, and housing satisfaction have the primary role in reducing the effect of persons per room.

The relationships between marital relations and both objective and subjective crowding, controlling for background measures, are shown in the second column of Table 6.2. As before, persons per room is unrelated to the marital relations measures. Perceived crowding, however, is significantly related to both marital instability and marital arguments.

The more crowded one feels, the more unstable one's marriage and the more reported arguments there are between spouses. This does not hold for marital companionship.

Stronger results are obtained when we use lack of privacy as the measure of subjective crowding. Lack of privacy is significantly related to all three measures of marital relations, and the beta for lack of privacy is larger than the beta for perceived crowding for all three measures.

Crowding, at least as subjectively experienced, has an impact on psychological distress, as we saw in the previous chapter. Additionally, we anticipated and found that crowding has an impact on felt demands. The impact of persons per room, perceived crowding, and lack of privacy on

Table 6.1 Zero-order Correlations among Crowding and Family Relations Measures

	1	2	3	4	5	6	7	8	9	10	11	12
1. Persons per room	1.000											
2. Perceived crowding	.193[c]	1.000										
3. Lack of privacy	.265[c]	.336[c]	1.000									
4. Felt demands	.133[c]	.201[c]	.402[c]	1.000								
5. Psychological distress	.129[c]	.221[c]	.322[c]	.367[c]	1.000							
6. Marital instability	.124[c]	.097[c]	.240[c]	.256[c]	.389[c]	1.000						
7. Marital arguments	.130[c]	.186[c]	.261[c]	.305[c]	.424[c]	.493[c]	1.000					
8. Marital companionship	-.107[c]	-.022	-.198[c]	-.066[b]	-.084[b]	-.231[b]	-.181[c]	1.000				
9. Parent-child tension	.125[c]	.119[c]	.224[c]	.285[c]	.358[c]	.247[c]	.253[c]	-.141[c]	1.000			
10. Supportive behavior	-.082[b]	.050	.011	.059[a]	.072[b]	-.011	-.024	.272[c]	-.024	1.000		

(continues)

Table 6.1 *(continued)*

	1	2	3	4	5	6	7	8	9	10	11	12
11. Discipline of children	.073[b]	.080[b]	.125[c]	.127[c]	.259[c]	.227[c]	.189[c]	-.087[c]	.371[c]	.104[c]	1.000	
12. Sibling conflict	.027-	.022	.073[a]	.099[b]	.153[b]	.119[b]	.115[b]-	.067[a]	.314[c]	.054	.383[c]	1.000
Mean	.5641	.769	.6013	.63811	.066-7	.18411	.9989	.0108	.0909	.2466	.4638	.513
Standard Deviation	.551	.470	.6772	.6006	.4161	.2384	.1743	.1383	.0372	.4002	.4256	.329

[a]$p<.05$ [b]$p<.01$ [c]$p<.001$

Note: The correlations are based on listwise deletion of cases with missing data. For rows 1-9, N=1993; for rows 10 and 11, N=1392; and for row 12, N=1184. The natural logs of persons per room, perceived crowding, and lack of privacy are used.

Table 6.2 Relationship Between Measures of Marital and Family Relations and Objective and Subjective Crowding, with Controls: Standardized Regression Coefficients

	Beta1	Beta2	Beta3
Marital Instability (N=1979)			
Persons per room	.036	.030	.030
Perceived crowding	----	.067[b]	-.012
Felt demands	----	----	.110[c]
Psychological distress	----	----	.311[c]
R^2	.072[c]	.076[c]	.190[c]
Lack of privacy	----	-.181[c]	-.069[b]
Marital Arguments (N=1985)			
Persons per room	.052	.039	.039
Perceived crowding	----	.161[c]	.071[c]
Felt demands	----	----	.156[c]
Psychological distress	----	----	.329[c]
R^2	.063[c]	.087[c]	.230[c]
Lack of privacy	----	.226[c]	.088[c]
Marital Companionship (N=1986)			
Persons per room	.005	.003	.003
Perceived crowding	----	.020	.029
Felt demands	----	----	.002
Psychological distress	----	----	-.047
R^2	.077[c]	.078[c]	.080[c]
Lack of privacy	----	-.140[c]	-.152[c]
Supportive Behavior (N=1386)			
Persons per room	-.030	-.038	-.037
Perceived crowding	----	.083[b]	.061[a]
Felt demands	----	----	.067[a]
Psychological distress	----	----	.065[a]
R^2	.053[c]	.059[c]	.069[c]
Lack of privacy	----	.054	.011
Parent-child tension (N=1983)			
Persons per room	.020	.012	.011
Perceived crowding	----	.090[c]	.013
Felt demands	----	----	.149[c]
Psychological distress	----	----	.271[c]
R^2	.109[c]	.116[c]	.222[c]
Lack of privacy	----	.167[c]	.046

(continues)

Table 6.2 (continued)

	Beta1	Beta2	Beta3
Discipline of children (N=1386)			
Persons per room	-.029	-.035	-.029
Perceived crowding	----	.057ᵃ	.016
Felt demands	----	----	.032
Psychological distress	----	----	.201ᶜ
R^2	.145ᶜ	.148ᶜ	.188ᶜ
Lack of privacy	----	.056ᵃ	-.011

ᵃp<.05; ᵇp<.01; ᶜp< .001

Note: When perceived crowding is in the model, lack of privacy is not, and vice versa. Controlling for sex of respondent, family income, education of the respondent, stage in the family life cycle, household control, number of generations, number of married couples in the household, and housing satisfaction. The natural logs of persons per room, perceived crowding, and lack of privacy have been used as explanatory variables in the models.

psychological distress and felt demands is examined by means of a regression model in which the former three variables are used as predictors, along with the control variables. The results (not presented in tabular form) indicate that both perceived crowding and lack of privacy have an effect on psychological distress and felt demands at the .001 level. The standardized regression coefficients for the effects of perceived crowding and lack of privacy on psychological distress are .130 and .216, respectively. The corresponding effects on felt demands are .115 and .321. If either subjective measure of crowding is used without the other, the corresponding effect is stronger. Persons per room, however, has no significant effect on either intervening variable, whether or not the subjective measures of crowding are included.

Column three in Table 6.2 displays the relationships between the dependent measures and both subjective and objective crowding, incorporating background variables and the two intervening variables, felt demands and psychological distress. Again, persons per room has no effect on any of the measures of marital relations. With psychological distress and felt demands added to the model, perceived crowding no longer has a significant effect on marital instability; it still has a significant effect on marital arguments, but the effect is muted. In sum, the effect of perceived crowding on marital instability is fully explained by the intervening variables, while it retains a significant, albeit reduced, effect on marital arguments after introducing the intervening variables. Once more, stronger results are obtained when lack of privacy is used as the measure of subjective crowding. Lack of privacy is significantly related to all three dependent measures even after the intervening variables are introduced.

Both psychological distress and felt demands have significant and relatively strong effects on marital instability and marital arguments. The effect of distress on each measure of marital relations is over .3, while that of felt demands is about .1 or .15.

Contrary to expectations, wives are not more reactive to crowding than husbands are. Although wives report higher marital instability and more marital arguments than husbands do, none of the interaction terms involving sex is statistically significant. While Booth and Edwards (1976) and Gove and Hughes (1983) present data suggesting that crowding has a greater effect on family relations for women, neither team reports significance tests for these differences. The main difference between their results and ours, then, may be simply that we used statistical tests.

Parent-Child Relations Outcomes

The zero-order correlations between objective household crowding and parent-child relations show that persons per room is modestly, but significantly, related to supportive behavior, parent-child tension, and discipline of children (Table 6.1). Parents who live in objectively more crowded households tend to provide less support to their children, have more tension in their interactions with their children, and discipline their children more frequently.

Neither perceived crowding nor lack of privacy is significantly related to supportive behavior, but both are significantly, though modestly, related to parent-child tension and the discipline of children. These relationships, too, are in the expected direction. Parents are likely to feel more tension with their children and discipline their children more to the extent that they feel crowded or lack privacy.

Returning to Table 6.2, the relationships between the dependent measures and objective crowding, after introducing relevant controls, are shown. Controlling for the background variables, persons per room is unrelated to any of the parent-child variables (Beta1 in Table 6.2). The explanation of why this is so varies somewhat depending on the specific dependent variable, but family income, education of respondent, and housing satisfaction again have the primary role in reducing the effect of persons per room.

The relationships between the dependent measures and both objective and subjective crowding, controlling for background measures, appear in the second column of Table 6.2 As before, objective crowding is not related to any of the measures of parent-child relations. Perceived crowding, on the other hand, is significantly related to supportive behavior and parent-child tension, but not to the disciplining of children. Parents who feel more crowded provide more supportive behavior and feel more tension in their interactions with their children. When lack of privacy, rather than perceived crowding, is included in the model, lack of privacy is significantly related to all three dependent variables and is more strongly related to parent-child tensions than is perceived crowding. These results suggest that subjective crowding has an important impact on parent-child relations. However, once the intervening variables have been added to the model (column three, Table 6.2), perceived crowding has an effect only on supportive behavior, while the effect of lack of privacy remains significant but is reduced in two of the three relationships. Hence, the effect of subjective crowding on parent-child relations is largely mediated by the two intervening variables, psychological distress and felt demands. Consistent with expectations, parents who feel that many demands are made on them or who exhibit more psychological distress have greater parent-child tension, and parents with more felt demands discipline their children more. Paralleling the results for perceived crowding and a lack of privacy, but contrary to our expectations, parents who feel that many demands are made on them or who report more psychological distress are more supportive of their children, perhaps reflecting some sort of a compensatory reaction.

With regard to gender differences, although mothers report more parent-child tension and discipline their children more than fathers do, none of the interaction terms involving sex and either objective or subjective crowding is statistically significant. In short, mothers are not more reactive to crowding than fathers are. Disaggregated analyses do reveal that perceived crowding increases parent-child tensions for mothers, but not fathers; however, the effect for mothers is not significantly greater than the effect for fathers. Since none of the differences between men and women is statistically significant, it does not appear that crowding affects parent-child relations more for mothers than for fathers.

The Effect on Sibling Relations

Just as we predicted that household crowding could have adverse consequences for the husband-wife relationship and the relations between parents and their children, we anticipated that it might affect sibling relations as well. To our knowledge, only one other crowding study has ever examined the effect of overcrowding on the relations between children, at least as these relations are perceived by parents. Booth (1976), in his Toronto study, included one question regarding sibling relationships, and this concerned the frequency of quarrels among the children in the seven days prior to the interview. Neighborhood congestion, he found, was not related to the amount of quarreling reported by the parents. On the other hand, objective household crowding (persons per room and a room deficit measure) was positively correlated with the number of reported quarrels, but only among the reports made by mothers. We included a similar item on sibling quarrels in the Bangkok survey.

With respect to the bivariate results, neither persons per room nor perceived crowding is significantly related to the degree of sibling conflict reported by parents (Table 6.1). Lack of privacy, however, is significantly related to sibling conflict; parents who feel they lack privacy report more sibling conflict.

Turning to the multivariate analyses, we find little support for the hypothesized link between household crowding and sibling conflict. As was true in the bivariate case, persons per room is not significantly related to sibling conflict after controlling for background variables (Table 6.3, column 1). Similarly, we find that neither perceived crowding nor lack of privacy has any significant effect on sibling conflict, once controls for background variables and objective crowding are added to the analysis. Psychological distress does have a significant impact on sibling conflict: parents who experience more psychological distress report more sibling conflict among their children. Curiously, and unexpectedly, when controls for felt demands and psychological distress are introduced, perceived crowding actually has a small but significant negative effect on sibling conflict. That is, parents who feel more crowded report less sibling conflict among their children. Interaction analyses show no significant sex difference.

Given that household crowding seems to have little or no effect on sibling conflict, as reported by parents, we wondered whether household crowding, nonetheless, might have some effect on one or more of the individual items comprising the sibling conflict scale. We replicated the analyses shown in Table 6.3 with each of the four items comprising the scale. We found virtually no support for the hypothesized relationship.

As is the case with parent-child relations, the stage of the family life cycle has an important effect on the amount of sibling conflict, as one might expect. In families with more preschool or elementary age children, more sibling conflict is reported. The number of high school age children appears to be unrelated to sibling conflict. High school age children are no doubt out of the home more often than younger children, which may explain why they are engaged in fewer fights and arguments. Another similarity with the analyses of parent-child relations is that fathers report less sibling conflict than do mothers, which may reflect the amount of time each parent is in the home and is around the children.

**Table 6.3 Relationship Between Sibling Conflict and Objective
and Subjective Crowding, with Controls:
Standardized Regression Coefficients**

	Beta1	Beta2	Beta3
Sibling Conflict (N=1380)			
Persons per room	.013	.017	.006
Perceived crowding	----	-.026	-.062[a]
Felt demands	----	----	.048
Psychological distress	----	----	.139[c]
R^2	.116[c]	.117[c]	.141[c]
Sibling Conflict (N=1381)			
Persons per room	.013	.004	-.001
Lack of privacy	----	.048	-.007
Felt demands	----	----	.044
Psychological distress	----	----	.129[c]
R^2	.116[c]	.118[c]	.137[c]

[a]$p<.05$; [b]$p<.01$; [c]$p<.001$

Note: Controlling for sex of respondent, family income, education of respondent, stage in family life cycle, household control, number of generations, and number of married couples in the household. The natural logs of persons per rooms, perceived crowding and lack of privacy are used.

Violence

One of the most consistent findings in the literature on animals is a positive association between crowding and aggressive behavior. If, as we have shown, crowding increases stress, it appears reasonable to assume that people in overcrowded situations are more likely to feel frustrated and thwarted in their aspirations. One way this frustration might be manifested is in terms of violent behavior, the human counterpart to the aggression exhibited by crowded animals.

Only a limited number of studies have dealt with this issue, particularly among those investigations using individual-level data. The Toronto survey included questions about physical aggression both inside the home and fights with people outside of the household (Booth, 1973). In the main, episodes of violence were unrelated to most of the crowding measures used in that study. The one exception to that general pattern was a positive relationship, for both men and women, with subjective crowding, a scale on which our perceived crowding scale is based. Even in this case, the relationship was a rather weak one.

The Chicago study also provides some limited information on the possible relationship between crowding and violence (Gove and Hughes, 1983). Following a screening question about the occurrence of arguments in the home, respondents who indicated there had been arguments were asked: "Did any of these arguments lead to physical blows? (yes, no)" Gove and Hughes found a statistically significant relationship between reports of fights and three indices of crowding, persons per room and their two subjective crowding measures. The relationships, however, were not as strong as some of their findings pertaining to other facets of marital and family relations. Gove and Hughes also observed rather weak relationships between the crowding measures and the occurrence of arguments outside the home.

Accumulating evidence in Western societies, particularly the United States, indicates that the family, contrary to our common image of it, is not a very harmonious group (Straus, Gelles, and Steinmetz, 1980; Lystad, 1986). Violence occurs in all socioeconomic classes, racial and ethnic groups, and at all educational levels. Family members, in fact, are the most likely perpetrators of physical violence on an individual, despite it being the most underreported crime, at least in the United States.

In their national survey of American couples, Straus and his associates (1980) found slapping to be the most frequent form of physical force, but there were numerous reports of much more serious forms of physical force, including severe beatings resulting in hospitalization and threats with a deadly weapon. Much of the violence is directed at the wife on the part of the husband, and much of the physical force emanating from the wife is thought to be an attempt at self-defense. Few such studies have been conducted in non-Western countries, but what little existing evidence there is suggests that across cultures the patterns of family violence are very similar (Gelles and Cornell, 1983).

Thailand, as a country, is said to have one of the lowest levels of wife-beating found anywhere. It is low both in terms of frequency and severity (Campbell, 1985). We would note, however, that the discussion of violence on the part of Thais is a very sensitive subject. In accordance with Buddhist principles, the family is expected to be harmonious, as is to be the case with all of one's relationships with others. Extremes in all matters are to be avoided, and the occurrence of any violent episode--no matter how mild--constitutes a clear violation of that cultural norm. It is no mere tourist slogan that Thailand is referred to as "The Land of Smiles."

Yet, in our focus groups, there was recurring mention made with reference to physical force being used against family members. In talking about their relations with their husbands, one wife indicated: "I was folding my clothes when he started to scold me. I scolded him back, so he walked over and kicked my mouth." "Maybe," another wife suggested, "he only wanted to kindly pull your tooth out for you," eliciting general laughter from the focus group. A third wife entered the discussion stating, "I tell you with no shame that we hit each other often," to which a fourth responded, "My husband and I do not hit very often, but when we do, we must see blood." A fifth respondent added, "I only fought seriously once. I got on top of him and strangled him. After that we never fought anymore!"

The husbands were not hesitant to mention violence either. When asked what actions they would take if they had problems with their wives, one male focus group member flatly stated, "I might hit her." Mostly the males mentioned slapping and kicking. Some of the husbands, though, were very wary of how their wives might respond if they hit or kicked their spouses. As one husband pointed out, "Some of the wives here have a trick to warn her man. She would be sharpening the knife everyday in his sight... that's a warning."

Both the men and women indicated physical force was sometimes necessary in disciplining children. This is contrary to the general characterization of Thai parent-child relations, which depicts these relationships as being warm and gentle. Thai parents, especially in the early years of a child's life, tend to pamper offspring and fuss over them (Cooper and Cooper, 1982), producing the pleasant, gentle personalities most Thais have. Thais are usually taught, moreover, that aggression is something to be avoided. When the question was raised in the focus groups as to what is the best method of discipline, one father indicated, "Teaching isn't the best method. They usually forget. Hitting is best... I think." Another father added, "Even hitting... children forget the next day." Another responded, "If they do and they repeat the behavior, then give them twice as hard punishment... and increase the punishment until they stop their bad behaviors." A few parents noted a good method of punishment was to hit the child with a stick. As one Thai saying puts it: "If you love your cow, tie it; if you love your child, beat it."

On the basis of these qualitative data, as well as theoretically, there was ample reason to suspect that we would find some evidence of physical force in our survey, particularly violence directed toward the wife. Due to limitations imposed by the length of an acceptable interview, as well as the sensitive nature of the subject, we were unable to extensively explore this issue. Three pertinent items, though, were included in the interview schedule. Following a screening question regarding the frequency of spousal arguments or fights, respondents were asked if these ever resulted in the slapping, hitting, or kicking of the wife. They were further queried about whether they ever had serious arguments or fights with any family members other than the spouse or children (yes, no). A third, and similar, question had to do with serious arguments and fights with people outside of the family (yes, no). The results of the multivariate analyses are contained in Table 6.4.

As may be seen in that table, objective crowding, unlike in some of the previous analyses, has a significant and persistent effect on wife abuse (see column three). Lack of privacy is also related to abuse. The significant sex interaction effect for perceived crowding suggests, and separate analyses confirm, that perceived crowding is related to reports of wife abuse only for wives, not for husbands. In the final equation, neither subjective crowding variable is significantly associated with the violence measure for either husbands or wives. These findings suggest that the effect of subjective crowding is mediated by felt demands and psychological distress, which are both significant in the final regression model. In that model, some of the control variables—notably income, education, and housing satisfaction—have a persistent effect on abuse, and all of these relationships are in the direction we would expect. The greater they are, the less the likelihood of abuse. One other noteworthy finding not shown in Table 6.4 concerns the effect of the sex of the respondent. While males and females were just as likely to admit the occurrence of violence (about 19 percent of both male and female respondents), in the multivariate model, wives report a greater frequency of abuse.

A somewhat more complex pattern of results concerning arguments or fights outside the home is shown in Table 6.4. As with wife abuse, persons per room has a significant and positive effect on the occurrence of this form of violence. Neither of the subjective crowding measures does so, however. The only intervening factor, in fact, that has a significant impact is psychological distress. There is some hint of a compositional effect of the household. Whereas wife abuse tends to be lower in three-generation households, serious arguments or fights with people outside the household are more likely to happen in these families. Here, again, wives more so than husbands report this form of violence.

Turning to arguments and fights with other, non-nuclear family members, we can see that, unlike the case with the other forms of violence, objective crowding does not have a significant impact (Table 6.4). The subjective crowding measures are positively related to quarreling and fighting, when introduced along with the control variables. This effect does not persist, though, it being mediated by felt demands and psychological distress (see column three), both of which are highly significant in the final regression model. As in the case of violence outside the household, there is a family composition effect here, too. Individuals in both three-generation households and dwellings comprised of two or more married couples are more likely to argue or fight with other family

**Table 6.4 Relationship Between Measures of Violence and Objective
and Subjective Crowding, with Controls:
Standardized Regression Coefficients**

	Beta1	Beta2	Beta3
Wife Abuse			
Persons per room	.055[a]	.053[a]	.053[a]
Perceived crowding	—	.075[b]	.035
Sex-perceived crowding	—	-.211[a]	-.197[a]
Felt demands	—	—	.052[a]
Psychological Distress	—	—	.149[c]
R^2	.042[c]	.047[c]	.073[c]
N	1986	1986	1986
Lack of privacy	—	.077[b]	.020
Arguments - Outside			
Persons per room	.062[a]	.061[a]	.061[a]
Perceived crowding	—	.013	-.018
Felt demands	—	—	.025
Psychological distress	—	—	.136[c]
R^2	.030[c]	.030[c]	.049[c]
N	1985	1985	1985
Lack of privacy	—	.016	-.032
Arguments - Nonnuclear			
Persons per room	.011	-.006	-.011
Perceived crowding	—	.108[b]	.042
Felt demands	—	—	.198[c]
Psychological distress	—	—	.115[c]
R^2	.088[c]	.098[c]	.157[c]
N	929	929	929
Lack of privacy	—	.066	-.036
Sex-Lack of privacy	—	.073	.064

[a]$p<.05$; [b]$p<.01$; [c]$p< .001$

Note: When Perceived Crowding is the model, Lack of Privacy is not, and vice
versa. Controlling for sex of respondent, family income, education of the respondent, stage in the family life cycle, household control, housing satisfaction,
number of generations, and number of married couples in the household. The
natural logs of persons per room, perceived crowding, and lack of privacy have
been used as expalnatory variables in the models.

members. It would appear that these complex types of households, in a general sense, increase the occurrence of violence, while at the same time suppressing violence specifically directed to the wife.

Conclusions

Although the findings presented in this chapter are complex, there is broad support for the notion that household crowding is detrimental to marital and family relations. We find the expected correlations between objective crowding and marital and family relations, but these relationships appear to be largely spurious, for they disappear once controls for background variables are introduced. Only in two of the relationships involving physical violence does persons per room have a persistent effect. This is a finding previously unobserved and may in part be accounted for by a ceiling effect that we discussed in Chapter 4.

Subjective crowding has a more reliable relationship with the dependent variables. Those who feel crowded are more likely to report marital instability, more marital arguments, feel greater tension in the parent-child relationship, and discipline their children more often. Using the alternate measure of subjective crowding, those who feel that they lack privacy are even more likely to experience marital instability and arguments, and report less companionship. They also report having a more adverse relationship with their children. Moreover, people who feel crowded by virtue of their lack of privacy are more likely to report wife abuse. Lack of privacy and perceived crowding both have a significant impact on arguments or fights with members of the family.

One consistent result concerns the importance of both felt demands and psychological distress as intervening variables affecting most measures of family relations. People who have more psychological distress or feel more demands experience more marital instability and marital arguments, and they experience greater parent-child tension. In a like vein, parents who feel more psychological distress discipline their children more frequently. This pattern largely holds for the measures of violence as well. The impact of subjective crowding on wife abuse and serious arguments or fights with other non-nuclear family members disappears when the effect of distress and/or felt demands is taken into account. Taken together, these findings strongly suggest that the effects of subjective crowding are largely mediated, and that distress and felt demands are important explanatory variables accounting for crowding outcomes.

While previous researchers have posited, and claim to have found, stronger crowding effects for wives than for husbands, we find no such differences in our data, except with regard to reports of physical violence.

Theoretically, the findings suggest strong support for the model proposed, other than for the efficacy of objective crowding. It appears, as we saw in Chapter 4, that there is a rather modest linkage between objective crowding and its subjective experience, contrary to logic and commonsensical notions about why people feel crowded. What is or is not perceived as crowding or as impinging on one's sense of privacy may vary significantly from one culture to the next. To put it differently, the threshold at which a person begins to feel crowded may depend on what, in a statistical sense, is normative for a culture, and the findings seem to suggest that the threshold is relatively high for Thais. Crucially, though the data indicate, even in the face of normative standards higher than those in the industrialized world, that the perception of being crowded is critical in explaining why people experience decrements in their marital relations and the relationships parents have with their children. As we have noted, the resulting elevated stress individuals experience largely mediates these effects.

Even with a history of high levels of household crowding, it thus does not appear to be the case that Bangkokians have adjusted to crowding to the extent that it has ceased to have any effect on their lives. In fact, compared to the findings of North American and European studies, the effects of crowding on Thai family life, at least as subjectively perceived, are far less selective and have even stronger detrimental consequences than have been found elsewhere.

7

Sexual Relations and Reproductive Behaviors

Sexual relations and reproductive behavior are plainly a central part of the crowding equation. Conceived in an objective sense, household crowding is simply a function of too many people occupying too small a space. By reducing the number of people present or increasing the amount of space, crowding is lessened or eliminated altogether.

Background: Prior Research

Somewhat ironically, as central as sex and reproduction are to the phenomenon of crowding, we have little theoretical guidance as to what to expect. All our general crowding model suggests is that, in comparison with less crowded people, individuals living in compressed dwellings will behave differently. What that difference may be, and whether any difference may be less or more of some activity, is not specified. Moreover, there is very little empirical research, as well, to guide us in the formulation of specific hypotheses.

Most of what is known about crowding and sexual behavior is derived from ethological research. Observations of crowded animals have suggested that such animals exhibit aberrant forms of sexual behavior, aberrant at least in terms of the respective patterns normally observed in those animal populations. Investigations of crowded house mice, voles, Mongolian gerbils, wild monkeys, fish, and laboratory as well as wild rats note a diverse set of sexual pathologies (Southwick, 1955; Louch, 1956; Jillings, 1967; Susiyama, 1967; Morris, 1952; Calhoun, 1962). In some cases, the observations are of interrupted copulation, such as among crowded house mice. Other studies report hypersexuality as a result of dense conditions. A high incidence of homosexuality has been noted, particularly among crowded fish. Some investigations indicate there is a combination of these aberrations, suggesting that crowding precipitates pansexual behavior on the part of certain animals.

Calhoun's classic study (1962), which we reviewed in Chapter 2, is one of the better controlled experiments on crowding effects. Under high and unchecked crowding conditions--what Calhoun refers to as a behavioral sink--several pathological behaviors developed among the rats in the experiment. These ranged from extreme withdrawal on the part of some animals to the frenetic overactivity of others. Cannibalism emerged. Sexual deviation was widespread. Hypersexuality was one such deviation. Females in estrus were relentlessly pursued by packs of males, unable to divert the unwanted attention of the males. Some males became pansexual, apparently unable to discriminate between appropriate and inappropriate sexual partners. Another group of male rats became completely passive, paying no attention to even the estrous females in their midst. Still other males became what Calhoun termed "probers," who engaged in both hypersexual and homosexual activities.

The evidence concerning the effects of crowding on the reproductive behavior of animals is somewhat more consistent, generally reporting an inverse relationship. Particularly among rats and mice, it has been observed, crowded conditions are related to smaller litter size and a higher incidence of spontaneous abortion (Calhoun, 1962; Davis, 1964; Snyder, 1968). Crowded females engage in ineffectual maternal care, raising the probability of infant mortality, and sometimes resort to cannibalism of the young. In one experiment where the animal population was allowed to reach a peak, 30 litters were subsequently born without any of the young surviving (Christian, Lloyd, and Davis, 1965). In reaction to high population density, declines in fertility also have been observed among birds, elephants, rabbits, wolves, chickens, and deer (Perrins, 1965; Laws and Parker, 1968; Lockley, 1961; Hoffman, 1958; Siegal, 1959; Christian, Flyger, and Davis, 1960).

While this body of ethological research is indeed suggestive, it must be interpreted very cautiously in extrapolating it to human populations. What looks to us as pathological and ultimately dysfunctional behavior among these various animals--and perhaps would be so among humans-- actually may have utilitarian value. Withdrawal, interrupted copulation, bisexuality, and homosexuality each serve to check population growth. Along with a high rate of infant mortality, which often occurs under extreme crowding conditions, sexually deviant behavior can be functional in serving as a population-reducing mechanism, bringing some measure of equilibrium back to the group.

Furthermore, the analogy between human behavior and that of other species breaks down at some crucial points. Environmentally, there is little similarity. Most of the evidence on sexual pathologies comes from the study of rodents, and some of the strongest evidence stems from experimental situations. For these animals, there is no escape from crowded conditions. Crowding is a constant part of their lives. Even among so-called free-roaming animals, territoriality may impose severe limitations on the ability to escape from crowding. Human habitats seldom have such limitations. There is, moreover, no cross-species analogue to the human experience of feeling crowded and a perceived lack of privacy. These are symbolically-conceived and may be symbolically-expressed experiences that are absent in other animals. Inasmuch as the subjective experiences of crowding for humans may be more important than the objective circumstances themselves, comparisons with other animals may be inappropriate altogether.

As far as natality and reproductive behavior are concerned, the analogy between humans and other species is incomplete. In other species, sex and reproduction are governed by the estrous cycle of females. As a result, the natality rate among most animals approximates the limits of their biological potential. Humans make choices as to when to have sexual intercourse and under what circumstances they will do so. While women are able to conceive 12 months of the year, most seek to limit their pregnancies, so that human natality is usually far below biological capacity.

It is also the case that the ethological research is not as unequivocal as it first appears. Significantly, most of the studies dealing with the effects of population densities on animal behavior are silent about the existence of any sexual deviations or unusual reproductive behavior. Some investigations even note that there are no significant relationships between high density, sexual behavior, and reproduction (Syme, 1973). Others suggest that fertility may actually increase as a result of crowding (Ludwig and Boost, 1939). As we mentioned, most of the attention has been focused on rodents in experimental situations. Until there are more observations of a broader range of animals in natural settings, we need to be wary of generalizing these findings to other animal species, let alone to humans.

What evidence we have regarding the impact of crowding on human sexual relations and reproductive behavior is quite limited and often inconsistent. Based on some of the ethological evidence, Galle and his associates (1972), using aggregate data, found crowding to be positively associated with a high fertility rate. This, they speculated, could stem from either the sort of hypersexuality observed in some other crowded animals or could result from the inability to plan carefully, which would be reflected in the inconsistent use of birth control. Galle and Gove (1979) later replicated the finding about high fertility using data from four different time periods.

In a rather unique study dealing with the residents of Ciudad Kennedy, a government-constructed satellite city of Bogata, Columbia,

Felson and Solaun (1975) found just the opposite. Two types of dwellings were available, individual houses and apartments. The apartments were close to three times the size of the houses. After controlling for key variables affecting fertility and possible self-selection factors, Felson and Solaun found that the apartment dwellers reduced their fertility, while occupants of the houses increased theirs. The house dwellers had the ability to increase needed space by adding rooms, whereas the apartment residents were unable to neutralize any increases in objective crowding. The response on the part of the latter, Felson and Solaun suggest, was simply to reduce the number of children they otherwise may have had.

The Toronto study (Booth, 1976) examined two aspects of reproduction: number of pregnancies and total infant mortality (which included induced abortion, spontaneous abortion, proportion stillborn, and proportion dying in the first year of life). Neither aspect of reproduction was related to any of the crowding measures, including persons per room.

In a related analysis, using the Toronto data, Edwards and Booth (1977) focused on the sexual behavior of those living in crowded circumstances. This involved an examination of marital relations, extramarital affairs, homosexual contacts, and incestuous experience. On the assumption that crowding interferes with privacy, one of the questions asked in regard to marital sex had to do with whether the respondents had ever refrained from having intercourse because of a lack of privacy. This, it turned out, was one of the strongest findings. Subjective crowding was strongly related to reports that a lack of privacy interfered with intercourse. The perceived lack of privacy was not followed, though, by any appreciable withdrawal from sexual activity. If anything, crowded individuals tended to have marital coitus somewhat more frequently than people living in less compressed conditions.

A similar tendency was observed with respect to the other forms of sexual behavior that were examined. Those in crowded households had slightly elevated levels of extramarital, homosexual, and incestuous activities. The differences between crowded and uncrowded people were small and, generally, not statistically significant. Crowding in itself, Edwards and Booth point out, explains a very modest portion of the variance in sexual behavior, and they contend (1977:805) that human sexual behavior--perhaps unlike that of other animals--"is not appreciably influenced by crowded conditions."

A parallel analysis of marital sexuality and reproductive behavior is contained in the Chicago study. Gove and Hughes (1983) found that both their objective and subjective indicators of crowding were related to reports that a lack of privacy sometimes prevents sexual intercourse, and there was a small--but statistically significant--negative relationship between persons per room and the frequency of marital intercourse. In short, neither the Toronto nor the Chicago study finds any evidence of hypersexuality, contrary to some of the reports contained in the ethological literature.

With regard to reproductive behavior, a series of questions was posed in the Chicago study asking about the desire for children, birth control practices, and the occurrences of miscarriages and abortions. Two indexes were used having to do with the desire for children. One was calculated by dividing the number of offspring the respondent already had, or expected to have, by the number desired. Overcrowded individuals generally had more children than they ideally wanted. The second index concerned simply a response as to whether the respondent currently was "purposely trying to have a child." Persons per room, as Gove and Hughes expected, was negatively associated with the desire for an additional child, but the subjective crowding measures were only weakly related to this variable. One subjective indicator (lack of privacy), in fact, was positively related to the attempt to have another child, which is contradictory to overcrowded people reporting that they presently have more children than they actually want.

If people who reside in crowded households indeed have more children than they think are an ideal number, on the surface they would seem to have a powerful incentive for practicing birth control. As we pointed out in the previous chapter, Thai fertility has in fact declined substantially in the last two decades, suggesting that the programs designed to educate and promote birth control have met with considerable success. However, for the adults who live in crowded households, there is a counter-hypothesis. Galle and his colleagues (1972) have argued that crowding in the household, simply because there are too many people around, makes it difficult to plan one's activities, and practicing birth control clearly requires planning and a conscious effort on thepart of the sexual partners. If crowded couples already have more children than they perceive as ideal, this is prima facie evidence that they tend to be poor family planners. Overall, Gove and Hughes found that crowding has little effect on whether individuals practice birth control, but it does have a small effect on sometimes forgetting to do so.

The Chicago investigation also explored the issue of the impact of crowding on fetal mortality, an issue raised in ethological research and found by Booth (1976) not to apply to the Toronto sample. Gove and Hughes (1983), however, did find a persistent relationship between persons per room and the occurrence of a miscarriage or abortion, even after a number of controls were introduced. The subjective crowding measures were not so related. Gove and Hughes are careful to point out, though, that they had no information on whether the death was spontaneous or induced, and that because the mortality was a past event, it was uncertain the respondent was residing in a crowded household at the time of the occurrence.

Given the very mixed and equivocal findings regarding crowding and human sexuality, these studies provided little guidance and no specific expectations of what we might find among our Thai respondents. The privacy--especially as it relates to sex--might be a major issue for those living in crowded households. The lack of privacy could lower the frequency of marital coitus and, if persistent, might lead to prolonged periods of sexual abstinence. As it happened, the focus group interviews lent us the most guidance as to what we might expect to find in the survey.

Privacy, or the lack thereof, was a recurrent theme in the focus groups, both for the male and female groups. The participants spoke of what it meant to them, the steps they took to try to achieve it, and especially mentioned how the lack of privacy affected their lives with their spouse, including the impact on their sex lives. This is a group of males talking:

Wattana: "I don't think people living here have the activity [sex] during the daytime."

Mongkol: "Yes, it's impossible. Our houses are not private. There is a path in front of the house."

Pen: "Many people keep passing by. If you close the door, neighbors would tease you loudly outside. Spoil the mood."

And here are excerpts from a discussion in one of the female groups when the subject of sex came up:

Chamnian: "When the kids sleep, we can make love."

Sriprai: "My husband is a nervous type. He is afraid the kids will wake up. He works at night, so he has time with me during the daytime."

Malee: "Why don't you just close your door?"

Sriprai: "Even with the door closed, we feel that there are children outside."

The problems posed by having children present came up time and again, particularly in the female focus groups. Many mentioned that at some point--usually by the age of four or five--children become aware of the sexual relationship between their parents. This had led to some wives trying to minimize the frequency of sexual intercourse, if not withdraw from the sexual relationship altogether.

Lamjai: "Long before, I wanted to be close to my husband. Now, it's dead."

Chamnian: "It's boring for us, not for them."

Malae: "During the Khao Phansa period [Buddhist Lent, a period of three months], I'll eat only vegetables. I told him not to have sex with me during that period. He said no. He thought that's crazy. It won't work for him--not to have sex for three months."

Sriprai: "I ask him not to have sex one day a week on Buddhist day. But more than that it's not possible for him."

Nim: "Not even one day off for my case."

Malee: "I don't want it with my husband. When he asked for it, I would take a long prayer and he would fall asleep while waiting for me to finish the prayer. In the morning, he would ask me 'Did I do it last night with you?' I would then answer 'Of course you did! How soon you forget!'"

It was evident from these conversations, mostly among slum dwellers, that privacy was an important issue, and its lack seemed to be very much implicated in how people conducted their daily lives, including having consequences for their sexual interaction with their spouse. These findings from the focus groups prompted us to explore how crowding, in both its objective and subjective dimensions, might affect the husband-wife sexual relationship and how it might relate to matters associated with their reproductive behavior.

The Analysis

In order to address the issue of sexual frequency, we asked our respondents, "How many times in the past month did you and your husband/wife have sexual relations?" For the minority of respondents who could not remember the number of times in the past month, we asked for the number of times they had sexual relations in the past week, and extrapolated this number to obtain a monthly estimate.

We were also interested in whether the respondents perceived that crowding had any effect on their frequency of sexual relations. We accordingly asked, "Are you ever reluctant to have sexual relations because the children or others are at home?"

Another issue that the literature sensitizes us to is whether crowding leads to the cessation of sexual relations (Edwards and Booth, 1977). To obtain information pertaining to this issue, respondents were asked, "Have you and your husband/wife ever stopped having sexual relations for a period of time for any reason other than pregnancy?" If so, we ascertained the reason for this cessation and how long it lasted.

As Gove and Hughes (1983) suggest, parents who are more crowded may be less likely to desire additional children. In order to examine this aspect of reproductive wishes, we inquired, "Do you want to have any more children in the future?" Closely related to the desire to have, or avoid, additional children is the use of birth control. Respondents were asked several questions pertaining to birth control. First, "Are you or your husband/wife currently using some family planning or doing something to avoid a pregnancy?" Those who were using some form of birth control were then asked, "How often do you forget to use your method of birth control?" (often, sometimes, rarely, never) and "Does a lack of privacy in your home ever prevent you from using your method of birth control?" The latter two questions did not apply to couples who were not using any form of birth control or who were relying on either a tubal ligation or a vasectomy to prevent pregnancy.

Finally, both the ethological and the human literatures on crowding suggest that crowding may affect child survival and fetal survival. To measure these aspects of reproductive behavior, we inquired, "Did you have any children who died?", "Have you (has your wife) ever had a miscarriage?", and "Have you (has your wife) ever had an abortion?" As Knodel and his associates have pointed out (1987:89), abortion is illegal under most circumstances in Thailand and is believed by most Thais to be contrary to the principles of Buddhism. For this reason, survey data on abortion must be interpreted with caution.

A number of control variables are included in the analyses because of their potential impact on various aspects of reproductive behavior. Inasmuch as reproductive behavior is related to the stage in the personal and family life cycle, we control for the age of the respondent, the age of the spouse, and the number of years the respondent has been married. Certain aspects of reproductive behavior are related to socioeconomic status, indicating the need to control for the respondent's level of education and family income. The desire for additional children is related to the number of children a person already has; hence, the number of children is controlled. Finally, controls are introduced for the wife's employment status and the overall health of the respondent.

The Impact on Sexual Relations

In the way of background, our respondents, on average, reported having sexual relations with their spouse 4.4 times per month, almost exactly once per week. The reported average varied significantly between husbands and wives. Husbands reported having sexual intercourse with their wives 5.2 times per month, while wives indicated having sexual relations with their husbands 4.1 times per month (Table 7.1). It is not clear whether husbands overreported or wives underreported, a pattern nonetheless consistent with American findings (Kinsey, 1953). Inasmuch as there is a systematic sex difference, sex of respondent becomes an important control variable.

The frequency of marital intercourse varies in a curvilinear fashion with the age of the respondent. Husbands and wives age 25-29 report the highest level of sexual relations (6.4 and 5.4 times per month, respectively). The frequency of sexual relations is slightly lower in the age group 20-24 (5.6 and 5.2), and declines to 2.6 and 2.4 in marriages where the respondent is 50 or older. Generally, the frequency of sexual relations is lower the longer a couple has been married. As the results from the focus group interviews suggested, frequency of sexual relations is related to the age of the oldest child. Focus group participants indicated that finding an opportunity to have sexual relations became more problematic after the children reached a certain age. We found that the frequency of sexual relations was significantly lower once the oldest child was at least four years old.

Husbands and wives who have relatively high, but not the highest, levels of education and income tend to have sexual relations more often. Moreover, the frequency of sexual relations tends to be higher for those in better health, especially for husbands. For wives, a similar, but smaller trend is evident. On the other hand, household structure--i.e., whether there are two or three generations in the household, whether there is only one or more than one married couple in the household--has no effect on the frequency of sexual relations.

The zero-order correlations between the crowding measures and the measures of reproductive behavior are reported in Table 7.2; the multivariate results are contained in Table 7.3. As the zero-order correlations show, none of the crowding measures is significantly related to the frequency of sexual relations (Table 7.2). Not surprisingly, the multivariate analyses confirm that neither objective crowding nor subjective crowding has any effect on frequency of sexual relations (Table 7.3).

Turning to the reluctance to engage in sexual relations because of the presence of children or others, a very different result is obtained. This is one area in which the objective level of crowding, as well as subjective crowding, decidedly have significant effects. Persons per room, lack of privacy, and psychological distress are all significantly correlated with such reluctance. Furthermore, the multivariate analyses confirm that all three variables have significant independent effects on the reluctance to engage in sexual relations.

**Table 7.1 Frequency of Sexual Relations Per Month
by Selected Characteristics**

	Husbands	Wives
Sex of respondent		
$F=27.0^c$	5.2	4.1
Age of respondent		
20-24	5.6	5.2
25-29	6.4	5.4
30-34	6.2	4.1
35-39	6.0	4.5
40-44	4.0	3.3
45-49	3.2	2.9
50 or more	2.6	----
$F=12.9^c$		
Interaction NS		
Years married		
Up to 5	6.4	4.6
6-10	6.1	4.5
11-15	5.2	3.8
16-20	3.5	3.2
More than 20	3.0	2.7
$F=15.8^c$		
Interaction NS		
Age of oldest child		
3 or younger	5.8	4.7
4 or older	5.3	3.9
$F=4.9^a$		
Interaction NS		
Education of respondent		
4 years or less	4.4	3.7
5-7 years	5.7	4.4
8-10 years	5.9	4.1
11-12 years	5.6	5.0
College graduate	5.2	4.2
$F=5.7^c$		
Interaction NS		
Family income		
Less than 3000 Baht	5.3	4.1
3000-4999 Baht	4.5	3.9
5000-7999 Baht	5.6	4.1
8000-13999 Baht	5.8	4.4
14000 or more Baht	5.1	3.9
$F=1.7$ (NS)		
Interaction NS		

(continues)

Table 7.1 *(continued)*

	Husbands	Wives
Number of generations		
Two	5.2	4.0
Three	5.3	4.2
F=0.53 (NS)		
Ineraction NS		
Number of married couples		
One	5.2	4.1
Two or more	5.2	4.0
F=0.06(NS)		
Interaction NS		
Overall health of respondent		
Not very good	3.8	3.9
Fair	4.8	3.8
Good	5.6	4.3
Very good	5.7	4.6
F=3.3[a]		
Interaction NS		

[a]p<.05; [b]p<.01; [c]p< .001

Table 7.2. Zero-order Correlations Among Crowding, Sexual Relations, and Reproductive Behavior

		Persons per room	Lack of privacy	Perceived crowding	Psychological distress
1.	Frequency of sexual relations	-.022 (1977)	-.008 (1977)	-.009 (1975)	.012 (1971)
2.	Reluctance to engage in sexual relations	.183[c] (2004)	.171[c] (2004)	.105[c] (2002)	.189[c] (1998)
3.	Temporary cessation of sexual relations	.097[c] (2010)	.070[b] (2010)	-.021 (2008)	.078[c] (2004)
4.	Desire additional child(ren)	-.047[a] (2014)	-.018 (2014)	-.039 (2012)	-.002 (2007)
5.	Using birth control	.035 (1833)	.015 (1833)	.042 (1831)	.029 (1828)
6.	Forget to use birth control	-.033 (2001)	-.051[a] (2001)	-.009 (1999)	-.026 (1994)
7.	Lack of privacy prevents use of birth control	-.038 (2001)	-.056[a] (2001)	-.003 (1999)	-.029 (1994)
8.	Child loss	.024 (2017)	.003 (2017)	-.041 (2015)	.024 (2010)
9.	Miscarriage	-.056[a] (2015)	-.049[a] (2015)	-.037 (2013)	.031 (2008)
10.	Abortion	.021 (2041)	.034 (2014)	-.026 (2012)	.082[c] (2007)

[a]p<.05; [b]p<.01; [c]p<.001

Note: The correlations are based on pairwise deletion of cases with missing data (N=1392). The natural logs of persons per room, perceived crowding, and lack of privacy are used in this analysis.

Table 7.3 Relationship Between Measures of Reproductive Behavior
and Objective and Subjective Crowding, with Controls:
Standardized Regression Coefficients

	Beta1	Beta2	Beta3
Frequency of Sexual Relations (N=1936)			
Persons per room	-.026	-.024	-.024
Lack of privacy	——	-.009	-.017
Psychological distress	——	——	.030
R^2	.066^c	.066^c	.067^c
Ever reluctant to have sex (N=1958)			
Persons per room	.171^c	.147^c	.149^c
Lack of privacy	——	.130^c	.091^c
Psychological distress	——	——	.148^c
R^2	.037^c	.052^c	.070^c
Temporary cessation of sexual relations (N=1964)			
Persons per room	.063^a	.057^a	.057^a
Lack of privacy	——	.031	.023
Felt demands	——	——	.033
R^2	.024^c	.025^c	.026^c
Want more children (N=1965)			
Persons per room	-.010	-.002	-.002
Lack of privacy	——	-.042	-.041
Psychological distress	——	——	-.005
R^2	.149^c	.151^c	.151^c
Using birth control (N=1788)			
Persons per room	.003	.003	.004
Lack of privacy	——	.001	-.009
Psychological distress	——	——	.035
R^2	.014^b	.014^a	.015^a
Forget to use birth control (N=833)			
Persons per room	.016	.010	.013
Lack of privacy	——	.032	-.009
Psychological distress	——	——	.156^c
R^2	.022	.022	.043^c

(continues)

Table 7.3 (*continued*)

	Beta1	*Beta2*	*Beta3*
Lack of privacy prevents use of birth control (N=833)			
Persons per room	-.011	-.021	-.017
Lack of privacy	----	.057	-.004
Psychological distress	----	----	.233c
R^2	.004	.007	.053c
Child loss (N=1968)			
Persons per room	.020	.021	.021
Lack of privacy	----	-.006	-.006
Psychological distress	----	----	.001
R^2	.030c	.030c	.030c
Miscarriage (N=1966)			
Persons per room	-.036	-.031	-.031
Lack of privacy	----	-.026	-.038
Psychological distress	----	----	.046
R^2	.017c	.018c	.020c
Abortion (N=1965)			
Persons per room	.012	.007	.008
Lack of privacy	----	.026	.006
Psychological distress	----	----	.073b
R^2	.011a	.011a	.016b

[a]$p<.05$; [b]$p<.01$; [c]$p<.001$

Note: controlling for sex of respondent, age of respondent and spouse, years married, family income, respondent's education, wife's employment status, overall health, and number of children. The natural logs of persons per room and lack of privacy are used in this analysis.

The zero-order correlations show that objective crowding, lack of privacy, and psychological distress also are all significantly related to the temporary cessation of sexual relations. However, objective crowding has the most robust effect on cessation. When lack of privacy and psychological distress are added to the multivariate model, they do not have a significant impact, but persons per room retains its significance.

Similar results are obtained when perceived crowding is used as a measure of subjective crowding instead of lack of privacy. Compared to the effects of lack of privacy, perceived crowding has a weaker effect on the reluctance to have sex due to the presence of others. Interestingly, while the correlation between perceived crowding and cessation of sexual relations is nonsignificant, in the full model perceived crowding slightly, but significantly, reduces the likelihood of cessation of sexual relations.

The Impact on Desire for Additional Children

Are crowded parents less likely to desire additional children? The correlations indicate that parents who are objectively crowded desire fewer children, while subjective crowding is not related to the non-desire for additional children. The multivariate analyses show, on the other hand, that parents who are objectively crowded are neither more nor less likely to want to have additional children. The multivariate analyses, in addition, confirm that neither perceived lack of privacy nor perceived crowding has any effect on the desired number of children.

Gove and Hughes found that "crowded respondents are less likely than most respondents to want more children" (1983:94). They did not control, however, for the number of children the respondent already had. Our analyses of the Thai data show that the number of children the respondent already has is the single most important predictor of whether the respondent wants additional children. Additional analyses of the Thai data indicate that if we omit the number of living children the respondent has, we, too, would conclude (spuriously) that objective crowding and both measures of subjective crowding have significant effects on the desire for additional children.

A related concern for those desiring to limit family size or increase the spacing between births is the effective use of birth control. Galle and his associates (1972) argued that crowding may impede the ability of individuals to plan and to execute their plans. It is thus possible that crowded parents may be more likely to forget to use birth control, or that the lack of privacy in their homes may more often prevent the use of their chosen method of birth control.

Nearly 80 percent (N=1584) of the married men and women in our sample reported currently using some form of birth control. Both the bivariate and multivariate analyses fail to show any relationship between use of birth control and either persons per room, or lack of privacy, or psychological distress. Nearly half of those using birth control (N=744) relied on either male or female sterilization, a method of birth control that, once obtained, does not require contraceptive planning. For the 840 married couples who were using other forms of birth control, the issue of the effective use of their method is relevant. We explored this issue by using the two items mentioned above, namely, how often the couple forgets to use birth control and whether a lack of privacy ever prevents the use of birth control. The multivariate analyses indicate that neither persons per room nor lack of privacy is significantly related to either item.

The results for perceived crowding are similar. In the multivariate analyses, perceived crowding is not related to wanting more children or forgetting to use birth control. It is the case, however, that perceived crowding is significantly related to reports that a lack of privacy more often prevents respondents from using birth control. Overall, though, there is little evidence to suggest that crowded parents are less able to carry out their plans to use some form of birth control.

The Impact on Child Loss

The ethological literature, as earlier mentioned, suggests that under conditions of extreme crowding, adult animals do not care for their young as effectively and higher levels of mortality result. We explored these issues by examining patterns in child mortality, miscarriages, and abortion.

The results provide no evidence that either objective crowding or subjective crowding increases fetal mortality or child mortality. Neither persons per room, nor felt lack of privacy, nor perceived crowding is significantly, positively correlated with any of the three dependent measures of mortality. The multivariate analyses, furthermore, do not reveal any positive, significant effects of crowding on fetal or child mortality.

Contrary to expectations, our findings suggest that crowding reduces the risk of fetal or child mortality. The zero-order correlations show that both persons per room and a felt lack of privacy are negatively correlated with miscarriage. While these particular effects are not found in the multivariate analyses, the analyses involving perceived crowding do suggest that parents who feel more crowded are less likely to have suffered child mortality and are less likely to report having had an abortion. It is not clear why crowding would have these apparent effects of reducing mortality. Note, however, that only two unanticipated effects are significant in the multivariate results, and one of these (that pertaining to reported abortions) must be viewed with caution. There is, in sum, little evidence that objective or subjective crowding affects fetal or child survival either positively or negatively.

As a final consideration, we looked at the possibility that men and women might react differently to household crowding in terms of their sexual and reproductive behavior. To examine this possibility, sex interaction terms were used. None of the sex interaction terms for persons per room, felt lack of privacy, or psychological distress was significant.

The effects of household crowding on sexual and reproductive behavior, it would appear, are similar for Thai men and women.

Conclusions

If household crowding has any effect on reproductive behavior, we might expect it to be especially discernible in a context with a high level of household crowding such as we find in Bangkok. The objective level of crowding--persons per room--does have a significant effect on certain aspects of sexual behavior. Although persons per room is not significantly related to reported frequency of sexual relations, those who live in objectively more crowded households do sometimes have greater reluctance to engage in sexual relations because of the presence of others and they are more likely to have had periods of temporary cessation of sexual relations with their spouse. However, those who live in objectively more crowded households are just as likely to want additional children, are neither more nor less likely to use birth control, are no more likely to forget to use their method of birth control, and do not feel that the lack of privacy prevents them from using birth control. Moreover, objective crowding, we find, has no effect on fetal and child survival.

The results pertaining to perceived crowding are similarly mixed. Parents who feel more crowded are more likely to report that they are sometimes reluctant to engage in sexual relations because of the presence of others and that lack of privacy sometimes prevents them from using birth control. Contrary to some prior research, those who feel more crowded are less likely to report that they have ever stopped engaging in sexual relations for a period of time and they are less likely to report having suffered a child loss.

Felt lack of privacy affects only one of the measures examined. Individuals who have a greater felt lack of privacy are more often reluctant to engage in sexual intercourse. Otherwise, a felt lack of privacy has no significant effects on any of the measures examined.

Perhaps more surprising than the effects that crowding has are the effects that crowding does not have. Our analyses show that where the fertility is at a relatively low level but where household crowding is high, household crowding does not reduce the desire for children. Fortunately, household crowding does not seem to impede the effective use of birth control, nor does crowding significantly affect fetal or child survival. Our findings suggest that, overall, household crowding, either in its objective or subjective dimension, has a very selective--and generally modest--impact on sexual and reproductive behavior, if it has any consequences at all.

8

Crowding and Health

Given the confined nature of the household and the amount of time most people spend in it, there are three compelling reasons to believe crowding may affect one's health in a deleterious way. First, as we discussed in the chapter on psychological well-being, compressed living conditions can be viewed as constituting a source of chronic stress. Thwarted daily routines and the sensory overload associated with overcrowding elevate the amount of stress the individual experiences, the latter ultimately being manifested in certain physiological symptoms. The link between stress and ill-health is, in fact, well-established (Cassel, 1970). Secondly, because in overcrowded situations there are several people occupying a finite amount of space, if any one of them contracts an infectious disease, it may be easily transmitted to others in the household. By definition, crowded households do not have private spaces where an infected person can be confined until a disease runs its course. Thirdly, stemming from the association between lower income and crowding, crowded housing units are more likely to be of poorer quality and be characterized by deficiencies that could have health consequences. Most prominently, the lack of proper sanitary facilities and an adequate water supply could have a direct impact on the state of their occupants' health.

Background: Previous Studies

Just as with sexual and reproductive behavior, some of the evidence concerning the connection between crowding and health is based on studies of lower animals. More than five decades ago, Allee (1938) concluded that overcrowding has serious detrimental consequences for a wide variety of animal populations. (Parenthetically, he noted that very low levels of crowding also were related to pathology.) Most striking, as population density increases, the mortality rate goes up. In one of the better known studies, Christian and his associates (1960) introduced a small herd of deer on an island, where they were free to breed. Once the population density reached one deer per acre, the mortality rate inexplicably soared, despite the fact there was abundant food and water and no indication of other diseases. Cyclical mortality has been observed among lemmings and snowshoe hares (Deevy, 1960). In other animal populations, high rates of mortality due to cannibalism are related to high population density (Crombie, 1943), as was the case among the rats in Calhoun's experiment (1962). The latter study, in addition, reported high levels of infant mortality resulting from poor nesting behavior and poor infant care under high-density conditions. Even prenatal and juvenile mortality have been found to be related to high-density situations (Helmreich, 1960; Paynter, 1949; Chitty, 1952).

As far as morbidity is concerned, animal studies have documented, for example, a higher incidence of hypoglycemia--sometimes leading to death--among crowded hares (Deevey, 1972). In mice, overcrowding seems to adversely influence the course of acute as well as chronic tuberculosis (Tobach and Block, 1956). Studies suggest that, among a variety of animals, high levels of crowding inhibit normal growth and affect the adrenal glands, which in turn alter blood pressure (Christian, 1959). Among mammals, Christian and Davis (1964) have noted drastic changes in body chemistry and decreases in the formation of antibodies that normally ward off diseases.

Because of the differences in the crowding circumstances of observed animals and humans, we again need to be cautious in extrapolating these ethological findings to humans. As we pointed out in the prior chapter, the analogy between animal behavior and human behavior is incomplete. However, what the ethological research does suggest in this case is that objective crowding can alter physiological processes which need not be mediated by other factors, such as whether crowding is perceived or not. In trying to account for the aberrant behavior of crowded animals, Christian (1950, 1965) has formulated a rather sophisticated physiological explanation. Crowding, he argues, creates stress, the stress producing increases in adrenal activity. With the increase in adrenal activity, the heart beats faster and metabolism is increased, making the animal excitable and tense. If the animal is always "hopped up," this can produce heart disease, ulcers, and a variety of other physical maladies. Eventually, either directly or indirectly, this will shorten the life span. All of this, we would be led to expect, has its counterpart in humans. Furthermore, as we suggested at the outset, there are ample logical, and other, grounds for expecting that crowding and ill-health will be linked.

Unfortunately, research on crowding and human morbidity and mortality is scanty, but there are a few such studies. For instance, Galle and his associates (1972, 1979), in using aggregate-level data, have found a positive relationship between crowding and mortality. They note, however, that structural variables (race, education, occupation, and income) tend to explain more of the variance in mortality than various crowding measures, though the two sets of variables are highly collinear (90 percent of the explained variance is held in common.)

Using individual-level data, Baldassare (1979), on the other hand, found there to be little relationship between either persons per room or persons per residential acre and two health measures assessing the respondent's general health and the satisfaction with health. Baldassare's analysis, it is worth recalling, is a secondary analysis of two previously conducted surveys, and in general the indicators used are less than ideal, as is the case with his health measures.

Perhaps the most detailed examination of the crowding-health linkage comes from the Toronto study, which included information obtained by interview and through physical examination, in which urine and blood samples were taken and later tested for symptomatogy (Booth and Cowell, 1976). The central focus of the analysis was on stress-related symptoms, based on the assumption that crowded respondents would experience more stress and exhibit more physiological symptoms known to be stress-related.

Although many of their measures were indirect, Booth and Cowell (1976) looked at three different endrocrine systems that are known to be sensitive to stress: the sympathetic-adrenal medullary system, the pituitary-adrenal cortical system, and the pituitary-thyroid system. Their measures included: blood pressure, proteinuria, catecholamine levels, eosinopenia, serum-free thyroxine, and serum cholesterol. In addition, Booth and Cowell obtained information on infectious and communicable disease, menstural problems among the female respondents, and signs of physical trauma, such as the presence of bruises. The latter was included predicated on Calhoun's suggestion (1962) that crowding may lead to aggression, which might result in physical fights.

In all, Booth and Cowell examined 136 possible relationships between four different crowding measures and the broad array of health indicators included in the survey and the evidence obtained from the medical examinations. They conclude that there is "little or no effect" of crowding on people's health. Only 14 of the relationships were statistically significant, crowding in all cases explaining a modest amount of the variance in health (8 percent or less in most instances). Booth and Cowell concede, however, that objective and subjective crowding--particularly the latter--may have small adverse consequences under some conditions. Men, they note, seem to be especially vulnerable in terms of their health to the impact of household crowding, a pattern that was quite prominent with respect to stress diseases, infectious, and communicable diseases.

While not nearly as extensive and thorough as the Toronto project, the Chicago study also contained some measures bearing on health, six indicators to be exact (Gove and Hughes, 1983). These had to do with the inability to get enough rest, catching a "bug" from others in the household, being able to get a "good rest" when sick, having to do chores when ill, not being cared for by others when sick, and a self-reported evaluation of the respondent's overall health. With a few exceptions, crowding, especially as subjectively experienced, had a consistent and negative impact on health. The crowding variables independently accounted for 38 percent of the explained variance, the remainder being attributable to the control variables used and collinearity. It is worth noting, however, that the amount of total variance explained tended to be relatively modest, seven percent or less with respect to three of the six health measures. The highest amount of explained variance (14 percent) was in regard to overall health, which was mainly due to the demographic variables used as controls. Gove and Hughes conclude, nonetheless, that their findings provide "fairly substantial support" for the link between crowding and ill-health (1983:85).

We had reason to believe that we, too, would find some relationship between household crowding and the state of our respondents' health. Although it was not a frequent occurrence, some focus group participants brought up various matters related to their health, as this brief exchange illustrates:

> Rattanaporn: "Yes, sure. When one has a cold, after a few days, everybody in the house will have it because the room is small. The ventilation is bad."
>
> Moderator: "A small room doesn't help with communicable disease."
>
> Rattanaporn: "Yes, it's like the disease can spread easily, especially the cold."

The Analysis

We, accordingly, included several questions in our survey to tap and be able to assay the potential impact crowding might have on physical well-being. The health measures, we hasten to note, are some of our least sophisticated indicators. Our original intent had been to duplicate the procedures of the Toronto study. In that study, respondents were asked in a face-to-face interview if they had exhibited various physical symptoms, involving a checklist of 42 different signs that had been documented previously as being stress-related. Following the interview, participants in the survey were requested to undergo—free of charge—a physical examination at a medical clinic, where blood and urine samples were collected. Together, these provided the data for the analysis discussed above.

Unfortunately, the duplication of these procedures proved to be impractical in our case. The logistics and expense of getting over 2,000 people to a location in Bangkok where blood and urine samples could be taken were insurmountable. Furthermore, we found that even employing the Toronto checklist of symptoms was infeasible. The standard of health care, as one might anticipate, is rather different in developing countries from that prevailing in industrialized nations. Health care is provided by a wide array of practitioners, including herbalists and lay healers in addition to physicians and nurses. Most critically, though, it is common practice in Thailand even for medically-trained personnel not to inform the patient of their diagnosis (Riley and Sermsri, 1974). Medical practitioners simply instruct the patient as to what needs to be done in order to bring about a cure. Thus, unlike in North America, people do not label their symptoms in medically meaningful terms. As a consequence, it was necessary to keep our interview questions regarding health fairly simple and general in nature.

We, nevertheless, obtained a variety of indicators of the physical well-being of the respondents. First, we elicited information concerning the occurrence of illness that prevented the respondents from following their normal daily routines. Specifically, we elicited information about (1) the number of times and (2) the number of days in the past month that the respondent was so ill that he or she could not (a) work, (b) get out of bed, or (c) eat for two or more consecutive days. A summary measure was created that places each respondent into one of four categories: (1) not sick during the last two months, (2) too sick to work at some point during the past two months, but never too sick to get out of bed or eat, (3) too sick to work and either too sick to get out of bed or too sick to eat, and (4) too sick to work, get out of bed, and eat at some point during the past two months.

Second, we obtained information about the frequency with which our respondents sought assistance from health care professionals. Respondents provided information about the number of times in the past 12 months they saw a health professional or received treatment in a hospital and the number of nights, if any, they spent in a hospital in the past 12 months.

Third, each respondent was asked to rate his or her overall health (not very good, fair, good, very good). Fourth, we asked a question about the respondent's susceptibility to illness: "If someone else at home is sick, do you often seem to get sick too?" (no, yes) Finally, for women, we obtained a measure of menstrual problems.

The control variables used in these particular analyses include: sex, age, socioeconomic status, and number of preschool children. Emotional support and role obligations are critical controls suggested by the sociology of health literature. Our measure of role obligations replicates three of the items used by Gove and Hughes (1979) in their analysis of sex differences in health in the U.S.: (1) "When you are really sick, are you almost always able to get a good rest?", (2) "Even when you are really sick, are there a number of chores that you just have to do?", and (3) "When you are really sick, is there someone to help take care of you?" All three items are used in the analysis, rather than forming a scale.

Emotional ties with one's spouse, neighbors, relatives, and friends are measured with one scale and several items. The quality of the relationship between spouses is measured with the scale we call "marital companionship". The quality of emotional ties with neighbors was assessed by a single item: "All in all, how well do you get along with your neighbors?" (not too well, well enough, pretty well, very well). For relatives, we asked the location of the nearest relatives (in the same neighborhood, elsewhere in Bangkok, outside Bangkok). Inasmuch as we can assume that one gets along well with one's friends, we asked: "How many really good friends do you have that you fairly regularly get to speak to?"

Turning to the multivariate analyses, we first examine the effects of housing quality and the objective level of household crowding, controlling for background variables. Subjective crowding is added as a second step, and finally psychological distress is added to the model.

One conclusion that can be reached immediately (Table 8.1) is that, contrary to hypothesis, the source of drinking water is not significantly related to any of the ten measures of health reported in Table 8.1, and the type of toilet facilities is significantly related to only one of these measures. Those who have access to exclusive toilet facilities are less likely to have visited a health professional in the past year. It is possible, of course, that our measures are not sufficiently sensitive to detect critical differences in housing quality that exist in Bangkok. But, overall, our data provide very little evidence that the health of Bangkokians is related to either of these two objective measures of housing quality.

Housing satisfaction is a different matter. Housing satisfaction is significantly related to half of the measures of health. People who are more satisfied with their housing are less likely to report curtailing their daily activities due to illness, they perceive that they are in better health, and, among women, they report fewer symptoms of menstrual problems. All of these relationships are in the expected direction, and all remain significant after subjective crowding and psychological distress are added to the model.

One reason why the subjective measure of housing quality has significant effects on health while the two objective measures of housing quality have little impact may be simply because the subjective measure refers to a broader range of aspects of housing, such as ventilation, sunlight, kitchen and laundry facilities, noise, heat, and smell.

Table 8.1 presents the total (nonspurious) effects, direct effects, and, by implication, the indirect effects of housing quality, persons per room, lack of privacy, and psychological distress on the health measures. The impact of perceived crowding will be discussed momentarily. The total effect of housing satisfaction is found in the column labelled Beta1. As mentioned above, several total effects of housing satisfaction are significant. Indirect effects (not shown) can be determined by subtracting the direct effects from total effects. The total effect of housing satisfaction on being too sick to work is -.100. As shown in the Beta2 column, the direct effect of housing satisfaction on being too sick to work, after introducing lack of privacy, is -.077, indicating that the indirect effect of housing satisfaction through lack of privacy is -.023 [i.e., -.100 - (-.077)]. The direct effect of housing satisfaction on being too sick to work, after adding both lack of privacy and psychological distress, is -.060, implying that the indirect effect of housing satisfaction, through lack of privacy and psychological distress combined, is -.400 [i.e.,-.100 - (-.060)].

In the initial model, persons per room has no significant effect on any of the ten health measures examined in Table 8.1. Significant effects of persons per room do emerge for two measures--visiting a health care professional at some point in the past 12 month and, specifically, visiting a nurse--in the second and third models, when lack of privacy and then psychological distress are added to the analysis. Importantly, these significant effects are contrary to expectation: individuals who live in more crowded households are less likely to visit health professionals. Persons per room has no discernible effect on reported illness, propensity to become ill if another member of the household is sick, or on self-reports of health.

The total effect of lack of privacy appears in the Beta2 column, with the direct effect of lack of privacy, after introducing psychological distress, shown in Beta3. Lack of privacy is significantly related to most of the health measures. Lack of privacy has significant total effects on being too sick to work, being too sick to eat, the summary measure of the degree of sickness, visiting health professionals, including nurses, self-reports of health, and, for women, menstrual problems. In most cases, the effect of lack of privacy is no longer significant after introducing psychological distress. Lack of privacy, however, continues to exert significant, though muted, effects on being too sick to work and, for women, on menstrual problems, after introducing psychological distress.

Table 8.1 Effects of Housing, Crowding, and Psychological Distress on Physical Health: Standardized Regression Coefficients

	Beta1	Beta2	Beta3
Too sick to work (N=1962)			
Drinking water	.025	.025	.022
Toilet facilities	.018	.015	.014
Housing satisfaction	-.100[c]	-.077[b]	-.060[a]
Persons per room	-.017	-.029	-.028
Lack of privacy	----	.091[c]	.057[a]
Psychological distress	----	----	.139[c]
R^2	.028[c]	.034[c]	.050[c]
Too sick to get out of bed (N=1964)			
Drinking water	.004	.004	.000
Toilet facilities	.012	.012	.010
Housing satisfaction	-.019	-.015	.000
Persons per room	-.039	-.041	-.040
Lack of privacy	----	.018	-.012
Psychological distress	----	----	.122[c]
R^2	.013	.013	.026[c]
Too sick to eat (N=1971)			
Drinking water	.007	.008	.006
Toilet facilities	-.012	-.013	-.014
Housing satisfaction	-.109[c]	-.095[c]	-.087[c]
Persons per room	-.020	-.027	-.026
Lack of privacy	----	.052[a]	.037
Psychological distress	----	----	.065[b]
R^2	.025[c]	.027[c]	.031[c]
Degree of sickness in past month (N=1949)			
Drinking water	.019	.019	.015
Toilet facilities	.012	.010	.008
Housing satisfaction	-.091[c]	-.073[c]	-.057[a]
Persons per room	-.026	-.035	-.034
Lack of privacy	----	.071[b]	.038
Psychological distress	----	----	.138[c]
R^2	.025[c]	.029[c]	.045[c]
Visited a health care professional in past 12 months (N=1973)			
Drinking water	.019	.020	.017
Toilet facilities	-.056[a]	-.058[a]	-.059[a]
Housing satisfaction	-.040	-.025	-.011
Persons per room	-.047	-.054[a]	-.053[a]
Lack of privacy	----	.057[a]	.029
Psychological distress	----	----	.114[c]
R^2	.029[c]	.031[c]	.042[c]
Visited a nurse in past 12 months (N=1964)			
Drinking water	.015	.015	.012
Toilet facilities	-.040	-.041	-.043
Housing satisfaction	-.044	-.030	-.015
Persons per room	-.050	-.057[a]	-.056[a]
Lack of privacy	----	.056[a]	.028
Psychological distress	----	----	.116[c]
R^2	.023[c]	.026[c]	.037[c]

(continues)

Table 8.1 *(continued)*

	Beta1	Beta2	Beta3
Admitted to hospital in past 12 months (N=1971)			
Drinking water	.026	.026	.027
Toilet facilities	.007	.007	.007
Housing satisfaction	-.013	-.010	-.011
Persons per room	-.023	-.025	-.025
Lack of privacy	—	.011	.013
Psychological distress	—	—	-.008
R^2	.099^c	.099^c	.099^c
Get sick too (N=1973)			
Drinking water	-.027	-.027	-.031
Toilet facilities	.006	.005	.006
Housing satisfaction	-.018	-.007	.004
Persons per room	.036	.030	.032
Lack of privacy	—	.043	.018
Psychological distress	—	—	.134^c
Sex-distress	—	—	-.092^a
R^2	.028^c	.029^c	.041^c
Self-report of health status (N=1965)			
Drinking water	.026	.025	.032
Toilet facilities	.004	.006	.008
Housing satisfaction	.118^c	.096^c	.068^c
Persons per room	-.010	.000	-.002
Lack of privacy	—	-.086^c	-.032
Psychological distress	—	—	-.223^c
R^2	.099^c	.104^c	.146^c
Menstrual problems (N=1365)			
Drinking water	-.035	-.030	-.028
Toilet facilities	-.022	-.018	-.018
Housing satisfaction	-.165^c	-.130^c	-.104^c
Persons per room	.043	.028	.032
Lack of privacy	—	.137^b	.071^a
Psychological distress	—	—	.273^c
R^2	.069^c	.084^c	.157^c

^{a}p<.05; ^{b}p<.01; ^{c}p< .001

Note: controlling for age and sex of respondent, family income, education of respondent, number of preschool children, emotional support, and role obligations. The natural logs of persons per room and lack of privacy are used in this analysis.

The last stage of the analysis involves psychological distress (Table 8.1, Beta3). Psychological distress has a significant effect on all but one of the health measures. In most cases, the effect of psychological distress is greater than the total effect of any of the other independent variables. For example, the total effect of psychological distress on the self-report of health is -.223, while that of housing satisfaction is .118. Similarly, the effect of psychological distress on being too sick to get out of bed is .122, while none of the other independent variables has a significant effect on being too sick to get out of bed.

The above results are based on analyses involving lack of privacy. These analyses were replicated using perceived crowding as an alternate measure of subjective crowding. Perceived crowding is a weaker predictor of health than is lack of privacy. Specifically, (1) the total effect of perceived crowding is significant only for visiting a nurse, being admitted to a hospital, and menstrual problems; and (2) perceived crowding has a significant direct effect, after controlling for psychological distress, only on being admitted to a hospital, self-reports of health, and menstrual problems. The effects of psychological distress on the health measures, though, are virtually identical when perceived crowding rather than lack of privacy is used as a measure of subjective crowding.

Gender Differences in Health

Higher rates of morbidity for women have been routinely observed in health surveys conducted in the United States, implying that women are "sicker" than men. Women report more daily symptoms of illness and experience a higher incidence of transient illnesses. They are more likely to have arthritis, chronic sinusitis, and digestive problems. In an apparent contradiction, however, these same studies note that men experience higher illness prevalence rates leading to fatal conditions. Men are more likely to have heart disease, atherosclerosis, emphysema, and other life-threatening illnesses. This parallels their shorter life expectancy (Hing, Kovar, and Rice, 1983; Nathanson, 1976; Verbrugge, 1976, 1985, 1989; Waldron, 1982; Wingard, 1984). In short, women get sick; men die earlier.

This morbidity-mortality puzzle has drawn extensive attention (Nathanson, 1975, 1976, 1977; Gove and Hughes, 1979; Mechanic, 1976). The morbidity disadvantage of women and the mortality disadvantage of men are widely thought to be a function of: (1) biological risks, (2) acquired risks, (3) psychosocial factors bearing on symptoms and care, (4) health-reporting behavior, and (5) prior health care (Verbrugge, 1989). Biological risks and less prior care disfavor men, while psychosocial factors and health-reporting behavior increase the morbidity experiences and reports of women. Some acquired risks (smoking, alcohol consumption, occupational hazards) work to the disadvantage of males; other aspects of lifestyle (less strenuous leisure activities, greater stress, role pressures) put females at greater risk. Thai wives are significantly more likely than husbands to report (see Table 8.2) that at some point in the past month, they had been too sick to work for two or more consecutive days (18.7% versus 11.7%), too sick to get out of bed (7.8% versus 4.0%),

**Table 8.2 Sex Differences in Health for
Married Men and Women in Bangkok**

Health Indicator	Husbands	Wives	p
Too sick to work in past month			
Percent	11.7%	18.7%	.001
Times	.16	.27	.001
Days	.63	.92	.07
Too sick to get out of bed in past month			
Percent	4.0%	7.8%	.002
Times	.05	.10	.002
Days	.33	.46	ns
Too sick to eat in past month			
Percent	2.4%	4.9%	.01
Times	.03	.06	.02
Days	.06	.25	.02
Degree of sickness in past month	1.18	1.31	.001
Utilized services of health care professional in the past 12 months			
Percent, all providers	45.7%	58.2%	.001
Times, all providers	1.77	2.31	.03
Percent, nurse	45.0%	54.7%	.001
Percent, physician	0.2%	1.2%	.03
Percent, traditional healer	0.00%	0.01%	.03
Percent, admitted to hospital	6.8%	21.8%	.001
Times, admitted to hospital	.11	.26	.001
Nights in hospital	.37	1.23	.001
Self-report of health status	2.71	2.46	.001

or too sick to eat (4.9% versus 2.4%). Significant differences are also found with respect to the number of times such sicknesses occurred. In addition, wives report significantly more serious sicknesses, as indicated by the summary measure.

Consistent with the more frequent reports of illness, wives were more likely than husbands to report that they had sought assistance from health care professionals. Wives were more likely to see a health care professional in the past twelve months (58.2% versus 45.7%), and they saw a health professional more often than did husbands (2.3 times versus 1.8). Both wives and husbands are far more likely to utilize the services of nurses than those of doctors or traditional healers. About 55% of the wives and 45% of the husbands were treated by a nurse in the past twelve months, while fewer than 2% of the wives and husbands went to a doctor and fewer than 1% visited a traditional healer.

Wives, moreover, were more likely than husbands to have been admitted to a hospital in the past twelve months (22% versus 7%). They were hospitalized more often in the past twelve months (.26 times versus .11) and spent more nights in the hospital (1.23 versus .37).

With respect to the self-report of overall health, wives generally report poorer health than do husbands. Specifically, the mean score for wives is 2.5 on a 4-point scale versus 2.7 for husbands. Of the seven symptoms of menstrual problems, wives indicate, on average, 1.4 symptoms. We thus routinely examined the possibility that husbands and wives may react differently to housing quality, household crowding, and psychological distress. This involved inspecting six sex interaction terms, one for each of the independent variables (with 1=male, 0=female). If a sex interaction term was nonsignificant, as was usually the case, we left it out. If the sex interaction term for, say, lack of privacy had a significant negative value in the equation for being too sick to work, this would indicate that lack of privacy had a significantly greater effect for husbands than for wives.

For the analyses reported in Table 8.1 only one significant sex interaction term was found, that involving the relationship between psychological distress and "get sick too". Psychological distress itself has a significant positive value, indicating that wives who are more distressed are more likely to get sick when other household members are ill. The sex interaction term has a significant negative value, indicating that this effect is significantly weaker for husbands than for wives. The magnitude of a standardized coefficient for an interaction term cannot be readily interpreted. However, the coefficient for the interaction term and for the distress term are similar in magnitude. This suggests, and separate analyses of husbands and wives confirm, that psychological distress has a significant detrimental effect on "get too sick" only for wives, but not for husbands.

Conclusions

Our results, at least in one respect, are quite consistent with Cassel's view. Cassel, contends: "The past century has witnessed a change from a complete conviction that there is a simple and direct relationship between the urban environment, particularly the quality of the housing, and health status, to one of considerable uncertainty and confusion. A review of the literature since 1920 reveals some studies showing a relationship between housing and various indicators of poor health, others showing no such relationship, and yet others showing an inverse relationship" (1979:129). Cassel further maintains: "One of the more widely held and cherished notions in medicine is that the spread of infectious disease is facilitated by crowding. This assumption underlies many of the research endeavors seeking to establish a relationship between housing and health, and has been accepted as a truism by policy makers. There is little question that under certain circumstances crowding may be linked to an increased incidence of communicable diseases, but ... under other circumstances no such relationship has been discovered" (1979:131).

While Cassel's skepticism was based on a review of the evidence in Western countries, we find that in Bangkok, objective aspects of housing quality and objective crowding have little effect on health. Inconsistent with his conclusion, however, we find that subjective aspects of housing and of crowding, especially housing satisfaction and a felt lack of privacy, do have detrimental effects on health. Furthermore, psychological distress is shown to have a potent influence on the physical health of Bangkokians. Subjective crowding and psychological distress are, of course, interrelated. Additional analyses suggest that a felt lack of privacy contributes to psychological distress. Importantly, our analyses suggest that both factors, as well as housing satisfaction, have independent effects on health outcomes.

Thai wives do appear to have poorer health than husbands. But there is little evidence to suggest that housing quality, household crowding, or psychological distress has a different effect for wives than for husbands. Our findings rather unequivocally suggest that subjectively inadequate housing, subjective crowding, and stress, though not the objective housing conditions or the level of congestion per se, do have detrimental effects on the health of married men and women.

9
Conclusions

Previous researchers have devoted considerable effort to determining the effects, if any, of household crowding. The results have been mixed, and different researchers have come to radically different conclusions. As Gove and Hughes rightly point out, this question has not only theoretical importance, but it also has substantial policy relevance. To the extent that social policy is based on social research, "making a mistake on this issue can have undesirable consequences by legitimizing policies whose implementation would either waste a great deal of money (if crowding has no effects) or have a substantial negative impact on the quality of life (if crowding does have serious effects)" (1980a:864). Gove and his associates conclude that crowding does have "substantial" detrimental effects, and, by way of advancing the research agenda, they argue that "it is time to turn away from the question of whether it ever has effects to the study of the factors which magnify or minimize effects" (1979:79).

Booth and his associates, however, reach very different conclusions based not only on their Toronto analyses, but also on their review of the results from Chicago. They conclude that "The findings support, not reject, the contention that household crowding is a variable of minimal importance in explaining pathology, at least in modern industrial society. On the basis of findings to date, pathology has little to do with crowding" (1980b:878).

In stating their conclusion in this way, Booth and his associates cautiously and quite rightly avoid any implication that their conclusion holds for the vast majority of the world's population living in less developed countries. Both research teams examined North American cities. And both teams, as well as other researchers, have suggested that reactions to crowding may be conditioned by the cultural context. While there have been several studies of the effects of household crowding in less developed countries, they are all fairly weak from a methodological point of view. Recognizing the paucity of knowledge about how household crowding affects the hundreds of millions of people living in the cities of the less developed world, who live in much more crowded circumstances than do the typical citizens of the industrialized cities, is what stimulated us to embark on the present study.

The average level of household crowding in Bangkok, and in our sample, is over two persons per room. The higher average level of household crowding and its greater dispersion in Bangkok than in North American or European cities might well lead one to expect that crowding would have stronger effects in Bangkok than in industrialized countries. There are several other reasons, however, for anticipating that, in the context of Thai culture, crowding effects might be relatively modest.

First, the typical household structure found in Bangkok suggests that there may be normative tolerance for household crowding. Very few Bangkokians live alone, extended families are fairly common, and the average household size is more than five persons. Whether these living arrangements are a matter of necessity or choice, social norms may facilitate harmonious relations among crowded family members. A second, and related, aspect of Thai normative structure is its emphasis on the avoidance of interpersonal conflict and the maintenance of harmonious relations (Klausner, 1972, 1981). The emphasis placed on self control may moderate any potential effects of crowding. Third, even in rural areas, where land is relatively abundant, similar levels of persons per room are found. This history of crowding may make it easier for Thais to accommodate to high levels of crowding in urbanized areas to which people have migrated. Fourth, the tropical climate of Thailand allows household members to be out-of-doors many hours every day, during all seasons of the year. Living space is not confined to the housing unit itself, but expands to adjacent communal areas. Moreover, in Bangkok, those who work outside the home often work long hours and may have a time-consuming commute to work. This means that some household members are absent during most of their waking hours. Hence, the effective level of crowding is sometimes lower than indicated by a simple "head count". Finally, Thais appear to value social interaction more than Americans or Europeans do, while placing less value on privacy. Where an American may wonder whether it is appropriate to disturb someone who is alone, Thais are more likely to think that a person who is alone may need companionship. For many Thais, high levels of household crowding may simply provide protection from loneliness and offer many opportunities for social interaction.

Thus, even if one thought that crowding had detrimental effects in North American or Europe, it was unclear at the outset whether to expect that crowding would have similar, stronger, or weaker effects in Bangkok. In brief summary, this is what we found.

Summary of Major Findings

Subjective Crowding

The relationship between objective and subjective crowding is a modest one. The major findings pertaining to this relationship, and other major analyses, are summarized in Table 9.1.

We closely examined the nature of the relationship between objective and subjective crowding, as discussed in Chapter 4, in an attempt to ascertain why it is not stronger. In the process, we utilized a number of alternative measures of objective crowding. After examining seven different measures of objective crowding and two alternative measures of subjective crowding, we find rather similar correlations between objective and subjective crowding, regardless of the specific operationalization used. This would rather emphatically suggest that the modest relationship between the two types of crowding is not an artifact of measurement, and that the explanation of its modest nature lies elsewhere.

A prime reason for the modest nature of the relationship may be that the link between objective congestion and the feeling of being crowded is contingent on various aspects of an individual's circumstances. The findings suggest, in sum, that while objective crowding may be a necessary condition, it is not sufficient to explain why people feel crowded. Why they feel crowded is largely a consequence of household circumstances and individual reactions to those circumstances.

Thinking that reactivity to crowding may depend, in part, on the particular characteristics and circumstances of different individuals, we examined several specific subgroups in our sample. Objective and subjective crowding might be more highly related, we speculated, among women, those living with their in-laws, and among people with low household control. But as we saw in Chapter 4, the results are mixed and even when the expected patterns emerge, the differences tend to be rather small. In sum, we could not detect any particular conditions under which objective and subjective crowding are strongly related.

Contrary to the assumptions of prior investigations, we find that the relationship between objective and subjective crowding is not entirely linear. The feeling of being crowded does not increase over the entire range of objective crowding. Instead, our results suggest that there is a ceiling effect. Those people living in the most extreme of congested circumstances feel no more crowded than individuals residing in households somewhat lower on the scale of residential crowding. The level of perceived crowding appears to peak when the number of persons per room is about 2.5, and the level actually declines to a minor degree

Table 9.1 Summary of Major Findings

	Independent Variables				
Dependent Variables	Persons per room	Perceived crowding	Lack of privacy	Felt demands	Psychological distress
Psychological Well-being					
Psychological distress	++/ns	+++/+++	+++/+++	+++	
Unhappiness	++/ns	++/ns	+++/+++	++	
Irritability	ns/ns	+++/+++	+++/+++	+++	
Psychological withdrawal	ns/ns	+++/+++	+++/+	+++	
Lethargy	+++/ns	+++/+++	+++/+++	+++	
Distraction	ns/ns	+++/+++	+++/+++	+++	
Loneliness	++/ns	+++/++	+++/+++	+++	
Lose your mind	ns/ns	+++/ns	+++/+++	+++	
Contemplate suicide	ns/ns	+++/+	+++/+++	+++	
Marital and Family Relations					
Marital instability	ns/ns	++/ns	--/-	+++	+++
Marital arguments	ns/ns	+++/+++	+++/+++	+++	+++
Marital companionship	ns/ns	ns/ns	--/--	ns	ns
Supportive behavior	ns/ns	++/+	ns/ns	+	+
Parent-child tension	ns/ns	+++/ns	+++/ns	+++	+++
Discipline of children	ns/ns	+/ns	+/ns	ns	+++
Sibling conflict	ns/ns	ns/-	ns/ns	ns	+++

Table 9.1 *(continued)*

| | Independent Variables | | | | |
Dependent Variables	Persons per room	Perceived crowding	Lack of privacy	Felt demands	Psychological distress
Violence					
Wife abuse	+/+	++/ns	++/ns	+	+++
Arguments - outside	+/+	ns/ns	ns/ns	ns	+++
Arguments - nonnuclear	ns/ns	++/ns	ns/ns	+++	+++
Reproductive Behavior					
Frequency of sexual relations	ns/ns		ns/ns		ns
Ever reluctant to have sex	+++/+++		+++/+++		+++
Temporary cessation of sexual relations	+/+		ns/ns		ns
Want more children	ns/ns		ns/ns		ns
Using birth control	ns/ns		ns/ns		ns
Forgot to use birth control	ns/ns		ns/ns		+++
Lack of privacy prevents use of birth control	ns/ns		ns/ns		+++
Child loss	ns/ns		ns/ns		ns
Miscarriage	ns/ns		ns/ns		ns
Abortion	ns/ns		ns/ns		++

(continues)

Table 9.1 (*continued*)

Dependent Variables	Independent Variables		Psychological distress
	Persons per room	Lack of privacy	
Physical Health			
Too sick to work	ns/ns	+++/+	+++
Too sick to get out of bed	ns/ns	ns/ns	+++
Too sick to eat	ns/ns	+/ns	++
Degree of sickness in past month	ns/ns	++/ns	+++
Visited a health care professional	ns/+	+/ns	+++
Visited a nurse in past 12 months	ns/+	+/ns	+++
Admitted to hospital in past 12 months	ns/ns	ns/ns	ns
Get sick too	ns/ns	ns/ns	+++
Self-report of health status	ns/ns	—/ns	—
Menstrual problems	ns/ns	++/+	+++

Note: Controlling for sex of respondent, family income, education of the respondent, state in family life cycle, household control, number of generations and number of married couples in the household. The natural logs of persons per room, perceived crowding, and the lack of privacy are used.

Note: The first symbol in each pair of symbols refers to the significance of the relationship after controlling for causally prior variables, while the symbol following the slash mark refers to the significance in the full model. Plus signs indicate a positive relationship; negative signs indicate a negative relationship; one such sign means the relationship is significant at the .05 level, two means .01, and three means .001; "ns" means not significant.

thereafter. Thus, in part, the strength of the objective-subjective crowding relationship is reduced by a ceiling effect, and the evidence clearly does not support the notion of a "tipping point" or a speculated threshold effect (Booth, Johnson, and Edwards, 1980a).

While the presence of others elevates a subjective sense of crowding, as one would anticipate, so does spending less time at home than elsewhere. This may be due to three possibilities, which require further exploration. Feeling crowded, although one is in the household less time, could stem from a contrast effect between the home and other settings or it could be that the subjective experience of crowding is the impetus to spend fewer hours in the household. Unfortunately, our data do not address these points. Alternatively, it could well be that those who spend long hours in the household simply become inured to its congestion. Given the evidence for a ceiling effect and the non-linearity of the objective-subjective crowding relationship, we are inclined to accept this latter explanation. If this is the case, it would help explain why other crowding researchers (Booth, Johnson, and Edwards, 1980a,b) have found the pathological effects of subjective crowding to be unexpectedly selective and the relationships to various aberrant behaviors relatively modest in strength.

To say objective crowding is a necessary but not sufficient condition to feeling crowded and to suggest that there is a relatively modest relationship between objective and subjective crowding should not lead us to conclude that neither of them has consequences for how people behave. On the contrary, objective crowding plainly has something to do with how individuals perceive a situation. And, as our theoretical model suggests, it is that perception which will trigger a chain of reactions, some perhaps being of an adverse nature.

Psychological Well-Being

For example, objective crowding has a small but significant effect on a number of aspects of psychological well-being, including psychological distress, unhappiness, lethargy, and loneliness, with the control variables included in the model. On the other hand, objective crowding has no effect on irritability, psychological withdrawal, the feeling that one may "lose one's mind", or whether the respondent has ever contemplated suicide. When subjective crowding is added to the model, objective crowding no longer has a significant effect on any of the measures of psychological well-being.

With regard to the effects of subjective crowding, a felt lack of privacy is significantly related to all nine measures of psychological well-being that we examined. People who feel that they lack privacy are more likely to experience psychological distress, be less happy, feel more irritable, more apt to withdraw psychologically, be lethargic and easily distracted, feel they are losing their minds, and are more likely to indicate that they have contemplated suicide. Perhaps surprisingly, but consistent with the hypothesis, people who feel that they lack privacy also feel lonelier. In this context, loneliness refers less to an objective state of isolation and more to a psychological frame of mind.

These findings are based on using lack of privacy as the indicator of subjective crowding. When the analyses are replicated using perceived crowding as the indicator of subjective crowding, the results are quite similar. Whether one uses the measure of subjective crowding from the Chicago study or the one from the Toronto study, the results are similar, but we can conclude that lack of privacy has a stronger and more consistent effect than does perceived crowding.

Felt demands also has a significant effect on each measure of psychological well-being. People who feel that other household members make many demands on them are more likely to display psychological distress, be less happy, feel more irritable, engage in psychological withdrawal, report that they sometimes feel that they are losing their mind, and indicate that they have contemplated suicide. As we noted in Chapter 5, felt demands partly mediates the effect of a lack of privacy on psychological well-being.

How strong is the effect of subjective household crowding on psychological well-being? The standardized coefficients provide us with a quantified answer, of course, but they do not indicate if these effects are small, moderate, or large. One can better answer this question by comparing the effects of crowding to the effects of income. In Bangkok, perhaps even more than in the United States, the poor have few support systems enabling them to survive. Poverty creates constant stresses, which surely take their toll in terms of psychological well-being and otherwise. In fact, though, we find in every case that the effect of a lack of privacy on well-being is greater than the effect of income.

Overall, objective household crowding—persons per room—has only weak and selective effects on psychological well-being, but the subjective experience of household crowding is a chronic stressor that has a strong and consistent detrimental effect on psychological well-being. These results pertain not simply to a single item or a single scale, but are documented by reference to a broad array of measures of psychological well-being. The effects are unmistakable for both men and women. At least in Bangkok, and possibly in other cities with comparable levels of household crowding, crowding constitutes a major threat to psychological well-being.

Marital and Family Relations

There is broad support for the notion that household crowding is also detrimental to marital and family relations. We find that objective crowding has significant detrimental effects on marital arguments and instability, as well as on parent-child tension, controlling for background variables. Furthermore, objective crowding has a significant deleterious effect on wife abuse and on arguments or fights outside the home.

Subjective crowding has detrimental effects on marital and family relations, too. Those who feel crowded are more likely to report higher levels of marital instability and more marital arguments. They also feel greater tension in the parent-child relationship and discipline their children more. More positively, and contrary to expectation, parents who feel crowded also report being more supportive of their children. Using the alternate measure of subjective crowding, those who feel that they lack privacy are more likely to experience marital instability and arguments, and report less companionship. They also report more tension in their interactions with their children and they discipline their children more.

Moreover, people who feel they lack privacy are more likely to report wife abuse, and wives who feel crowded are more likely to report that they are victims of wive abuse. Perceived crowding, furthermore, has significant impacts on the frequency of arguments and fights with members of the family.

One consistent result we find concerns the importance of both felt demands and psychological distress as intervening variables affecting most measures of family relations. People who have more psychological distress or feel more demands experience more marital instability and marital arguments, and they experience greater parent-child tension. In a like vein, parents who experience more psychological distress discipline their children more frequently. This pattern largely holds for the measures of violence as well. The impact of subjective crowding on wife abuse and serious arguments or fights with other non-nuclear family members disappears when the effect of distress and/or felt demands is taken into account. Taken together, these findings strongly suggest that distress and felt demands are important explanatory variables accounting for crowding outcomes.

Sexual Relations and Reproductive Behaviors

If household crowding has any effect on reproductive behavior, one might expect it to be especially discernible in a context with a high level of household crowding such as we find in Bangkok. The objective level of crowding—persons per room—does have a significant effect on certain aspects of sexual behavior, but the effects are quite selective. Although objective crowding is not significantly related to the reported frequency of sexual relations, those who live in objectively more crowded households do sometimes have greater reluctance to engage in sexual relations because of the presence of others and they are more likely to have had periods of temporary cessation of sexual relations with their spouse. However, those who live in objectively more crowded households are just as likely to want additional children; they are neither more nor less likely to use birth control. They are no more likely to forget to use their method of birth control, and they do not feel that the lack of privacy prevents them from using birth control. Contrary to the report of one study (Gove and Hughes, 1983), objective crowding has no effect on fetal and child survival among the Bangkok sample.

The results pertaining to subjective crowding are similarly selective. Parents who feel more crowded are more likely to report that they are sometimes reluctant to engage in sexual relations because of the presence of others and that lack of privacy sometimes prevents them from using birth control. Felt lack of privacy affects only one of the measures examined. Individuals who have a greater felt lack of privacy are more often reluctant to engage in sexual intercourse. Other than the effects mentioned here, perceived crowding and a felt lack of privacy have no significant effects on any of the measures examined.

Perhaps more surprising than the effects that crowding has are the effects that crowding does not have. Our analyses show that, in Bangkok, where the fertility rate is at a relatively low level but where household crowding is high, household crowding does not reduce the desire for children. Fortunately, household crowding does not seem to impede the effective use of birth control, nor does crowding significantly affect fetal or child survival. Our findings suggest that, overall, household crowding, either in its objective or subjective dimension, has a very selective—and generally modest—impact on sexual and reproductive behavior, if it has any consequences at all.

Physical Health

Cassel has written, "One of the more widely held and cherished notions in medicine is that the spread of infectious disease is facilitated by crowding. This assumption underlies many of the research endeavors seeking to establish a relationship between housing and health, and has been accepted as a truism by policy makers. There is little question that under certain circumstances crowding may be linked to an increased incidence of communicable diseases, but ... under other circumstances no such relationship has been discovered" (1979:131).

While Cassel's skepticism was based on a review of the evidence in Western countries, we find that, in Bangkok, objective aspects of housing quality and objective crowding have little effect on health. We do find, on the other hand, that subjective aspects of housing and of crowding, especially housing satisfaction and a felt lack of privacy, do have detrimental effects on health. Furthermore, psychological distress is shown to have a potent influence on the physical health of Bangkokians. Importantly, our analyses suggest that both factors, as well as housing satisfaction, have independent effects on health outcomes. Our results rather unequivocally suggest that subjectively inadequate housing, subjective crowding, and stress, though not the objective housing conditions or the level of congestion per se, do have detrimental effects on the health of married men and women.

Gender Differences

In light of reports from prior crowding studies, we hypothesized that the effects of crowding on psychological well-being, as well as on marital and family relations, would be greater for women than for men. There is some—but very little—evidence in our data to support such a conclusion for Bangkok. With respect to psychological well-being, a total of 36 sex interaction terms were examined, and only two were significant. At least as far as psychological well-being is concerned, in most of the comparisons, men and women respond in quite similar ways to both objective and subjective crowding. Likewise, in our examination of marital and family relations, we found no gender differences in reactivity to either objective or subjective crowding, except with respect to reports of physical violence.

While previous researchers have posited, and claim to have found, stronger reactivity to crowding for wives than for husbands, we find very little evidence of such differences in Bangkok. There are at least two possible explanations for the differences between our results and those of earlier researchers. First, of course, there may be cultural differences. Perhaps North American women are more reactive to crowding than are North American men, while no such differences occur in Bangkok. Second, different methodologies may account for the difference in conclusions. We explicitly tested statistically for sex differences in the reactivity to crowding, while neither of the North American studies reporting such differences had explicit tests for differences between men and women.

Crowding and Culture: Theoretical Implications

Most crowding research, either implicitly or explicitly, has been guided by a basic, and often simplistic, stress model, where stress is seen as an intervening mechanism between crowding and a variety of behavioral outcomes. Our study, conducted as it was in a major Asian city where the level of household crowding is much greater than that typically found in cities of the industrialized world, affords an opportunity to test the generality of the theory that a high level of household crowding has detrimental effects on psychological well-being, on marital and family relations, and on physical health—an opportunity to see, in short, how well this theory holds up in a cultural context very different from the one in which it has previously been tested.

Prior researchers, who have focused primarily on North America and Europe, could never overcome one serious limitation of their studies, no matter how rigorous their methodologies. Namely, in their chosen research sites, families enjoy what are, by world standards, remarkably low levels of crowding. In the United States, household crowding for the vast majority of families falls somewhere between 0.25 and 1.0 persons per room. In Bangkok, and in most cities in developing countries, by contrast, the level of household crowding typically ranges from 1 person per room to 4 persons per room, with relatively few people living in circumstances at either extreme. Subjectively, the difference between 1 and 4 persons per room may be much greater than the difference between 0.25 and 1 person per room. The theory of household crowding has been on shaky empirical grounds precisely because we knew nothing about the validity of the theory in the circumstances in which most of the world's urban dwellers live.

With some notable exceptions, our findings support many aspects of the more elaborate proposed model. The most important exception pertains to the impact of objective crowding. It appears that there is a rather modest linkage between objective crowding and its subjective experience, contrary to logic and commonsensical notions about why people feel crowded. What is or is not perceived as crowding or as impinging on one's sense of privacy may vary significantly from one culture to the next. To put it differently, the threshold at which a person begins to feel crowded may depend on what, in a statistical sense, is normative for a culture, and the findings seem to suggest that threshold is relatively high for Thais. Crucially, though, the data indicate that, even in the face of normative standards higher than those in the industrialized world, the perception of being crowded is critical in accounting for differences in psychological well-being and in explaining why people experience decrements in their marital and family relations. And, while the effects of objective crowding are weaker and more selective than those of subjective crowding, objective crowding does have some important detrimental effects in the context of Bangkok. As we have observed, the elevated stress that individuals experience largely mediates the effect of crowding on marital and family relations.

Thus, even with a history of high levels of household crowding, it appears to be the case that Bangkokians have not adjusted to crowding to the extent that it has ceased to have any effect on their lives. In fact, compared with the findings of North American and European studies, the effects of crowding on well-being and Thai family life, at least as subjectively perceived, are far less selective and have even stronger detrimental consequences than have been found elsewhere.

We would argue for a conclusion somewhere between that reached by Booth and his colleagues—"pathology has little to do with crowding" (1980b:878)—and that reached by Gove and his colleagues, who flatly state that "crowding does have substantial effects ..." (1979:79). Like Booth and his associates, we find that the effects of objective and subjective crowding are "selective," but we cannot conclude that poor mental health or poor marital and family relations have "little to do with crowding." In some respects, despite the cultural differences, our empirical results in Bangkok are similar to those found in Chicago. But, like Gove and Hughes, we find that the effects of persons per room on mental health, on marital and on family relations, controlling for background variables but not controlling for lack of privacy or felt demands, are modest, and that these effects disappear when controls for lack of privacy and felt demands are added. Also as in the Chicago study, we find that lack of privacy and felt demands have substantial effects on mental health and marital and family relations.

One difference between our results and those found in North America pertains to the consequences of crowding at the upper range of crowding. The comparatively low levels of household crowding in industrialized cities means that finding cases above a "threshold," a point beyond which crowding begins to have detrimental effects, is problematic. Finding families above such a threshold is not problematic in Bangkok, where crowding frequently reaches the level of two, three, or even four persons per room. The converse problem, a "ceiling effect," where additional crowding has little incremental effect, may be more of a problem. Indeed, our data suggest that, within the range of household crowding found in Bangkok, there is a "ceiling effect." That is something that we did not previously know, and which studies in cities of the industrialized world could not have told us.

One possible concern in interpreting our findings has to do with the relationship between household crowding and socioeconomic status, making it difficult to separate the effects of these two variables. We do have more multicollinearity between socioeconomic status and household crowding than did Gove and Hughes, but the level of multicollinearity is acceptable.

While our results indicate that, up to certain limits, household crowding produces stronger detrimental effects than have previously been found in similar studies in industrialized countries, they also suggest that people in Bangkok have adjusted to a level of household crowding that many North Americans probably would find intolerable. There are few families in North America who have two, three, or four persons per room, but extrapolating from the Toronto and Chicago data suggests that North American families would have considerable difficulty adjusting to such high levels of household crowding. Families in Bangkok, by contrast, routinely cope with such levels of crowding, even if they do have adverse consequences for their mental well-being and various social relations.

How do they do this? There appear to be a number of coping mechanisms. One is the strategy of physical withdrawal. People may leave their housing unit to socialize with others outside their home, or leave simply to be alone. Another strategy is psychological withdrawal. Family members sometimes ignore the demands of others. It should be remembered, of course, that many people are out of the home for long hours every day. In addition to the work day, a commute of an hour or two is not unusual; even longer commutes are common. Although such long commutes are not a coping mechanism per se, they may reduce the impact of household crowding. A more thorough investigation of coping mechanisms is an important topic for further investigation.

Implications for Public Policy

Our results plainly suggest that the task of housing ever larger numbers of people cannot be approached complacently. The earth, to our misfortune, does not expand. The population, perhaps to our ultimate misfortune, does. And it continues to do so at an extremely rapid pace. As more than an additional billion people are added to the world's population over the next decade, societies will be evermore hard-pressed to provide adequate housing. This will be especially the case in developing countries, where much of that increase will be concentrated. Despite ongoing industrialization and the wealth it brings, the governments of developing nations already are experiencing great difficulties in providing the infrastructure required by urbanization. The net result, in all probability, will be cities of ever higher density, with the likelihood of more intense crowding at the household level. As our findings attest, there will be numerous "social costs" to pay.

While the provision of more commodious housing may be ideal, for most developing countries it is an impractical solution. There are, however, relatively simple measures that could be undertaken. One policy implication that follows from our findings is that residential areas should have ample communal space. In flats, for example, the space beneath and around the flats appears to be an important congregating area, one that can provide a respite from the crowded conditions in the housing units themselves. This opportunity for physical withdrawal seems to be helpful in ameliorating the effects of crowding. Private housing developers, as well as housing authorities providing public housing, should take care to provide such opportunities, and agencies regulating private housing should encourage private developers to provide such communal areas.

Beyond these architectural considerations, our results suggest that the manner in which household members interact with each other is also important, perhaps even more important. The demands that household members make on each other have an important effect on psychological well-being, as well as on marital and family relations. If other family members "are always making demands", or if one is "almost always interrupted" when one tries to do something at home, this is detrimental to mental health and to family relations. The implication is that people may find it easier to cope with crowding if others don't make such strong demands on them. While governments cannot dictate how family members interact, social work agencies, armed with this information, may be able to suggest to their clients ways of interacting within the home that may be less harmful.

Appendix A: Questionnaire

FAMILY RELATIONS AND HEALTH IN BANGKOK

Institute for Population and Social Research
Mahidol University
Bangkok

Questionnaire Number _____
Name of respondent _____
House number _____ Lane _____ Street _____
Subdistrict _____ District _____
Date _____
Starting time _____ Ending time _____
Total time _____
Appointment time _____ 1 _____ 2 Substitute house _____
Reason for substitution
1.   No eligible couple
2.   No eligible person available
3.   Refusal
4.   Interview terminated prematurely
Interviewer's name _____
Supervisor's name _____ Date _____
Coder's name _____
Coding supervisor _____ Date _____
Data Entry Person _____ Date _____

1.   Obtain information on the age, sex, relationship, and marital status of all
        household members.

Number	Name	Age	Sex	Marital Status	Relation to Respondent
1					
2					
3					
4					
5					
6					
7					
8					
9					
10					

2.   Are there any other people who sometimes live in the household?
        _____   yes
        _____   no
        (If yes, add this person above. Indicate "PT" for "part-time" next to
        person number.)
        How many days per month is your husband/wife in Bangkok? _____
        days
        What is the relationship of the respondent to the head of household?
        _____

3.   What is the highest grade in school you have ever attended?
        _____   never attended school (0)
        _____   Primary. Years completed _____
        _____   Secondary. Years completed _____
        _____   Diploma (13)
        _____   College graduate (14)
        _____   Post-graduate (15)
        _____   Religious training (16)

4.	Are you currently working?	Respondent	Spouse
	_____ Yes (1)	_____	_____
	_____ No (2) Are you	_____	_____
	_____ looking for work (1)	_____	_____
	_____ unable to work (2)	_____	_____
	_____ taking care of house/		
	children (3)	_____	_____
	_____ student (4)	_____	_____
	_____ retired (5)	_____	_____
	_____ other (6) _____	_____	_____

5. (If employed or looking for work)
What is your occupation? _____
(Interviewer: Write the specific job title and indicate the occupational group.)

		Respondent	Spouse
_____	Professional, technical, and related (1)	_____	_____
_____	Administrative, executive, managerial, and government officials (2)	_____	_____
_____	Clerical and related (3)	_____	_____
_____	Sales workers (4)	_____	_____
_____	Transport equipment operators and related (5)	_____	_____
_____	Craftsmen, production workers, and laborers (6)	_____	_____
_____	Service worker (7)	_____	_____
_____	Agricultural, fishermen, and related (8)	_____	_____
_____	Miners, quarrymen, well drillers and related	_____	_____
_____	Other (10) _____		

6. Are you renting your housing, do you own it, are you buying it, is your housing provided as payment-in-kind, or is your housing free? Do you _____?

_____ Rent (1)
_____ Own (2)
_____ Rent land, but own house (3)
_____ Other (4)

How long have you lived in this house? _____ years

7. How much is the monthly payment for your housing?
_____ Baht

8. Does your household have any of the following items?

_____ Electric fan (1)
_____ Refrigerator (2)
_____ Television (3) _____ number
_____ Video (VCR) (4)
_____ Radio (5)
_____ Sewing machine (6)

_____ Bicycle (7)
_____ Motorcycle (8)
_____ Truck (9)
_____ Automobile (10) _____ number
_____ Telephone (11)
_____ Air conditioner (12) _____ number

9.   How many rooms are there in your housing unit?
     _____ rooms (permanent construction)
     Do not count bathroom or toilet, but do count kitchen, all-purpose room,
     and bedrooms.

10. How many of these rooms are used for sleeping?
     _____ rooms

11. Have you partitioned any of these rooms?
     _____ yes (1)   _____ (2)   _____ (Skip to 12)
     (If yes)

11.1 How many rooms are there altogether, including all rooms formed by
     partitions?
     _____ rooms

12. How many square meters are there in your dwelling? _____ sq. meters
     (Include only the area used by the respondent's household)

13. Normally, what is your source of drinking water? (check only one)
     _____ Piped, inside house (1)
     _____ Piped, outside (2)
     _____ Well (3)
     _____ Bottled (4)
     _____ Rain (5)
     _____ Other (6) _____

14. What type of bathroom do you have?
     _____ Bathroom, exclusive (1)
     _____ Bathroom, shared (2)
     _____ Bathroom, public or community (3)
     _____ Public place (e.g. terrace, veranda, river, canal) (4)
     _____ None (i.e. outdoors) (5)
     _____ Other (6)

15. Do you have an exclusive toilet or a shared toilet?
     _____ Exclusive (1)
     _____ Shared (2)

15.1 How many exclusive toilets do you have? _____ number

16. Do your children (does your child) have a place to play at home without
     getting in anyone's way?
     _____ Usually (1)
     _____ Sometimes (2)
     _____ Never (3)

17. Sometimes people don't invite friends into their home because they feel
     they don't have enough space to entertain them. Have you ever felt this
     way about your present home?
     _____ Often (1)

_____ Sometimes (2)

_____ Never (3)

18. Housing satisfaction, specific.

I would like to ask how satisfied you are with various features of your home.

Could you indicate whether you are strongly satisfied, satisfied, dissatisfied, or strongly dissatisfied with these features of your home? Strongly satisfied = 1; Satisfied = 2; Dissatisfied = 3; Strongly dissatisfied = 4

18.1	Drinking water	1	2	3	4
18.2	Water supply	1	2	3	4
18.3	Ventilation	1	2	3	4
18.4	Bathroom	1	2	3	4
18.5	Kitchen	1	2	3	4
18.6	Toilet	1	2	3	4
18.7	Brightness-sunlight	1	2	3	4
18.8	Number of rooms	1	2	3	4
18.9	Size of rooms	1	2	3	4
18.10	Kitchen	1	2	3	4
18.11	Laundry	1	2	3	4
18.12	Noise	1	2	3	4
18.13	Smell	1	2	3	4
18.14	Heat	1	2	3	4

19. What do you think about your housing conditions? Overall, is your housing safe (physically)?

_____ Good (1)

_____ OK (2)

_____ Not good (3)

20. Housing satisfaction, general.

20.1 How satisfied are you with where you are living now? Would you say you are:

_____ Very satisfied (1)

_____ Good enough (2)

_____ Satisfied (3)

20.2 If you could, do you want to move to a larger house?

_____ yes, want (1)

_____ Not sure (2) (skip to 21)

_____ No, don't want (3) (skip to 21)

20.3 (If yes) Do you think you will move to a larger house in the next year? (PROBE: IS THAT DEFINITELY OR PROBABLY)

_____ definitely will move (1)

_____ probably will move (2)

_____ will not move (3)

		Respondent	Spouse
21.	Did you grow up in Bangkok?		
	_____ Yes (1)	_____	_____
	_____ No (2)	_____	_____
21.1	(If No) Where did you grow up?		
	_____ Changwat town (1)	_____	_____

    _____   Amphur town (2)   _____   _____

    _____   Village (3)   _____   _____

    _____   Outside Thailand (4)   _____

21.2   (If No) How many years have you lived in Bangkok?   _____   _____

22.   With what ethnic or cultural group do you identify yourself?

        _____   Thai (1)

        _____   Part Thai, Part Chinese (2)

        _____   Chinese (3)

        _____   Other (4) _____

23.   We would like to know how you spent your time yesterday. (Note: If yesterday was Saturday or Sunday, obtain for last Friday.)

We want to know when you got up, how much time you spent at home, and who else was at home with you. What time did you get up yesterday (or Friday)? Find out when the person was home during the day, record for each hour, and find out who was home with them. Continue record for 24 hours, noting when the respondent went to bed.)

Time person got up _____

Time person went to bed _____

Time	At home?	Not at home	Number of others present
5 am			
6 am			
7 am			
8 am			
9 am			
10 am			
11 am			
12 noon			
1 pm			
2 pm			
3 pm			
4 pm			
5 pm			
6 pm			
7 pm			
8 pm			

9 pm
10 pm

---

11 pm
12 midnight

---

1 am
2 am

---

3 am
4 am

23.1	Today is: SU M TU W TH F SA
23.2	Time budget is for: SU M TU W TH F SA
24.	According to the information you gave me, yesterday (last Friday) you spent about _____ hours awake at home, right?

_____ Right
_____ Not right

(If not right, check time budget, correct the information, and record the number of hours the person spent awake at home.)

25. During a normal weekday, how many hours a day on the average do you spend away from home, including time when you are working?
_____ hours

26. During a normal night, how many hours do you spend sleeping?
_____ hours

27. During a normal day, how many hours do you spend resting or napping? _____ hours

28. Are you ever bothered by the noise made by your neighbors?
_____ Yes (1)
_____ No (2)

(If yes) How many times were you bothered in the last week?
_____ times

(If no) Is that because you never heard noise made by your neighbors or because you heard some noise but you didn't mind?
_____ Did not hear any noise (1)
_____ Heard noise, but did not mind (2)

29. All in all, how well do you get along with your neighbors? Would you say:
_____ Very well (1)
_____ Pretty well (2)
_____ Well enough (3)
_____ Not too well (4)

30. Do you have any relatives living elsewhere in Bangkok?
_____ Yes
_____ No (3)

(If yes) Do these relatives live in this neighborhood or elsewhere in Bangkok?

_____ In this neighborhood (1)
_____ Elsewhere in Bangkok (2)

30.1   (If yes) All in all, how well would you say you get along with your
       relatives? Would you say:
       _____ Very well (1)
       _____ Pretty well (2)
       _____ Well enough (3)
       _____ Not too well (4)

31.   How many really good friends do you have that you fairly regularly get
       to speak to?
       _____ number of friends

32.   Now I am going to ask a few questions about your neighborhood.

32.1   When you go outside and look at your neighborhood, how do you feel
       about your neighborhood?
       _____ Good (1)
       _____ OK (2)
       _____ Not Good (3)
       _____ Uncertain (4)

32.2   How do you feel about the level of noise in your neighborhood?
       _____ A lot of noise (1)
       _____ Some noise (2)
       _____ No noise (3)

32.3   How do you feel about the level of crowding in your neighborhood?
       _____ A lot of crowding (1)
       _____ Some crowding (2)
       _____ No crowding (3)

32.4   Do you feel most people in your neighborhood care about the neighbor-
       hood?
       _____ A lot of people care (1)
       _____ Some care (2)
       _____ No one cares (3)

32.5   How happy are you with your neighborhood? Are you:
       _____ Very happy (1)
       _____ Fairly happy (2)
       _____ A little happy (3)
       _____ Not happy (4)

33.   Within the past month, was there any time when you were so sick that
       you could not work for two or more consecutive days?
       _____ Yes (1)
       _____ No (3)
       _____ Don't know (2)
       _____ Delivery (4)
       (If yes) How many times did that happen, and how many days in the
       past month were you so sick you could not work?
       _____ times   _____ days could not work (total)

34.   Within the past month, was there any time when you were so sick that
       you could not even get out of bed for two or more consecutive days?
       _____ Yes (1)

_____ No (3)
_____ Don't know (2)
_____ Delivery (4)
(If yes) How many times did that happen, and how many days were you so sick you could not get out of bed in the past month?
_____ times _____ days could not get out of bed (total)

35. Within the past month, was there any time when you were so sick that you could not even eat for two or more consecutive days?
_____ Yes (1)
_____ No (3)
_____ Don't know (2)
(If yes) How many times did that happen, and how many days were you so sick you could not eat in the past month?
_____ times _____ days could not eat (total)

36. Do you have any health problem or illness that you have had for more than three months?
_____ Yes (1)
_____ No (3)
_____ Don't know (2)
(If yes) What is the health problem or illness? _____

37. Have you seen a doctor during the last twelve months?
_____ Yes (1) How many times? _____ Times
_____ No (2)
(If ever) Did you go to _____? (multiple answers allowed)
_____ a physician
_____ a nurse
_____ a traditional healer

38. Have you ever received treatment in the hospital in the last twelve months?
_____ Yes (1)
(If received treatment) How many times were you admitted and how many nights did you spend in the hospital in the last twelve months?
_____ Never (2) _____ Number of night _____ Number of times

39. Would you say that your overall health is:
_____ Very good (1)
_____ Good (2)
_____ Fair (3)
_____ Not very good (4)

40. (For women only) During the past three months, have you had any of these symptoms?
Yes No
(1) (2)
40.1 _____ _____ irregular periods
40.2 _____ _____ bleeding between periods
40.3 _____ _____ heavy bleeding during your period
40.4 _____ _____ unusually painful periods
40.5 _____ _____ unusually tense or jumpy just before or during your period

40.6   _____   _____excessive vaginal discharge
40.7   _____   _____ pain during intercourse
41.   Next, I would like to ask a few questions about times when you are sick.
41.1   When you are really sick, are you almost always able to get a good rest?
          _____   Yes (1)
          _____   No (2)
41.2   Even when you are really sick, are there a number of chores that you just have to do?
          _____   Yes (1)
          _____   No (2)
41.3   When you are really sick, is there someone to help take care of you?
          _____   Yes (1)
          _____   No (2)
41.4   If someone else at home is sick, do you often seem to get sick too?
          _____   Yes (1)
          _____   No (2)
42.   Here are things some people say when they are talking about their home. Tell me whether you strongly agree, agree, disagree, or strongly disagree with each item.
42.1   At home, there are too many people around.
          _____   strongly agree (1)
          _____   agree (2)
          _____   disagree (3)
          _____   strongly disagree (4)
42.2   At home, I like having lots of people around.
          _____   strongly agree (1)
          _____   agree (2)
          _____   disagree (3)
          _____   strongly disagree (4)
42.3   In this house, I have almost no time alone.
          _____   strongly agree (1)
          _____   agree (2)
          _____   disagree (3)
          _____   strongly disagree (4)
42.4   In my home, people get in each other's way.
          _____   strongly agree (1)
          _____   agree (2)
          _____   disagree (3)
          _____   strongly disagree (4)
42.5   At home, I don't have enough room to do things conveniently.
          _____   strongly agree (1)
          _____   agree (2)
          _____   disagree (3)
          _____   strongly disagree (4)
43.   Household control
43.1   When I am tired or busy, I can tell anyone in the household to help me with household chores.
          _____   Strongly agree (1)

_____ Agree (2)
_____ Disagree (3)
_____ Strongly disagree (4)

43.2 When I want to move a piece of furniture in the all-purpose room, I can go ahead and move it without asking if others agree.
_____ Strongly agree (1)
_____ Agree (2)
_____ Disagree (3)
_____ Strongly disagree (4)

43.3 If I want to invite a friend to visit my house and be entertained (have a good time), I can go ahead and invite him without asking if others agree.
_____ Strongly agree (1)
_____ Agree (2)
_____ Disagree (3)
_____ Strongly disagree (4)

43.4 If one of my relatives comes to visit from up-country, I feel free to invite him to stay here for several days. I don't have to ask others if they agree.
_____ Strongly agree (1)
_____ Agree (2)
_____ Disagree (3)
_____ Strongly disagree (4)

43.5 Other household members often move my things.
_____ Strongly agree (1)
_____ Agree (2)
_____ Disagree (3)
_____ Strongly disagree (4)

43.6 When I am working in the house, I often have to move to make room for someone else.
_____ Strongly agree (1)
_____ Agree (2)
_____ Disagree (3)
_____ Strongly disagree (4)

44. Privacy.
Usually = 1   Sometimes = 2   Rarely = 3   Never = 4

44.1	At home, do you have as much privacy as you want?	1	2	3	4
44.2	At home, do you have a place where you can get away from the children?	1	2	3	4
44.3	At home, if you want to relax or work quietly at some task without interruption, do others leave you alone?	1	2	3	4
44.4	At home, if you want to talk quietly to someone in the family (e.g. husband/wife) without others listening to your conversation, are you able to do that?	1	2	3	4

44.5   At home, does it seem as if you can never be yourself?

_____   Yes (1)

_____   No (2)

44.6   At home, if you want to be alone, is there someplace you can go to be alone?

_____   Yes (1)

_____   No (2)

_____   Never want to be alone (if volunteered) (3)

44.7   Do others in your house sometimes make so much noise that you can't sleep?

_____   Often (1)

_____   Sometimes (2)

_____   Rarely (3)

_____   Never (4)

45.   Felt demands

45.1   Does it seem as if others are always making demands on you?

_____   Yes (1)

_____   No (3)

_____   Undecided (2)

45.2   At home, does it seem as if you almost never have any peace and quiet?

_____   Yes (1)

_____   No (3)

_____   Undecided (2)

45.3   At home, does it seem as if you always are having to do something for someone else?

_____   Yes (1)

_____   No (3)

_____   Undecided (2)

45.4   When you try to do something at home, are you almost always interrupted?

_____   Yes (1)

_____   No (3)

_____   Undecided (2)

46.   Physical withdrawal

46.1   Do you sometimes go out of the house just to get away from it all? Would you say:

_____   Often (1)

_____   Sometimes (2)

_____   Rarely (3)

_____   Never (4)

46.2   (If rarely or never) Do you often wish you could get out of the house just to get away from it all? Would you say:

_____   Often (1)

_____   Sometimes (2)

_____   Rarely (3)

_____   Never (4)

46.3 Do you sometimes go shopping or go on an errand just to get out of the house? Would you say:

_____ Often (1)
_____ Sometimes (2)
_____ Rarely (3)
_____ Never (4)

46.4 Do you ever go into another room to get away from other members of the family? Would you say:

_____ Often (1)
_____ Sometimes (2)
_____ Rarely (3)
_____ Never (4)

47. Psychological withdrawal

47.1 Do you sometimes try to ignore the demands of others? Would you say:

_____ Often (1)
_____ Sometimes (2)
_____ Rarely (3)
_____ Never (4)

47.2 Do you sometimes pretend to be busy even though you are not? Would you say:

_____ Often (1)
_____ Sometimes (2)
_____ Rarely (3)
_____ Never (4)

47.3 At home, when someone asks you to do something, do you sometimes agree to do it even though you don't think you will really do it? Would you say:

_____ Often (1)
_____ Sometimes (2)
_____ Rarely (3)
_____ Never (4)

47.4 At home, when others are talking to you, do you sometimes pretend that you don't hear them? Would you say:

_____ Often (1)
_____ Sometimes (2)
_____ Rarely (3)
_____ Never (4)

48. "Washed out" scale

Often=1   Sometimes=2   Rarely=3   Never=4

48.1	Is there often so much going on about you that you have trouble thinking straight?	1	2	3	4
48.2	Is there often so much going on that it is impossible to finish things that you have set out to do?	1	.2	3	4
48.3	Is there often so much going on about you that you never do what you plan to do?	1	2	3	4
48.4	Do you often feel lonely?	1	2	3	4

48.5	Do you almost always feel tired?	1	2	3	4

48.6 Do you often feel no one really
understands you and no one cares about
your needs?   1   2   3   4

49. Self concept.
The next questions deal with how you feel about yourself. After I read
a statement, please tell me whether you strongly agree, agree, disagree,
or strongly disagree. (TRY TO GET DECISION. USE UNDECIDED
ONLY AS A LAST RESORT.)
Strongly Agree=1   Agree=2   Disagree=3   Strongly Disagree=4

49.1 I feel that I am a person of worth, at
least equal to others.   1   2   3   4

49.2 At times I am not as good as I want to be.   1   2   3   4

49.3 I have a positive feeling about myself.   1   2   3   4

49.4 I think of myself as a person who has
self-respect.   1   2   3   4

49.5 I feel I no not have much to be proud of.   1   2   3   4

49.6 All in all, I am inclined to feel that I
am a failure.   1   2   3   4

49.7 I certainly feel useless at times.   1   2   3   4

49.8 On the whole, I am satisfied with myself.   1   2   3   4

49.9 I feel that I have a number of good
qualities.   1   2   3   4

49.10 I am able to do things as well as most
people.   1   2   3   4

50. How long have you been living with your present spouse?
_____ years

51. Have you ever been married before?
_____ Yes (1)
_____ No (2) (Skip to 52)

51.1 (If yes) How did your last marriage end?
_____ Death of spouse (1)
_____ Divorce (2)
_____ Disappearance of spouse (3)
_____ Other (4) _____

51.2 (If yes) How long ago did your previous marriage end?
_____ years

52. Good Marital relations.
I'm going to read you some things that married couples sometimes do
together. Please tell me how often you and your husband/wife have
done them in the past month.
Often=1   Sometimes=2   Rarely=3   Never=4

52.1 Had a good laugh together or shared a joke.   1   2   3   4

52.2 Showing love, affection, and caring toward
each other.   1   2   3   4

52.3 Have small talk with each other.   1   2   3   4

52.4 Did something the other particularly
appreciated.   1   2   3   4

53.   Marital Understanding and Attachment

53.1   How well do you think you know your husband/wife? Would you say:
- _____ very well (1)
- _____ fairly well (2)
- _____ not too well (3)
- _____ not at all well (4)

53.2   How well do you think your husband/wife knows you? Would you say:
- _____ very well (1)
- _____ fairly well (2)
- _____ not too well (3)
- _____ not at all well (4)

53.3   How emotionally attached are you and your husband/wife? Would you say:
- _____ very close (1)
- _____ fairly close (2)
- _____ not too close (3)
- _____ not at all close (4)

54.   Poor marital relations

Now I'm going to read you some things that husbands and wives sometimes agree about and sometimes disagree about. Would you tell me how often each of these caused differences of opinion or were problems in your marriage during the past few weeks?

Often=1   Sometimes=2   Rarely=3   Never=4

54.1	Being too tired and not wanting to do anything.	1 2 3 4
54.2	Irritating habits?	1 2 3 4
54.3	Spending money?	1 2 3 4
54.4	Being away from home?	1 2 3 4
54.5	Talking to other men/women too often?	1 2 3 4
54.6	Drinking alcohol or gambling?	1 2 3 4
54.7	Doing household chores?	1 2 3 4
54.8	How to discipline the children?	1 2 3 4

54.9   Is there anything else that caused problems between you and your husband/wife in the past few weeks?

---

55.   Arguments between husband and wife.

In many households, bad feelings, arguments or fights occur from time to time.

55.1   How often do you and your husband/wife have serious arguments or fights? Would you say:
- _____ Often (1)
- _____ Sometimes (2)
- _____ Rarely (3)
- _____ Never (4) (skip to Question 56)

55.2   In these arguments or fights, did you ever slap, hit or kick your husband/wife? (CHECK ALL THAT APPLY)
- _____ yes, ever slapped

_____ yes, ever hit
_____ yes, ever kicked
_____ no, never slapped, hit or kicked

55.3 In these arguments or fights, did your husband/wife ever slap, hit, or kick you? (CHECK ALL THAT APPLY)

_____ yes, ever slapped me
_____ yes, ever hit me
_____ yes, ever kicked me
_____ no, never slapped, hit, or kicked me

56. A lot of people have quarrels with their husband/wife and get so angry that they ask them to leave home or they threaten to leave home themselves.

56.1 Has this ever happened in your marriage?

_____ yes (1)
_____ no (2)

56.2 (If yes) How long ago did this last occur?

_____ months _____ years

56.3 Even people who get along quite well with their spouse sometimes wonder whether their marriage is working out. Have you ever thought your marriage might be in trouble?

_____ yes (1)
_____ no (2)

56.4 Has the thought of getting a divorce or separation crossed your mind in the past three years?

_____ yes (1)
_____ no (2)

56.5 Have you or your husband/wife ever seriously suggested the idea of divorce within the last three years?

_____ yes (1)
_____ no (2)

56.6 Have you discussed divorce or separation with a close friend?

yes (1)
no (2)

57. Positive affect
Now I'm going to ask you some questions about how you have been feeling. When I read a question, I'd like you to tell me whether you've felt that way often, sometimes, rarely, or never during the past few weeks.

Often=1   Sometimes=2   Rarely=3   Never=4

57.1	Something particularly enjoyable happened to you?	1	2	3	4
57.2	Felt good because someone complimented you on something you had done	1	2	3	4
57.3	In a good mood?	1	2	3	4
57.4	That things were going your way (smoothly)?	1	2	3	4
57.5	Satisfied with your life?	1	2	3	4

58.   Manifest irritation
       Everybody, at least occasionally, gets frustrated or angry. I'm going to
       read you some statements about how people feel and behave when they
       are frustrated or angry. Would you tell me if the statements are true of
       you or not? Please tell me if these statements are true often, sometimes,
       rarely, or never.
       Often=1   Sometimes=2   Rarely=3   Never=4

58.1   When you get mad, you speak harshly.   1   2   3   4
58.2   You sometimes get so mad that you kick
       things, break things, or slam doors.   1   2   3   4
58.3   At times you let small things upset you.   1   2   3   4
58.4   When you get angry, you sometimes yell
       at people.   1   2   3   4
58.5   You sometimes get mad enough to throw
       things.   1   2   3   4
58.6   You sometimes make threats that you don't
       mean to carry out.   1   2   3   4

59.   Relations with children
       Now I'd like to ask you some questions about your children. (PROBE
       TO FIND OUT IF THEY FEEL THESE THINGS OFTEN, SOMETIMES,
       RARELY, OR NEVER)
       Often=1   Sometimes=2   Rarely=3   Never=4

59.1   How often is it a relief when your children
       are out of the house?   1   2   3   4
59.2   How often do your children get in the way
       (physically)?   1   2   3   4
59.3   How often do you get upset because your
       children are too noisy?   1   2   3   4
59.4   How often do you feel as if your children
       are making too many demands?   1   2   3   4
59.5   How often do you wish you could get away
       from your children?   1   2   3   4
59.6   How often do you feel you can't do what
       you want to do because you have children?   1   2   3   4

60.   Next we would like to ask some specific questions about one of your
       children. (CHECK LIST OF FAMILY MEMBERS TO FIND THE
       RESPONDENT'S CHILD WHO IS CLOSEST TO AGE 13. RECORD
       NAME, AGE, SEX BELOW).
       Name _____ Age _____ Sex _____
       (If the child is less than 5 years old, skip parts 1 and 2 and ask parts 3
       and 4.)
       (FOR EACH QUESTION, PROBE FOR OFTEN (1), SOMETIMES (2),
       RARELY (3), OR NEVER (4))

60.1   How often do you have a long talk with _____?1   2   3   4
60.2   How often do you compliment ("chom
       chuey") _____, that is, tell him how good he
       is, or what a good job he has done?   1   2   3   4

60.3   How often are you able to cheer up
        ("phlob cay") _____ when he is unhappy?   1   2   3   4
60.4   How often do you show love toward
        _____? ("sadaeng khwaam rak taw luuk")   1   2   3   4
61.   Discipline of children
        Sometimes children do things they are not supposed to do and their
        parents discipline or punish them.
        (OFTEN (1), SOMETIMES (2), RARELY (3), NEVER (4))
        (If the children are less than 5 years old, skip parts 1 and 2 and ask parts
        3 and 4.)
61.1   How often do you have to talk to your
        child(ren) to explain what behavior is
        appropriate and what behavior is not
        appropriate?   1   2   3   4
61.2   How often do you have to scold your
        child(ren)?   1   2   3   4
61.3   How often do you have to punish your
        child(ren) by pinching or slapping him?   1   2   3   4
61.4   How often do you have to punish your
        child(ren) by hitting him severely?   1   2   3   4
61.5   When you punish your child do you use
        your hand, your foot, or a piece of wood? (CHECK ALL THAT APPLY)
        _____   hand
        _____   foot
        _____   piece of wood
        _____   never hit child (if volunteered)
62.   All in all, how well would you say you get along with your child(ren)?
        Would you say:
        _____   Very well (1)
        _____   Well (2)
        _____   Well enough (3)
        _____   Not too well (4)
63.   Child interaction (IF THERE IS ONLY ONE CHILD IN THE HOUSE-
        HOLD, SKIP THIS QUESTION)
63.1   When children get to a certain age, it's normal for them to quarrel with
        each other. How many quarrels have your children had in the last seven
        days?
        _____   number of quarrels
63.2   It's also common for children to hit each other when they get angry.
        How many times did your children hit each other in the past seven
        days?
        _____   number of times
63.3   Do you or your husband/wife ever have to intervene to make them stop
        fighting?
        _____   Often (1)
        _____   Sometimes (2)
        _____   Rarely (3)
        _____   Never (4)

63.4 Do you feel that your children quarrel and fight with each other more than other children do, less than other children do, or about as much as other children do?

_____ less than other children do (1)
_____ about as much as other children do (2)
_____ more than other children do (3)

64. Arguments between the respondent and people outside the family. Have you ever had any serious arguments or fights with any person outside the family?

_____ yes (1)
_____ no (2)

65. Arguments between family members (ASK THE FOLLOWING QUESTION IF THE HOUSEHOLD INCLUDES ADULT RELATIVES OTHER THAN THE HUSBAND AND WIFE).

In many households, bad feelings, arguments, or fights occur from time to time. Have you ever had any serious arguments or fights with any family members other than your husband/wife and children?

_____ yes (1)
_____ no (2)

66. Fertility, desired family size, contraceptive use

66.1 How many of your children are living with you now?

_____ number

66.2 Do you have any children that are not living with you now?

_____ yes (1)
_____ no (2)

(If yes) How many? _____ number

66.3 Did you have any children who died?

_____ yes (1)
_____ no (2)

(If yes) How many? _____ number

What were their ages when they died? (Specify years or months)

_____

66.4 Have you/has your wife ever had a still birth?

_____ yes (1)
_____ no (2)

66.5 Have you/has your wife ever had a miscarriage?

_____ yes (1)
_____ no (2)

66.6 Have you/has your wife ever had an abortion?

_____ yes (1)
_____ no (2)

66.7 Do you want to have any more children in the future?

_____ yes (1)
_____ no (2)

(If yes) How many more children do you want to have in the future?

_____ number

66.8 Are you/is your wife currently pregnant or trying to become pregnant?

_____ currently pregnant (1)

_____ trying to become pregnant (2)
_____ neither (3)

66.9   (IF NOT PREGNANT OR TRYING TO BECOME PREGNANT) Are you
        or your husband/wife currently using some family planning or doing
        something to avoid a pregnancy?
        _____ yes (1)
        _____ no (2) (IF NO, PROBE FOR MALE OR FEMALE STERILIZA-
                     TION)

66.10   (If yes) What method are you currently using?
        _____ pill (1)
        _____ female sterilization (2)
        _____ injectable (3)
        _____ implant (4)
        _____ IUD (5)
        _____ rhythm (6)
        _____ withdrawal (7)
        _____ condom (8)
        _____ male sterilization (9)

66.11   (Skip to 67 for those who are not using birth control or are using
        sterilization.)
        How often do you forget to use your method of birth control?
        Would you say:
        _____ often (1)
        _____ sometimes (2)
        _____ rarely (3)
        _____ never (4)

66.12   Does a lack of privacy in your home ever prevent you from using your
        method of birth control?
        _____ often (1)
        _____ sometimes (2)
        _____ rarely (3)
        _____ never (4)
        _____ not currently using birth control (8)

67.   Sexual relations

67.1   How many times in the past month did you and your husband/wife
        have sexual relations?
        _____ times

67.2   NOTE: IF RESPONDENT CANNOT ANSWER OR IS NOT SURE, ASK:
        How many times in the past week did you and your husband/wife have
        sexual relations?
        _____ times

67.3   (After either question) Would you say this is typical for you?
        _____ yes (1) (Skip to 68)
        _____ no (2)

67.4   (If no) Do you usually have sexual relations more often than this or less
        often?
        _____ usually more often (1)
        _____ usually less often (3)

68. Are you ever reluctant to have sexual relations because the children or others are at home?

   _____ often (1)
   _____ sometimes (2)
   _____ rarely (3)
   _____ never (4)

69.1 Have you and your husband/wife ever stopped having sexual relations for a period of time for any reason other than pregnancy?

   _____ yes (1)
   _____ no (2) (skip to 70)

69.2 (If yes) Why? _____

69.3 (If yes) How long did you stop having sexual relations?

   _____

   (Indicate months or years)

70. Psychiatric symptoms

   Now I'm going to ask you some questions about how you have been feeling. When I read a question, I'd like you to tell me whether you've felt that way often (1), sometimes (2), rarely (3), or never (4) during the past few weeks.

   During the past few weeks, how often have you felt:

70.1 Anxious about something or someone?   1   2   3   4

70.2 That people are trying to pick quarrels
   or start arguments with you?   1   2   3   4

70.3 So depressed that it interferes with
   your daily activities?   1   2   3   4

70.4 That personal worries were getting you
   down physically, that is, making you
   physically ill?   1   2   3   4

70.5 Moody?   1   2   3   4

70.6 Felt you were confused, frustrated, and
   under a lot of pressure?   1   2   3   4

71. Langner Scale (Often (1), Sometimes (2), Rarely (3), Never (4))

71.1 Do you ever wonder if anything is
   worthwhile anymore?   1   2   3   4

71.2 Are you ever bothered by nervousness,
   i.e. by being irritable, fidgety, or
   tense?   1   2   3   4

71.3 Do you ever feel that nothing ever turns out
   for you the way you want it to?   1   2   3   4

71.4 Do you ever have periods of days, weeks,
   or months when you couldn't take care of
   things because you couldn't "get going"?   1   2   3   4

71.5 Do you ever have periods of such great
   restlessness that you cannot sit for long?   1   2   3   4

71.6 Do you ever feel somewhat apart or alone
   even among friends?   1   2   3   4

71.7 Are you the worrying type—you know,
   a worrier?

_____ yes (1)
_____ no (2)

71.8   Do you have trouble concentrating or
        keeping your mind on what you are doing?   1   2   3   4

71.9   In general, would you say that most of the time you are in very low
        spirits, low spirits, high spirits, or very high spirits?
        _____ very low spirits (1)
        _____ low spirits (2)
        _____ high spirits (3)
        _____ very high spirits (4)

72.   Health Opinion Survey (Often (1), Sometimes (2), Rarely (3), Never (4))

72.1   Do your hands tremble enough to bother you? 1   2   3   4

72.2   Do your hands and feet often sweat so that
        you feel damp and clammy?   1   2   3   4

72.3   Are you bothered by your heart beating hard,
        even when you are resting?   1   2   3   4

72.4   When you get up in the morning, do you ever
        feel bored or hopeless?   1   2   3   4

72.5   Do you have any trouble getting to sleep or
        staying asleep?   1   2   3   4

72.6   How often are you bothered by having an
        upset stomach, abdominal pain, or diarrhea? 1   2   3   4

72.7   Are you troubled by nightmares that
        sometimes frighten and wake you up?   1   2   3   4

72.8   How often do you have "cold sweat,"
        "feeling cold" when you are apprehensive?   1   2   3   4

72.9   Do you ever have loss of appetite?   1   2   3   4

72.10   Do you ever feel weak all over?   1   2   3   4

72.11   Do you have spells of dizziness?   1   2   3   4

72.12   When not exercising or exerting yourself,
        are you ever bothered by shortness
        of breath?   1   2   3   4

73.   Nervous breakdown

73.1   Have you ever felt that you were about to lose your mind (go crazy)?
        _____ Yes (1)
        _____ No (2) (Skip to 74)

73.2   (If yes) Was that during the past year or more than a year ago?
        _____ During the past year (1)
        _____ More than a year ago (2)

74.   Suicide

74.1   Have you ever seriously thought about committing suicide?
        _____ yes (1)
        _____ no (2) (skip to 75)

74.2   Was that during the past year or more than a year ago?
        _____ during the past year (1)
        _____ more than a year ago (2)

75.   Drinking behavior

75.1 Do you ever drink alcohol?

_____ Yes (1)

_____ No (2)

75.2 Does your spouse ever drink alcohol?

_____ Yes (1)

_____ No (2)

(If the respondent never drinks alcohol, skip 75.3, 75.4, 75.5.)

If the spouse never drinks alcohol, skip 75.6, 75.7, 75.8.)

75.3 During the past month, did you ever end up drinking more than you planned to drink?

_____ often (1)

_____ sometimes (2)

_____ rarely (3)

_____ never (4)

75.4 During the past month, did you ever fail to do some thing you should have done or do something you were not supposed to do because of drinking?

_____ often (1)

_____ sometimes (2)

_____ rarely (3)

_____ never (4)

75.5 During the past month, did you ever have any arguments with any household member because of your drinking?

_____ often (1)

_____ sometimes (2)

_____ rarely (3)

_____ never (4)

75.6 Does your husband/wife ever drink too much?

_____ Often (1)

_____ Sometimes (2)

_____ Rarely (3)

_____ Never (4)

75.7 During the past month, did your husband/wife ever fail to do something they should have done or do something they were not supposed to do because of drinking?

_____ Often (1)

_____ Sometimes (2)

_____ Rarely (3)

_____ Never (4)

75.8 During the past month, did your husband/wife ever have any arguments with any household member because of your spouse's drinking?

_____ Often (1)

_____ Sometimes (2)

_____ Rarely (3)

_____ Never (4)

76. Next, I would like to ask you about your usual family income for one month. I realize that you may not know exactly what your income is, but it will be very useful if you can say approximately what your

monthly family income is. Please look at this card and tell me which income range best describes your usual monthly family income from all sources.

1 = below 2000 baht per month
2 = 2000 baht - 2999 baht per month
3 = 3000 baht - 3999 baht per month
4 = 4000 baht - 4999 baht per month
5 = 5000 baht - 5999 baht per month
6 = 6000 baht - 7999 baht per month
7 = 8000 baht - 9999 baht per month
8 = 10,000 baht - 13,999 baht per month
9 = 14,000 baht - 19,999 baht per month
10= 20,000 baht or more per month
(NOTE: IF THE INTERVIEWEE CANNOT SAY WHICH INCOME RANGE IS APPROXIMATELY CORRECT, ASK FOR HIM TO INDICATE TWO CATEGORIES.)

77.   INTERVIEWER OBSERVATION
77.1   The respondent's skin color is:
         _____   very dark (1)
         _____   dark (2)
         _____   medium (3)
         _____   light (4)
         _____   very light (5)
77.2   Was anyone over 4 years old present during the interview besides yourself and the respondent?
         _____   yes (1)
         _____   no (2)
         (If yes) Who? (LIST RELATION TO RESPONDENT)

         _____

77.3   In general was the respondent's attitude toward the interview:
         _____   Friendly and eager (1)
         _____   Cooperative, but not particularly eager (2)
         _____   Indifferent and bored (3)
         _____   Hostile (4)
77.4   Was the respondent's understanding of the questions:
         _____   good (1)
         _____   fair (2)
         _____   poor (3)
77.5   What best describes the type of housing of this respondent?
         _____   slum   For slum or construction site:
                   _____   high density (1)   Is there a porch or balcony?
                   _____   low density (2)
         _____   construction site   _____ yes
         _____   flat (4)   _____ no
                   _____   respondent's floor
                   _____   total number of floors
         _____   single family dwelling
                   _____   suburban housing development (5)

     _____   mixed commercial/residential area (6)

_____   concrete shop house (7)

_____   wooden shop house (8)

_____   town house, apartment, court, condo (9)

     _____   respondent's floor

     _____   total number of floors

_____   other (10)_____

77.6   Are there holes, open cracks, or rotted, loose or missing materials:

     _____   over a considerable area of the floors, walls or ceiling (1)

     _____   over a small area of the floors, walls or ceiling (2)

     _____   over none of the floors, walls or ceiling (3)

     _____   unable to observe (4)

77.7   Are there shaky or unsafe sidewalks, porches, steps, or railings?

     _____   Yes (1)

     _____   No (2)

77.8   Large house or small house

     _____   Large house (1)

     _____   Small house (2)

77.9   Number of households in housing unit _____

77.10   Number of eligible couples in household _____

Appendix B: Description of Scales

1. Perceived Crowding

(This introduction was used for items [a] through [d].)
Here are things some people say when they are talking about their home. Tell me whether you agree or disagree with each item. (The response categories are strongly disagree, disagree, agree, strongly agree).

(a) At home, there are too many people around.
(b) In this house, I have almost no time alone.
(c) In my home, people get in each other's way.
(d) At home, I don't have enough room to do things conveniently.

Alpha for this unweighted scale is .80.

2. Lack of Privacy

The response categories for [a] through [c] are usually, sometimes, rarely, never.

(a) At home, do you have as much privacy as you want?
(b) At home, if you want to relax or work quietly at some task without interruption, do others leave you alone?
(c) At home, if you want to talk quietly to someone in the family (e.g. husband/wife) without others listening to your conversation, are you able to do that?
(d) At home, does it seem as if you can never be yourself? (No, Yes)
(e) At home, if you want to be alone, is there someplace you can go to be alone? (Yes, No)

Alpha for this unweighted scale is .70.

3. Psychological Distress

(This introduction was used for items [a] through [f].)
Now I'm going to ask you some questions about how you have been feeling. When I read a question, I'd like you to tell me whether you've felt that way

during the past few weeks. (The response categories are never, rarely, sometimes, and often.)

(a) Anxious about something or someone?
(b) That people are trying to pick quarrels or start arguments with you?
(c) So depressed that it interferes with your daily activities?
(d) That personal worries were getting you down physically, that is making you physically ill?
(e) Moody?
(f) Felt you were confused, frustrated, and under a lot of pressure?
(g) Are you ever bothered by nervousness, i.e. by being irritable, fidgety, or tense? (No, Yes)
(h) Do you ever feel that nothing ever turns out for you the way you want it to? (No, Yes)
(i) Do you have trouble concentrating or keeping your mind on what you are doing? (No, yes)
(j) Are you the worrying type—you know, a worrier? (No, Yes)

Alpha for this unweighted scale is .84.

4. Felt Demands

The response categories are no, undecided, yes.

(a) Does it seem as if others are always making demands on you?
(b) At home, does it seem as if you almost never have any peace and quiet?
(c) At home, does it seem as if you always are having to do something for someone else?
(d) When you try to do something at home, are you almost always interrupted?

Alpha for this unweighted scale is .68.

5. Unhappiness

(This introduction was used for the items [a] through [c].)
Now I'm going to ask you some questions about how you have been feeling. When I read a question, I'd like you to tell me whether you've felt that way often, sometimes, rarely or never during the past few weeks.

(a) In a good mood?
(b) That things were going your way (smoothly)?
(c) Satisfied with your life?

Alpha for this unweighted scale is .74.

6. Irritability

(This introduction was used for the items [a] through [f].)
Everybody, at least occasionally, gets frustrated or angry. I'm going to read you some statements about how people feel and behave when they are frustrated or angry. Would you tell me if the statements are true of you or not? Please tell me if these statements are true often, sometimes, rarely or never.

(a) When you get mad, you speak harshly.
(b) You sometimes get so mad that you kick things, break things, or slam doors.
(c) At times you let small things upset you.
(d) When you get angry, you sometimes yell at people.
(e) You sometimes get mad enough to throw things.
(f) You sometimes make threats that you don't mean to carry out.

Alpha for this unweighted scale is .62.

7. Psychological Withdrawal

(a) Do you sometimes try to ignore the demands of others?
(b) Do you sometimes pretend to be busy even though you are not?
(c) At home, when others are talking to you, do you sometimes pretend that you don't hear them? (The response categories are never, rarely, sometimes, and often.)

Alpha for this unweighted scale is .54.

8. Lethargy

(a) Do you ever have periods of days, weeks, or months when you couldn't take care of things because you couldn't "get going"?
(b) When you get up in the morning, do you ever feel bored or hopeless?
(c) Do you have any trouble getting to sleep or staying asleep?
(d) Do you ever have a loss of appetite?
(e) Do you ever feel weak all over? (The response categories are never, rarely, sometimes, and often.)

Alpha for the unweighted scale is .63.

9. Distraction

(a) Is there often so much going on about you that you have trouble thinking straight?
(b) Is there often so much going on that it is impossible to finish things that you have set out to do?

(c) Is there often so much going on about you that you never do what you plan to do? (The response categories are never, rarely, sometimes, and often.)

Alpha for the unweighted scale is .86.

10. Loneliness

(a) Do you often feel lonely?
(b) Do you often feel no one really understands you and no one cares about your needs?
(c) Do you ever wonder if anything is worthwhile anymore?
(d) Do you ever feel somewhat apart or alone even among friends? (The response categories are never, rarely, sometimes, and often.)

Alpha for the unweighted scale is .71.

11. Marital Instability

(This introduction was used for the following item.)
A lot of people have quarrels with their husband/wife and get so angry that they ask them to leave home or they threaten to leave home themselves.
(The response categories are yes and no.)

(a) Has this ever happened in your marriage?

(This introduction was used for items [b] through [d].)

Even people who get along quite well with their spouse sometimes wonder whether their marriage is working out.

(b) Has the thought of getting a divorce or separation crossed your mind in the past three years?
(c) Have you or your husband/wife ever seriously suggested the idea of divorce within the last three years?
(d) Have you discussed divorce or separation with a close friend?

Alpha for this unweighted scale is .79.

12. Marital Arguments

(This introduction was used for items [a] through [f].)
Now I'm going to read you some things that husbands and wives sometimes agree about and sometimes disagree about. Would you tell me how often each of these caused differences of opinion or were problems in your marriage during the past few weeks?
(The response categories are never, rarely, sometimes, and often.)

(a) Being too tired and not wanting to do anything?
(b) Irritating habits?
(c) Spending money?
(d) Being away from home?
(e) Talking to other men/women too often?
(f) Drinking alcohol or gambling?

(This introduction was used for the following item.)
In many households, bad feelings, arguments or fights occur from time to time.

(g) How often do you and your husband/wife have serious arguments or fights?

Alpha for the unweighted scale is .70.

13. Marital Companionship

(This introduction was used for items [a] through [d].)
I'm going to read you some things that married couples sometimes do together.
Please tell me how often you and your husband/wife have done them in the past
month.
(The response categories are never, rarely, sometimes, and often.)

(a) Had a good laugh together or shared a joke?
(b) Showing love, affection, and caring toward each other?
(c) Have small talk with each other?
(d) Did something the other particularly appreciated?

Alpha for this unweighted scale is .77.

14. Marital Knowledge and Understanding

The response categories for [a] through [b] are: 1, not at all well; 2, not too well;
3, fairly well; 4, very well.

(a) How well do you think you know your husband/wife?
(b) How well do you think your husband/wife knows you?
(c) How emotionally attached are you and your husband/wife?

1, not at all close; 2, not too close; 3, fairly close; 4, very close

Alpha for this unweighted scale is .82.

15. Supportive Behavior

(This introduction was used for the items [a] through [d].)

Next we would like to ask some questions about one of your children. (The interviewer selected the respondent's child closest to age 13. If the child was less than 5 years old, items a and b were skipped.)
(The response categories are never, rarely, sometimes, and often.)

(a) How often do you have a long talk with _____?
(b) How often do you compliment _____, that is, tell him how good he is, or what a good job he has done?
(c) How often are you able to cheer up _____ when he is unhappy?
(d) How often do you show love toward _____?

Alpha for this unweighted scale is .68.

16. Parent-Child Tension

(This introduction was used for the items [a] through [e].)
Now I'd like to ask you some questions about your children. (The response categories are never, rarely, sometimes, and often.)

(a) How often is it a relief when your children are out of the house?
(b) How often do your children get in the way (physically)?
(c) How often do you get upset because your children are too noisy?
(d) How often do you wish you could get away from your children?
(e) How often do you feel you can't do what you want to do because you have children?

Alpha for this unweighted scale is .69.

17. Discipline of Children

(This introduction was used for the items [a] through [d].)
Sometimes children do things they are not supposed to do and their parents discipline or punish them. (If the children were less than 5 years old, items a and b were skipped.)
(The response categories are never, rarely, sometimes, and often.)

(a) How often do you have to talk to your child(ren) to explain what behavior is appropriate and what behavior is not appropriate.
(b) How often do you have to scold your child(ren)?
(c) How often do you have to punish your child(ren) by pinching or slapping him?
(d) How often do you have to punish your child(ren) by hitting him severely?

Alpha for this unweighted scale is .61.

18. Sibling Conflict

(If there was only one child in the household, these questions were skipped.)

(a) When children get to a certain age, it's normal for them to quarrel with each other. How many quarrels have your children had in the last seven days? (Reported number of quarrels coded.)

(b) It's also common for children to hit each other when they get angry. How many times did your children hit each other in the past seven days? (Reported number of times coded.)

(c) Do you or your husband/wife ever have to intervene to make them stop fighting? (Never, rarely, sometimes, or often.)

(d) Do you feel that your children quarrel and fight with each other more than other children do, less than other children, or about as much as other children do?

Alpha for this unweighted scale is .68.

19. Household Control

(The response categories are strongly disagree, disagree, agree, or strongly agree.)

(a) When I want to move a piece of furniture in the all-purpose room, I can go ahead and move it without asking if others agree.

(b) If I want to invite a friend to visit my house and be entertained (have a good time), I can go ahead and invite him without asking if others agree.

(c) If one of my relatives comes to visit from up-country, I feel free to invite him to stay here for several days. I don't have to ask others if they agree.

Alpha for this unweighted scale is .85.

20. Housing Satisfaction

(The response categories are strongly dissatisfied, dissatisfied, satisfied, and strongly satisfied.)

The eleven specific aspects of housing are: drinking water, water for washing, ventilation, bathroom, kitchen, toilet, brightness-sunlight, laundry, noise, smell, and heat. Factor analyses suggest that these 11 items could be divided into four factors. However, for current purposes we form a single scale for these items.

Alpha for the unweighted scale is .85.

21. Family Income

There are ten response categories from below 2000 baht to more than 20,000 baht per month. At the time of the survey, U.S.$ = 25 Baht.

References

Aiello, J. R., Y. M. Epstein, and R. A. Karlin. 1975. "Field Experiment Research on Human Crowding." Paper presented at the annual meeting of the Eastern Psychological Association, New York.

Allee, W. C. 1938. *The Social Life of Animals*. Boston: Beacon Press.

Altman, I. 1974. "Privacy: A Conceptual Analysis," in D. H. Carson, ed., *Man-Environment Interactions: Evaluations and Applications (Volume 6)*. Pp. 3-28. New York: Halsted Press.

Altman, I. 1975. *The Environment and Social Behavior: Privacy, Personal Space, Territory, and Crowding*. Monterey, California: Brooks/Cole.

_____. 1976. "Privacy: A Conceptual Analysis." *Environment and Behavior* 8:7-29.

Aries, P. 1962. *Centuries of Childhood: A Social History of Family Life*. New York: Knopf.

Baldassare, M. 1978. "Human Spatial Behavior," in R. H. Turner, J. Coleman and R. C. Cox, eds., *Annual Review of Sociology*. Pp. 29-56. Palo Alto, California: Annual Review, Incorporated.

_____. 1979. *Residential Crowding in Urban America*. Berkeley: University of California Press.

_____. 1981. "The Effect of Household Density on Subgroup." *American Sociological Review* 46:110-118.

Baum, A. and Y. M. Epstein (eds). 1978. *Human Response to Crowding*. Hillsdale, New Jersey: Lawrence Erlbaum Associates.

Booth, A. 1976. *Urban Crowding and its Consequences*. New York: Praeger.

Booth, A. and J. Cowell, 1976. "The Effects of Crowding upon Health." *Journal of Health and Social Behavior* 17:204-220.

Booth, A. and J. N. Edwards. 1976. "Crowding and Family Relations." *American Sociological Review* 41:308-321.

Booth, A., D. Johnson, and J. N. Edwards. 1980a. "Reply to Gove and Hughes." *American Sociological Review* 45:870-873.

_____. 1980b. "In Pursuit of Pathology: The Effects of Human Crowding (Comment on Gove, Hughes, and Galle, *American Sociological Review*, February 1979)." *American Sociological Review* 45:873-878.

_____. 1983. "Measuring Marital Instability." *Journal of Marriage and the Family* 45:387-394.

Booth, A., D. Johnson, L. White, J. N. Edwards. 1984. "Women, Outside Employment, and Marital Instability." *American Journal of Sociology* 90:567-583.

Bryant, F. B. and J. Veroff. 1984. "Dimensions of Subjective Mental Health in American Men and Women." *Journal of Health and Social Behavior* 25:116-135.

Calhoun, J. B. 1962. "Population Density and Social Pathology." *Scientific American* 206:139-148.

Campbell, J. C. 1985. "Beating of Wives: A Cross-Cultural Perspective." *Victimology: An International Journal* 10:174-185.

Cassel, J. 1970. "Physical Illness in Response to Stress," in S. Levine and H. Scotch, eds., *Social Stress.* Pp. 189-209. Chicago: Aldine.

_____. 1979. "The Relation of the Urban Environment to Health: Toward a Conceptual Frame and a Research Strategy," in L. E. Hinkle and W. C. Loring, eds., *The Effects of the Man-made Environment on Health and Behavior.* Pp. 129-142. London: Castle House.

Chapin, S. F. 1951. "Some Housing Factors Related to Mental Hygiene." *Journal of Social Issues* 7:161-164.

Chayovan, N., P. Kamnuansilpa, and J. Knodel. 1988. Thailand: Demographic and Health Survey. Bangkok, Thailand: Institute of Population Studies, Chulalongkorn University.

Chitty, D. 1952. "Mortality among Voles (Microtus agresitis) at Lake Vyrnwy, Montgomershire in 1936-1939." *Philosophical Transactions of the Royal Society of London* B236:505-552.

Choldin, H. 1978. "Urban Density and Pathology," in R. H. Turner, J. Coleman, and R. C. Cox, eds., *Annual Review of Sociology.* Pp.91-113. Palo Alto, California: Annual Reviews, Incorporated.

Choldin, H. and D. Roncek. 1976. "Density, Population Potential and Pathology: A Block Level Analysis." *Public Data Use* 4:19-30.

Chombart de Lauwe, P. H. 1961. "The Sociology of Housing Methods and Prospects of Research." *International Journal of Comparative Sociology* 2:23-41.

Christian, J. J. 1950. "The Adreno-Pituitary System and Population Cycles in Mammals." *Journal of Mammalogy* 31:247-259.

_____. 1959. "The Roles of Endocrine and Behavioral Factors in the Growth of Mammalian Population," in A. Gorbman, ed., *Comparative Endocrinology.* New York: Wiley.

_____. 1971. "Population Density and Reproductive Efficiency." *Biology of Reproduction* 4:248-294.

Christian, J. J. and D. E. Davis. 1964. "Endocrines, Behavior and Population." *Science* 146:1550-1560.

Christian, J. J., V. Flyger, and D. E. Davis. 1960. "Factors in the Mass Mortality of a Herd of Sika Deer." *Chesapeake Science* 1:79-95.

Christian, J. J., J. Lloyd, and D. E. Davis. 1965. "The Role of Endocrines in Self Regulation of Mammalian Populations." *Recent Progress in Hormone Research* 21:501-578.

Cockerman, W. C. 1986. *Medical Sociology.* Englewood Cliffs, New Jersey: Prentice-Hall.

Cooper, R. and N. Cooper. 1982. *Culture Shock: Thailand.* Singapore: Times Books International.

Cox, R., P. Paulus, G. McCain, and J. Schkade. 1979. "Field Research on the Effects of Crowding in Prisons on Off-Shore Drilling Platforms," in J. R. Aiello and A. Baum, eds., *Residential Crowding and Design.* Pp. 99-106. New York: Plenum.

Crombie, A. C. 1943. "The Effect of Crowding upon the Natality of Grain-infesting Insects." *Proceedings of the Zoological Society (London Zoological Society)* 113:77-98.

D'Atri, D. A. 1975. "Psychophysiological Responses to Crowding." *Environment and Behavior* 7:237-252.

de Tocqueville, A. [1835] 1945. *Democracy in America* (Volume 1). New York: Vintage Books.

Davis, D. E. 1964. "The Physiological Analysis of Aggressive Behavior," in W. Etkin, ed., *Social Behavior and Organization among Vertebrates*. Pp.53-74. Chicago: University of Chicago Press.

Dean, L., W. Pugh, and E. K. E. Gunderson. 1975. "Spatial and Perception Components and Crowding: Effects on Health and Satisfaction." *Environment and Behavior* 7:225-236.

Deevey, E. S. 1960. "The Hare and the Haruspex: A Cautionary Tale." *The Yale Review* 49:161-179.

_____. 1972. "The Equilibrium Population," in W. Peterson, ed., *Readings in Population*. Pp.2-16. New York: Macmillan.

Demos, J. 1970. *A Little Commonwealth*. New York: Oxford University Press.

Desor, J. A. 1972. "Toward a Psychological Theory of Crowding." *Journal of Personality and Social Psychology* 21:79-83.

Dohrenwend, B. P. 1975. "Sociocultural and Social-psychological Factors in the Genesis of Mental Disorders." *Journal of Health and Social Behavior* 25:116-135.

Dohrenwend, B. P. and D. Cranwell. 1970. "Psychiatric Symptoms in Community, Clinic, and Mental Hospital Groups." *American Journal of Psychiatry* 126:1611-1615.

Dohrenwend, B. P. and B. P. Dohrenwend. 1981. "Life Stress and Illness: Formulation of the Issues," in B. S. Dohrenwend and B. P. Dohrenwend, ed., *Stressful Life Events and Their Contexts*. Pp. 1-27. New York: Prodist.

Dohrenwend, B. P., P. E. Shrout, G. G. Egri, and F. S. Mendelson. 1980. "Nonspecific Psychological Distress and other Dimensions of Psychopathology." *Archives of General Psychiatry* 37:1229-1236.

Durkheim, E. [1893] 1947. *The Division of Labor in Society*. Translated by George Simpson. Glencoe: The Free Press.

Edwards, J. N. and A. Booth. 1977. "Crowding and Human Sexual Behavior." *Social Forces* 55:791-808.

Edwards, J. N., D. Johnson, and A. Booth. 1987. "Coming Apart: A Prognostic Instrument of Marital Breakup." *Family Relations* 36:168-170.

Eechaute, W., G. Demeester, E. LaCroxi, and I. Leusen. 1962. "The Adrenal Cortex Activity during Experimental Renal Hypertension in Rats." *Archives Internationales de Pharmacodynamie et de Therapie* 136:161-173.

Ehrlich, P. 1968. *The Population Bomb*. New York: Ballantine.

Faris, R. and W. Dunham. 1939. *Mental Disorders in Urban Areas*. Chicago: University of Chicago Press.

Felson, M. and M. Solaun. 1975. "The Fertility-inhibiting Effect of Crowded Apartment Living in a Tight Housing Market." *American Journal of Sociology* 80:1410-1427.

Firebaugh, G. 1978. "A Rule for Inferring Individual-level Relationships from Aggregate Data." *American Sociological Review* 43:557-572.

Flaherty, D. H. 1972. *Privacy in Colonial New England*. Charlottesville: University of Virginia Press.

Freedman, J. L. 1975. *Crowding and Behavior*. San Francisco: Freeman.

Fuller, T. D. 1990. "Internal Migration in Thailand," in C. B. Nam, W. J. Serow, and D. F. Sly, eds., *International Handbook on Internal Migration*. Pp. 345-369. New York: Greenwood.

Galle, O., W. R. Gove, and J. McPherson. 1972. "Population Density and Pathology: What Are the Relationships for Man?" *Science* 176:23-30.

Galle, O. and W. R. Gove. 1979. "Crowding and Behavior in Chicago, 1940-1970," in J. Aiello and A. Baum, eds., *Residential Crowding and Design*. Pp. 23-29. New York: Plenum.

Gasparini, I. 1973. "Influences of the Dwelling on Family." *Ekistics* 216:344-348.

Gelles, R. J. and C. P. Cornell (eds). 1983. *International Perspectives on Family Violence*. Massachusetts: D.C. Heath and Company.

Gist, N. and S. F. Fava. 1971. *Urban Society*. New York: Thomas Y. Crowell Company.

Goffman, E. 1959. *Presentation of Self in Everyday Life*. New York: Doubleday.

Gove, W. R. 1979. "Sex Differences in the Epidemiology of Mental Disorder," in E. Gomberg and D. Franks, eds., *Gender and Psychopathology: Sex Differences in Disordered Behavior*. Pp. 23-68. New York: Brunner/Manzel.

Gove, W. R. and M. Hughes. 1979. "Possible Causes of the Apparent Sex Differences in Physical Health: An Empirical Investigation." *American Sociological Review* 44:126-146.

_____. 1980a. "Reexamining the Ecological Fallacy: A Study in Which Aggregate Data are Critical in Investigating the Pathological Effects of Living Alone." *Social Forces* 58:1157-1177.

_____. 1980b. "The Effects of Crowding in the Toronto Study: Some Methodological and Empirical Questions (a comment on Booth, Johnson, and Edwards, 1976)." *American Sociological Review* 45:864-870.

_____. 1983. *Overcrowding in the Household: An Analysis of Determinants and Effects*. New York: Academic Press.

Gove, W. R., M. Hughes, and O. Galle. 1979. "Overcrowding in the Home: An Empirical Investigation of Its Possible Pathological Consequences." *American Sociological Review* 44:59-80.

Hall, E. 1966. *The Hidden Dimension*. New York: Doubleday.

Hammond, J. L. 1973. "Two Sources of Error in Ecological Correlation." *American Sociological Review*. 38:754-777.

Hanushek, J., J. Jackson, and J. Kain. 1974. "Model Specification, Use of Aggregate Data, and the Ecological Correlation Fallacy." *Political Methodology* 1:89-107.

Hargens. L. L. 1976. "A Note on Standardized Coefficients as Structural Parameters." *Sociological Methods and Research* 5:247-256.

Hassen, R. 1977a. "Social and Psychological Implications of High Population Density." *Civilizations* 27:228-244.

_____. 1977b. "Social and Psychological Consequences of Household Crowding." *Southeast Asian Affairs* 11:230-236.

Hawley, A. 1972. "Population Density and the City." *Demography* 9:521-29.

Helmreich, R. L. 1960. "Regulation of Reproductive Rate by Intrauterine Morality in the Deer Mouse." *Science* 132:417.

Hillery, G. A. 1982. *A Research Odyssey: Developing and Testing a Community Theory*. New Brunswick: Transaction Books.

Hing, E., M. G. Kovar, and D. P. Rice, 1983. "Sex Differences in Health and Use of Medical Care." *Vital and Health Statistics* Series 3, No. 24, DGGS Publication Number (PHS) 83-1408. Hyattsville, Maryland: National Center for Health Statistics.

Hoffman, R. S. 1958. "The Role of Reproduction and Mortality Fluctuations of Wolves." (Microtus) *Ecological Monographs* 28:79-109.

Holmes, T. H. and M. Masuda. 1974. "Life Change and Illness Susceptibility," in B. S. Dohrenwend and B. P. Dohrenwend, eds., *Stressful Life Events*. Pp. 45-77. New York: Wiley.

Hoskins, W. G. 1963. *Provincial England: Essays in Social and Economic History*. London: Macmillan.

Jain, U. 1987. *The Psychological Consequences of Crowding*. California: Sage.

Jillings, L. 1967. "A Behavioral Analysis of the Mongolian Gerbil." Unpublished manuscript.

Kahn R., and S. Perlin. 1967. "Dwelling-unit Density and Use of Mental Health Services." Paper presented at the 75th annual convention of the American Psychiatric Association, New York.

Kinsey, A. C. 1953. *Sexual Behavior in the Human Female*. Philadelphia: Saunders.

Kessler, R. C. 1982. "A Disaggregation of the Relationship between Socioeconomic Status and Psychological Distress." *American Sociological Review* 47:752-764.

Kessler, R. C., R. H. Price and C. B. Wortman. 1985. "Social Factors in Psychopathology: Stress, Social Support, and Coping Processes." *Annual Review of Psychology* 36:531-572.

Klausner, W. J. 1987. *Reflections on Thai Culture*. Bangkok, Thailand: Siam Society.

Knodel, J., A. Chamratrithirong, and N. Debavalya. 1987. *Thailand's Reproductive Revolution: Rapid Fertility Decline in a Third-World Setting*. Madison: University of Wisconsin Press.

Krueger, R. A. 1989. *Focus Groups: A Practical Guide for Applied Research*. California: Sage.

Landon, K. P. [1939] 1968. *Siam in Transition*. New York: Greenwood Press.

Langer, E. and S. Saegert. 1977. "Crowding and Cognitive Control." *Journal of Personality and Social Psychology* 35:175-182.

Langner, T. 1962. "A Twenty-two Item Screening Score of Psychiatric Symptoms Indicating Impairment." *Journal of Health and Social Behavior* 3:269-276.

LaRocco, J. M. J. S. House, and J. R. P. French. 1980. "Social Support, Occupational Stress, and Health." *Journal of Health and Social Behavior* 3:202-218.

Laws, R. and I. Parker. 1968. "Recent Studies on Elephant Populations in East Africa." *Symposium of the Zoological Society* 21:319-359.

Levi, L. and L. Anderson. 1975. Psycho-social Stress: *Population, Environment and Quality of Life*. New York: Halsted.

Limanonda, B. 1979. *Nuptiality Patterns in Thailand*. Chulalongkorn University, Bangkok: Institute of Population Studies.

Lloyd, J. 1975. "Effects of Crowding among Animals: Implications for Man." *Sociological Symposium* (Fall):7-23.

Lockley, R. M. 1961. "Social Structure and Stress in the Rabbit Warren." *The Journal of Animal Ecology* 30:385-423.

Loo, C. and P. Ong. 1984. "Crowding Perceptions, Attitudes, and Consequences among the Chinese." *Environment and Behavior* 16:55-87.

Louch, C. D. 1956. "Adrenocortical Activity in Relation to the Density and Dynamics of Three Confined Populations of Microtus." *Ecology* 37:710-713.

Ludwig, W. and C. Boost. 1939. "Uber das Wachstum von Protistenpopulationen und den Allelokatalytischen Effekt." *Archiv Prostistenkunde* 92:453-484.

MacKintosh, E., S. West, and S. Saegert. 1975. "Two Studies of Crowding in Urban Public Places." *Environment and Behavior* 7:159-184.

Marsella, A., M. Escudero, and P. Gordon. 1970. "The Effects of Dwelling Density on Mental Disorders in Filipino Men." *Journal of Health and Social Behavior* 11:288-294.

Martindale, D. 1960. *The Nature and Types of Sociological Theory*. Glencoe: Free Press.

Mayhew, H. [1861] 1968. "Housing in London, 1851," in S. F. Fava, ed., *Urbanism in World Perspective*. Pp. 474-484. New York Thomas Y. Crowell Company.

McCarthy, D. P., and S. Saegert. 1979. "Residential Density, Social Overload, and Social Withdrawal," in J. R. Aiello and A. Baum, eds., *Residential Crowding and Design*. New York: Plenum.

Mechanic, D. 1976. "Sex, Illness, Illness Behavior, and the Use of Health Services." *Journal of Human Stress* 2:29-40.

Milgram, S. 1970. "The Experience of Living in Cities." *Science* 167:1461-1468.

Mirowsky, J. and C. Ross. 1989. *Social Causes of Psychological Distress*. New York: Aldine.

Mitchell, R. 1971. "Some Social Implications of High Density." *American Sociological Review* 36:18-29.

Montgomery, D. C. and E. A. Peck. 1982. *Introduction to Linear Regression Analysis*. New York: Wiley.

Morgan, D. L. 1988. *Focus Groups as Qualitative Research*. California: Sage.

Morgan, L. H. 1965. *Houses and House-in-life of the American Aborigines*. Chicago: University of Chicago Press.

Morris, D. 1969. *The Human Zoo*. New York: McGraw-Hill.

———. 1952. "Homosexuality in the Ten-spined Stickleback." *Behavior* 4:233-261.

Moss, G. E. 1973. *Illness, Immunity, and Social Integration*. New York: Wiley.

Mumford, L. 1961. *The City in History*. New York: Harcourt Brace and World.

———. 1968. *The Urban Prospect*. New York: Harcourt, Brace and World.

Myers, J. K., J. J. Lindenthal, and M. P. Pepper. 1971. "Life Events and Psychiatric Impairment." *Journal of Nervous and Mental Disorders* 152:149-157.

Nathanson, C. 1975. "Illness and the Feminine Role: A Theoretical Review." *Social Science and Medicine* 9:57-62.

———. 1977. "Sex, Illness, and Medical Care: A Review of Data, Theory, and Method." *Social Science and Medicine* 11:13-25.

National Statistical Office. 1983. *Population and Housing Census: Bangkok Metropolis*. Bangkok, Thailand: National Statistical Office.

Newsom, R. K. 1973. *Population Proxemics and Mortality*. Ph.D. dissertation, University of Texas.

Parsons, T. 1965. "The Normal Family," in S. M. Farber, P. Mustacchi, and R. H. L. Wilson, eds., *Man and Civilization: The Family's Search for Survival*. New York: McGraw-Hill.

Paynter, R. A. 1949. "Clutch-size and the Egg and Chick Mortality of Kent Island Herring Gulls." *Ecology* 30:146-166.

Pearlin, L. I., M. A. Lieberman, E. G. Meneghan, and J. T. Mullen. 1981. "The Stress Process." *Journal of Health and Social Behavior* 22:337-356.

Perrins, C. M. 1965. "Population Fluctuations and Clutch-Size in the Great Tit." *Journal of Animal Ecology* 34:601-647.

Phillips, H. P. 1965. *Thai Peasant Personality*. Los Angeles: University of California Press.

Reimer, S. 1945. "Maladjustment to the Family Home." *American Sociological Review* 5:201-209.

Riley, J. N. and S. Sermsri. 1974. The Variegated Thai Medical System as a Birth Control Service. Working Paper No. 6. Bangkok: Mahidol University, Institute for Population and Social Research.

Rodin, J. and A. Baum. 1978. "Crowding and Helplessness: Potential Consequences of Density and Loss of Control," in A. Baum and Y. Epstein, eds., *Human Response to Crowding*. Pp. 389-401. Hillsdale: Lawrence Erlbaum Associates.

Saegert, S., E. MacKintosh, and S. West. 1975. "Two Studies of Crowding in Urban Public Places." *Environment and Behavior* 7:159-184.

Sangsingkeo, V., B. Leoprapai, and A. Sriburatham. 1988. Voluntary Sterilization in Thailand. Bangkok, Thailand: Thai Association for Voluntary Sterilization.

Schmitt, R. 1966. "Density, Health and Social Disorganization." *Journal of the American Institute of Planners* 32:37-40.

Selye, H. 1950. *The Physiology and Pathology of Exposure to Stress*. Montreal: Acta.

_____. 1952. *The Story of the Adaptation Syndrome*. Montreal: Acta.

Sherrod, D. and S. Cohen. 1979. "Density, Personal Control, and Design," in J. Aiello and A. Baum, *Residential Crowding and Design*. Pp. 217-227. New York: Plenum.

Shorter, E. 1977. *The Making of the Modern Family*. New York: Basic Books.

Siegal, H. A. 1959. "Egg Production Characteristics and Adrenal Function in White Leghorns Confined at Different Floor Space Levels." *Poultry Science* 38:893-898.

Simmel, G. [1903] 1971. "The Metropolis and Mental Life," in D. Levine, *On Individuality and Social Forms*. Pp. 324-339. Chicago: University of Chicago Press.

Snyder, R. L. 1968. "Reproduction and Population Pressures," in E. Stellar and J. M. Sprague, *Progress in Physiological Psychology* (Volume 2). New York: Academic.

Southwick, C. 1955. "Regulatory Mechanisms of House Mouse Populations: Social Behavior Affecting Litter Survival." *Ecology* 36:72-83.

Srole, L., T. S. Langner, S. T. Michael, M. K. Opler, and T. A. C. Rennie. 1962. *Mental Health in the Metropolis: The Midtown Manhattan Study* (Volume 1 and 2). New York: McGraw-Hill.

Statistical Abstract of the United States. 1988. Washington D.C.: Government Printing Office.

Sternstein, L. 1984. "The Growth of the Population of the World's Pre-eminent "Primate City": Bangkok at its Bicentenary." *Journal of Southeast Asian Studies* 15:43-68.

Stokols, D. 1972. "A Social-psychological Model of Human Crowding Phenomena." *Journal of the American Institute of Planners* 38:72-83.

_____. 1976. "The Experience of Crowding in Primary and Secondary Environments." *Environment and Behavior* 6:49-86.

_____. 1978. "A Typology of Crowding Experiences," in A. Baum and Y. M. Epstein, eds., *Human Response in Crowding*. Pp. 219-255. Hillsdale, New Jersey: Lawrence Erlbaum Associates.

Straus, M. A., R. J. Gelles, and S. K. Steinmetz. 1980. *Behind Closed Doors: Violence in the American Family*. New York: Anchor Press.

Sundstrom, E. 1975. "Toward an Interpersonal Model of Crowding." *Sociological Symposium* 14:129-144.

Susiyama, Y. 1967. "Social Organization of Hanrman Langurs," in S. Altmann, *Social Communication among Primates*. Chicago: University of Chicago Press.

Syme, L. A. 1973. "Social Isolation at Weaning: Some Effects on Two Measures of Activity." *Animal Learning and Behavior* 1:161-895.

Thoits, P. A. 1983. "Dimensions of Life Events that Influence Psychological Distress: An Evaluation and Synthesis of the Literature," in H. B. Kaplan, ed., *Psychological Stress: Trends in Theory and Research*. Pp. 33-103. New York: Academic.

Timasheff, N. 1963. *Sociological Theory: Its Nature and Growth*. New York: Random House.

Tobach, E. and H. Block. 1956. "Effect of Stress by Crowding Prior to and Following Tuberculosis Infection." *American Journal of Physiology* 187:399.

Todaro, M. P. 1989. *Economic Development in the Third World*. New York: Longman.

Tonnies, F. [1887] 1957. *Community and Society*. East Lansing: Michigan State University Press.

United Nations. 1980. *Compendium of Housing Statistics, 1975-1977* (Third Edition). New York: United Nations Department of International Economic and Social Affairs, Statistical Office.

United Nations. 1985. *Compendium of Housing Statistics, 1983* (Fourth Edition). New York: United Nations Department of International Economic and Social Affairs, Statistical Office.

Valins, S. and A. Baum. 1973. "Residential Group Size, Social Interaction and Crowding." *Environment and Behavior* 5:421-440.

Varon, H. H. 1966. "Biological Conditions Modifying Quantity of 17 Hydroxycorticoids in Mouse Adrenal." *Acta Endocrinologica* 51:488-496.

Verbrugge, L. 1976. "Females and Illness: Recent Trends in Sex Differences in the United States." *Journal of Health and Social Behavior* 17:387-403.

_____. 1985. "Gender and Health: An Update on Hypotheses and Evidence." *Journal of Health and Social Behavior* 26:156-182.

_____. 1989. "The Twain Meet: Empirical Explanations of Sex Differences in Health and Mortality." *Journal of Health and Social Behavior* 30:282-304.

Waldron, E. 1982. "An Analysis of Causes of Sex Differences in Mortality and Morbidity," in W. R. Gove and G. R. Carpenter, eds., *The Fundamental Connection between Nature and Nurture*. Pp. 69-115. Massachusetts: Lexington Books.

Welford, A. T. 1974. "Stress and Performance," in H. T. Welford, ed., *Man Under Stress*. Pp. 1-14. New York: Halsted.

White, M. and L. White. 1962. *The Intellectual Versus the City: From Jefferson to Frank Lloyd Wright*. Cambridge: Harvard University and M.I. T. Press.

Wichiencharoen, A. 1972. *Social Values in Thailand*. Bangkok, Thailand: Thammasart University.

Wingard, D. L. 1984. "The Sex Differential in Morbidity, Mortality, and Lifestyle," in L. Breslow, J. E. Fielding, and L. B. Lave, eds., *Annual Review of Public Health* (Volume 5). Pp. 433-458. Palo Alto, California: Annual Reviews, Incorporated.

Winsborough, H. 1965. "The Social Consequences of High Population Density." *Law and Contemporary Problems* 30:120-126.

Wirth, L. 1938. "Urbanism as a Way of Life." *American Journal of Sociology* 44:1-24.

About the Book and Authors

As we move into the twenty-first century, the effects of human crowding loom as an ever larger and more pressing issue. In the next ten years alone, it is estimated that 1.1 billion people will be added to a world population already exceeding 5 billion. Much of this increase will take place in the less developed regions of the world, where the provision of adequate housing is already difficult. The result, in all likelihood, will be cities of ever higher density, with more intense crowding at the household level.

How does household crowding affect human behavior? Ethological studies have documented numerous and often extreme aberrations among lower animals. However, sociological and psychological investigations of humans have produced very mixed results. North American and European studies, in particular, generally have suggested that the consequences of crowding are highly selective and mild.

Prior research has relied mainly on surveys of cities with limited crowding. Here, an international team of researchers examines the impact of household congestion in a context more typical of the developing world. Their findings are based on a large representative sample of Bangkok, Thailand, where the average number of persons per room is over four times that found in North America.

Relying on both qualitative and quantitative data, the analyses reported are far-reaching, including an examination of psychological well-being, marital and family relations, sibling relations, violence within the family, the impact on marital sex and reproductive behavior, and the consequences for physical health. The results show that household crowding has a wide range of detrimental social and psychological effects.

John N. Edwards is a Professor of Sociology at Virginia Polytechnic Institute and State University. He received his Master's and Ph.D. degrees from the University of Nebraska (1962 and 1965). His primary research interests concern issues related to marriage and the family. He is currently a co-investigator on a U.S. longitudinal project dealing with marital change and instability over the life course. He has written several books and numerous journal articles.

Theodore D. Fuller, Associate Professor of Sociology at Virginia Polytechnic Institute and State University, received his Master's and Ph.D. degrees from the University of Michigan (1972 and 1977). Since 1974, Dr. Fuller has worked extensively in Thailand, primarily in the area of rural-to-urban migration. He has published one book, several chapters, and numerous articles based on his research in Thailand.

Sairudee Vorakitphokatorn is an Assistant Professor of Psychology at the Institute of Population and Social Research, Mahidol University, Bangkok, Thailand. Dr. Vorakitphokatorn received her Master's and Ph.D. degrees from the University of Illinois (1975 and 1979). She has conducted several research projects on AIDS. She is the author of numerous papers and reports.

Santhat Sermsri, Associate Professor of Sociology and the former Dean of the Faculty of Social Sciences and Humanities, Mahidol University, Bangkok, Thailand, received his Master's and Ph.D. degrees from Brown University (1978 and 1980) with concentrations in demography and medical sociology. His research interests include health care utilization and the impact of urbanization on health. He is the author of numerous articles, chapters, and technical reports.

Inasmuch as the contributions of each of the authors were essential to the successful completion of the research reported, the order of authorship should not be construed as indicating differential contribution.

Index

Aberrant responses
  animal studies, relevance to human crowding, 18
  size of an animal population, 20
Animal studies
  crowding and health, 149
  crowding and sexual behaviors, 131
  crowding and violence, 124
  research tradition, 18-21
Area deficit measure
  construction, 66
Bangkok study, 34-36
  hypotheses, 34
Birth control
  fertility and crowding, 135, 145, 146, 171, 172
Buddhism
  effect on Thais, 108
Child mortality
  and crowding, 146
City
  and family lives, 17-18
  central focus of early theorizing, 15
  critics, 1-3
  principal characteristics, 17
  residential crowding, 3,
  social integration, 15-16
  social solidarity, 16
Control variables, 94, 115, 138, 154
Coping mechanisms, 89, 177
Crowding
  and desire for additional children, 145
  and family relations, 112-130, 171
  and health, 152-158, 172-173

  and parent-child relations, 121-122
  and privacy, 13
  and psychological well-being, 92-100, 169-170
  and sibling relations, 122-123
  and specialized rooms, 13
  and stress, 36, 90-91, 157-158
  and violence, 127
  definition, 3
  effects on lower animals, 18
  effects on sexual relations and reproductive behavior, 137-145, 171-172
  feeling of being crowded, 65-83
  felt demands, 122
  history lessons, 11-15
  in the context of Thai culture, 164
  objective indicator, 3-4, 33
  regularities of behavioral change, 20
  socioeconomic level, 25, 102
  stress model, 4
  subjective indicator, 4, 33
  territoriality, 3
Culture and crowding, 56-57, 164, 174-176
Density definition, 3
  conception of space, 14
  objective measure of crowding, 3-4
Ecological approach, 22-25
Ecological fallacy, 23
Extended families, 49, 105, 164
Felt demands, 43, 61
  and marital relations, 114-115, 129, 171

and parent-child relations, 121-
122, 129, 171
and psychological well-being,
98, 100, 103, 169-170
and sibling relations, 123
and violence, 127
scale, 61
Fertility
and crowding among animals,
135
rate and crowding, 138-139
Fetal mortality, 145, 149
Focus group interviews, 40-48
Gender differences
in family relations, 115-116, 123
in health, 158-161
in parent-child relations, 121
in psychological well-being, 95,
100
interaction terms, 99, 100
lack of privacy interaction, 99
reactivity to crowding, 69, 78,
173
reproductive and sexual behavior, 147
General Adaptation Syndrome, 19
Homeostatic theory, 19
Household conflict, 43
Household control
and crowding, 78, 84
scale, 68-69, 94
Household structure
and crowding, 164
Housing
and specialized rooms, 12
evolution, 11-12
in rural areas, 12
provision of, 1
Housing quality, 155, 161
Housing satisfaction
and health, 155
Husband-wife quarrels, 29
Hypersexuality (animals), 132
Infectious disease, 152, 173
Interaction terms, 94, 99, 100, 160

Irritability
and crowding, 95
scale, 93
Laboratory experiments
advantage, 26
deficiencies, 26-27
external validity, 27
Lack of privacy
and family violence, 126
and fetal and child mortality,
147
and gender, 78
and health, 158
and marital relations, 116
and parent-child relations, 120
and psychological well-being,
87, 95, 98, 169
and reproductive behavior, 147
and sexual activity, 139
relationship with perceived
crowding, 59, 71
scale, 59
variance explained by objective
crowding, 70
Marital companionship
relationship with crowding, 116
scale, 114
Marital arguments
and felt demands, 116
and psychological distress, 116
relationship with crowding, 116
scale, 114
Marital instability
and felt demands, 116
and psychological distress, 116
relationship with crowding,
116, 171
scale, 114
Marital relationship
and crowding, 171
background in Thailand, 108
scales, 112-115
Mate selection
in Thailand, 108

Mental health (see Psychological distress)

Mode of analysis, 61-62

Objective crowding (see also Persons per room)
and desire for children, 145
and fetal or child mortality, 146
and frequency of sexual relations, 138-139, 171-172
and health, 154
and marital relations, 115-121
and parent-child relations, 121-122
and psychological well-being, 87, 101
and sibling relations, 123
and subjective crowding, 35, 63-65, 69
and violence, 124
gender differences, 78
indicators, 3-4, 32, 58, 65-67

Others per room measure construction, 66-67

Parent-child relationships
and crowding, 29
scales, 114

Pathology
among animals, 131
and crowding, 169
and stress, 89
definition, 6
manifestation, 6
within ecological framework, 23

Perceived crowding
and birth control, 145-146
and desire for children, 145-146
and family violence, 124
and fetal or child mortality, 146
and health, 155
and marital relations, 116
and parent-child relations, 121
and psychological well-being, 95, 99-102, 169
and sexual relations, 139

and sibling relations, 122
relationship with perceived lack of privacy, 59, 71
scale, 59
variance explained by objective crowding, 70

Persons per room
and birth control, 145
and ceiling and threshold efforts, 101
and density measure, 3
and family violence (wife abuse), 127
and fetal or child mortality, 146
and health, 155
and marital relations, 116
and parent-child relations, 121
and psychological well-being, 95, 98
and sexuality (sexual relations), 136-137
and sibling relations, 122
and socioeconomic status, 102
and subjective experience of crowding, 69
in the United States and other countries, 6
objective indicator of crowding, 3-4
relationship with hospitalization, 91
variance explained by, 70
virtues and weaknesses, 83

Power
effects on feeling crowded, 78

Primary environment
and household, 2, 87
definition, 2

Privacy
and sexual behaviors, 137
effects of crowding, 58

Psychological distress
and crowding, 95
and health, 157
and marital relations, 116

and parent-child relations, 122
and sibling relations, 123
and violence, 127
forms of, 60
interaction with sex, 160
scale, 60, 93
Psychological withdrawal
and crowding, 91, 95, 99, 169
scale, 93
Public policy
implications for, 176
Reproductive behaviors (also see fertility)
Rooms deficit measure
construction, 66
correlation with other measures, 69, 76
Sample design, 48-49
Scales, present study (see also Appendix B)
felt demands, 61, 93, 114
household control, 68-69, 94, 115
housing satisfaction, 115
irritability, 93
lack of privacy, 59
marital arguments, 114
marital companionship, 114
marital instability, 113
parent-child relationship, 114
perceived crowding, 59
psychological distress, 60, 92-93
psychological withdrawal, 93
unhappiness, 93
Sex (see Gender)
Sexual behavior
frequency, 137
impact of crowding, 131-137, 171-172
of animals, 131-133
of humans, 138-145, 171-172
pathologies, 131
previous research, 131-136
Sibling relations
and crowding, 122-123

Social integration and urban life, 15-16
Social pathology
and ecological approach, 23-25
Socioeconomic status
relationship with persons per room, 102
Stimulus overload
and crowding, 88
and coping strategy, 88,89
Stress
and crowding, 34
and general adaptive syndrome, 19
and pathology, 89
Stress model, 5, 28, 34
Subgroup differences in feeling crowded, 78
Subjective crowding
and birth control, 135
and desire for children, 145
and fetal or child mortality, 146
and family violence, 124
and frequency of sexual relations, 139, 172
and health, 155, 158
and marital relations, 120, 171
and parent-child relations, 121-122, 171
and psychological well-being, 95, 98, 99-102, 169
and sibling relations, 123
and stress, 87
factors affecting, 4, 35
relationship with objective crowding, 65, 69-78, 165
scales, 59, 67
Thai family, 105-110
Unhappiness
scale, 93
Urban life (see City)
Violence
and crowding, 124
Wife abuse
and crowding, 125, 171